Hiking Kansas City

The Complete Guide to More Than 125 Hiking and Walking Trails in the Kansas City Area

Updated & Expanded Fifth Edition

William B. Eddy &
Richard O. Ballentine

Pebble Publishing, Inc.
Rocheport, Missouri

Pebble Publishing Inc.
P.O. Box 2 • Rocheport, MO 65279
(573) 698-3903 • www.pebblepublishing.com

ISBN 1-891708-32-5 $16.95

Editor & Publisher: Brett Dufur
Editor: Kimberly Small
Assistant Editor: Emily Kinder
Cover Artwork: Gary Mehl
Interior Artwork: Jeremy Collins
Cover & Interior Design: Brett Dufur & Kimberly Small
Photographs: Richard Ballentine, Terry Barner, Brett Dufur, William Eddy, Ken Hightower, Phillip Ratterman & Richard Stigall.
Maps: Karen Ballentine McKenna

First Edition: First Printing March 1989. Fourth Printing April 1990. Second Edition: First Printing November 1991. Fourth Printing November 1994. Third Edition: First Printing June 1995. Fourth Printing August 1999. Fourth Edition: First Printing April 2001. Fifth Edition: April 2007.

CONTENTS

TRAIL SITES

Note: ( ) denotes the number of trails at that location

ET CETERA

Note: ( ) denotes the number of trails at that location

DEDICATION

This book is dedicated first to our wives Linda and Emily, hikers in their own right, but Saturday hiking widows for the most part during this project. They have also been invaluable cheerleaders, proofreaders and tick-checkers.

This book is also dedicated to the administrators and rangers in the parks and nature preserves where these trails are located. They have conceived, built and maintained these wonderful trails so that the rest of us can enjoy them. We hope this book provides them additional encouragement.

We would also like to extend our thanks to Steve Rhoades of the Mid-American Regional Council MetroGreen program and Bill Maasen of the Johnson County Parks and Recreation District, as well as several volunteers from the Kansas City Outdoor Club, including Joe Mariani, Lynne Beatty, Dan Iott, Kevin Otterman and Dave Brackey, who helped us locate new trails and check out existing ones.

INTRODUCTION

LET'S GO FOR A WALK

Hiking trails in Kansas City! There are more than 125 trails and paths through hardwood forests, prairie grasslands, river valleys and rugged hills. You can hike along lake shores, past limestone formations, through marshes, and find yourself atop lookout points. You may see deer, wild turkey, fox, beaver and bluebirds. And you will enjoy fresh air, the smell of woods, good exercise, tranquility and an escape from the phone. You will find that some of these trails are literally in your backyard, and most are easily accessible on a weekend afternoon.

Are we putting you on? Not at all. Within one or two hours from midtown is a varied assortment of pleasant trails to be explored. They range from 1 to more than 200 miles in length. Most are easy, but a few are quite challenging. So come along with us. We'll show you how to find the trails and how to follow them. Also, we'll suggest what to look for on your journey and provide hints for a pleasant and safe outing.

WHY THIS BOOK?

We and our families have long enjoyed hiking while vacationing in the mountains or at the seashore. But back home we've had to hang up our boots, since it seemed the opportunities for real hiking were sparse. In spite of the fun, comradery and good exercise that hiking provides, it has not until recently been popular in Kansas City. As a hobby (and a way of reminiscing about our pleasant vacation treks), we began collecting newspaper clippings about trails in the area, talking with park rangers, investigating nature preserves and reading materials from outdoors groups. As our list of trails developed, and as we began to explore, we were amazed to find so many interesting and challenging trails so close to home. Each has its own special characteristics and points of interest.

Local government, state parks and conservation departments have been active in recent years in developing many new hiking trails, and we have them to thank for many of the walks in this book. Many private organizations are also committed to preserving nature and making it accessible to all of us. All of these agencies and foundations are listed inside the back cover of this guidebook. If you enjoy hiking these trails, please let the sponsoring organizations and representatives know. It's important that they hear how appreciative we are.

Hikes around Kansas City, and this book *Hiking Kansas City,* have come a long way. The first edition of this book, published in 1989, contained 45 trails. We are gratified that many new trails have been developed in the Kansas City area and beyond over the last 18 years. In order to provide our readers with the most current information on additions and changes, we are pleased to publish this revised and enlarged fifth edition, which now features more than 125 hikes and walks. For more trail updates, please visit www.pebblepublishing.com and click on the *Hiking Kansas City* page.

TRAIL STEWARDSHIP

The trails are there for everyone to enjoy. A major factor in their attraction is their freedom from the unsightly debris of civilization. Keeping them pristine and free of debris is up to all of us. Please don't litter on the trails. Leave them as you found them—or even better. Don't cut limbs, pick flowers or damage the ecology. Remember the Sierra Club motto: "Take only pictures... Leave only footprints..."

We hope that this book will stimulate more interest in hiking, and thus lead to the creation of even more trails. And we hope that it will help provide you many pleasant hours of walking. Happy Trails!

Dick Ballentine

Bill Eddy

HINTS FOR HAPPY & SAFE HIKING

Here are a few pointers that are important to briefly mention, especially for those who are new to trail hiking. We recommend you browse bookstores, outdoors stores and magazines for more complete information to make your hiking experience more enjoyable.

Clothing: Comfortable shoes are the most crucial item. Tennis or running shoes are okay for most Kansas City trails. Walking shoes or boots are better because of stiffer soles for rocky paths. Take a hat or sunscreen, or both, for protection from the sun. Experienced hikers wear layers of clothing that can be added or removed as weather conditions change. Long pants or high socks, even in summer, may provide needed protection against brambles, poison ivy and ticks.

Safety Points: A little preparation can prevent a miserable aftermath to a pleasant hike. Poison ivy is thick in the woods in summer. Learn to recognize it and stay away from it. Remember the phrase "Leaves of three—let it be." A hot, soapy shower afterwards may also help.

Bugs: Bugs are another category of menace, especially ticks. These tiny creatures may jump from weeds onto your skin and burrow in if not removed. Check carefully during and after hikes. Mosquitoes, flies and gnats are also ever-present. Insect repellent can ward off all of these pests.

Water: A must in hot weather. A water bottle or two is highly desirable at all times. Plenty of water helps guard against dehydration and heat exhaustion. A lightweight water bottle or canteen is a good investment. Even before you leave your car, be sure and hydrate as well as possible by drinking extra water. Be sure and take enough water with you to comfortably complete your hike. Don't drink from springs, streams or wells without treating the water.

Other Safety Concerns: These may include sunburn, overexertion, heat and accidents. Prepare for your hike, know your physical limits, take proper clothing and equipment and stay alert to protruding roots, low hanging limbs and dangerous footing such as loose rocks or ditches. Packing a first aid kit is a good idea. Never hike alone.

Disclaimer: We have walked all the trails in this book and described them as accurately as we could at the time of our visit, using maps, pedometers and park information. However, distances are estimates, trails change with time due to development or use and directions may become inaccurate. Always be sure you know how to get back to your starting point if you lose the trail.

HOW TO USE THIS BOOK

For each trail described in this book, we provide a short description that tells how to locate the trailhead (the beginning of the trail), how to follow it and some of the trail's main features. We also provide a trail map for many of the longer trails. Most of the descriptions begin with five items of information:

Time: Approximate time to hike the trail round-trip (unless otherwise noted) at a pace of about 2 miles per hour, which is a steady, but not rushed, rate and includes rest stops.

Distance: Round-trip distance, unless otherwise noted, is estimated by map or pedometer.

Rating: Our judgment of the difficulty level, including such factors as steepness, trail surface, distance, obstacles or hazards, and ease of following the trail or trail markers.

Water Availability: Public drinking fountains or other treated water sources. Some may be turned off in winter.

Accessibility: Hard-surfaced trails are more likely to accommodate strollers and the less mobile. We suggest contacting sponsoring organizations if you require more information on determining a trail's suitability for your outing.

KEY TO MAP SYMBOLS

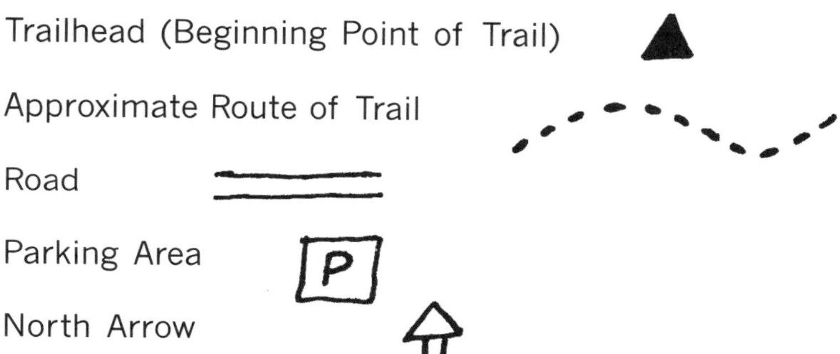

Rivers, Lakes & Other Significant Features are labeled.

Note: Maps and trail routes drawn in this book are general guides to the locations. For more exact information, contact the appropriate county, state or private agency for official maps.

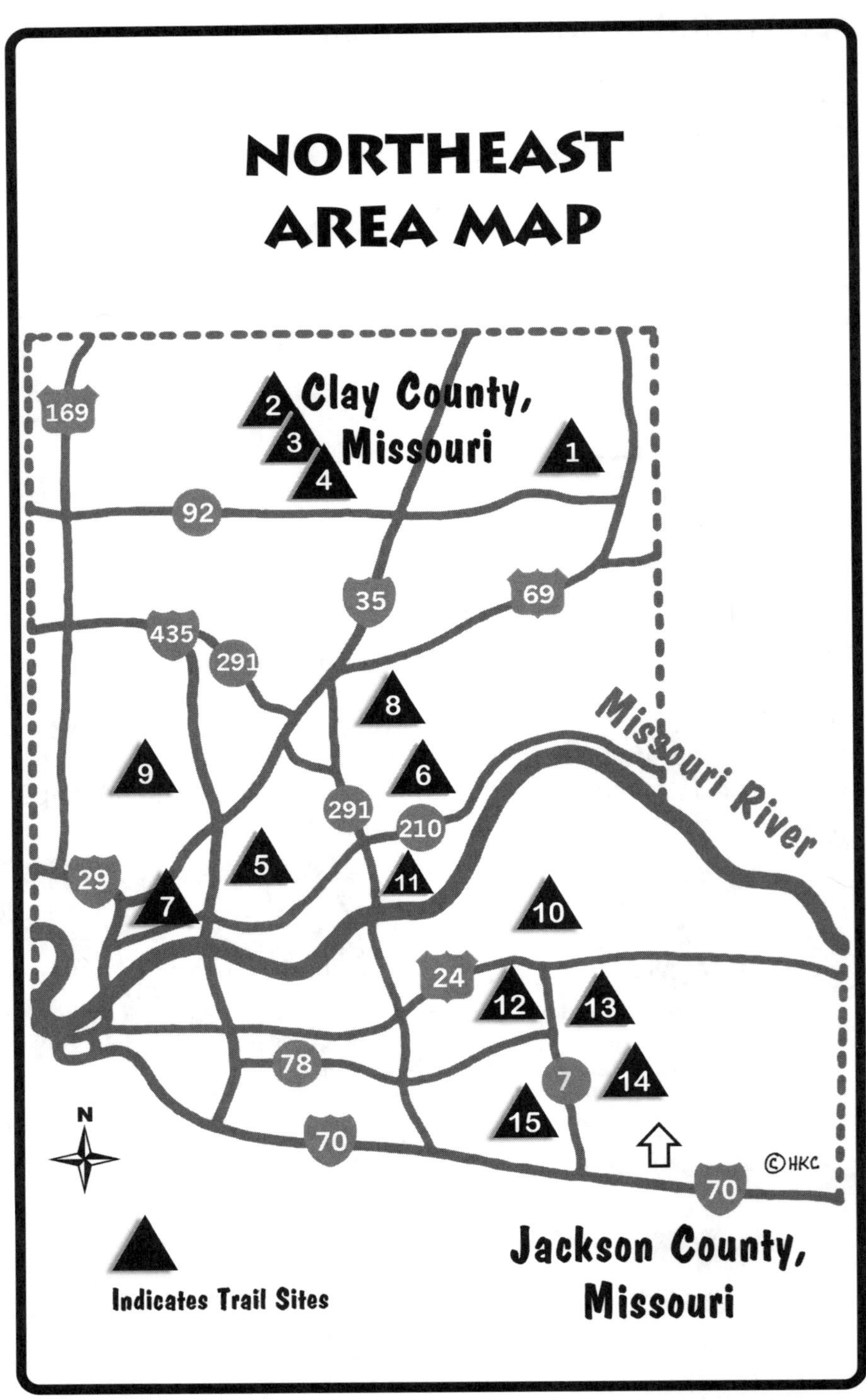
NORTHEAST
AREA MAP
Clay County,
Missouri
1
2
3
4
169
92
35
69
435
291
8
9
6
291
210
5
29
7
11
10
Missouri River
24
12
13
78
7
14
15
70
N
70
©HKC
Indicates Trail Sites
Jackson County,
Missouri

TRAIL SITES IN NORTHEAST AREA

Updated maps and other information for trails in the northern parts of the Kansas City metropolitan area can be found at www.northlandtrails.org.

Note: ( ) denotes the number of trails at that location

1
WATKINS MILL STATE PARK
Missouri Department of Natural Resources

Time: 2 Hours
Distance: 4.5 Miles
Rating: Easy

Drinking Water: Yes
Accessible: Yes, But Difficult

This asphalt hiking and bicycle trail follows the shoreline of Williams Creek Lake. The trail proceeds through rolling terrain with white oak, sycamore, burr oak, shagbark hickory, walnut and slippery elm. One may see several varieties of woodpecker, beaver and a beaver lodge. The restored Watkins Woolen Mill State Historic Site is nearby.

Directions: This park is 34 miles north of Kansas City. Take I-35 north past Liberty and exit on Hwy 92 (Exit 26). Take Hwy 92 east for 6 miles to Route RA. Turn left on RA. Go 1.1 miles to the south entrance to Watkins Mill State Park. Follow the signs to the Bike Trail.

The Watkins Mill State Park Trail: This is a 4.5-mile circuit trail around a 100-acre lake. The trailhead is well-marked. The path goes through woods and meadows, up some moderate inclines and along the lake. It is suitable for wet weather and winter hiking. Numerous restrooms, water fountains, benches, and picnic tables are located near the trail. Maps and information are available. Several great side trips include the Mt. Vernon Church, Franklin School, the Watkins Home and, of course, Watkins Mill.

Before or after your hike, visit the Watkins Home and Mill. Re-enactors are often present to demonstrate old-time skills.

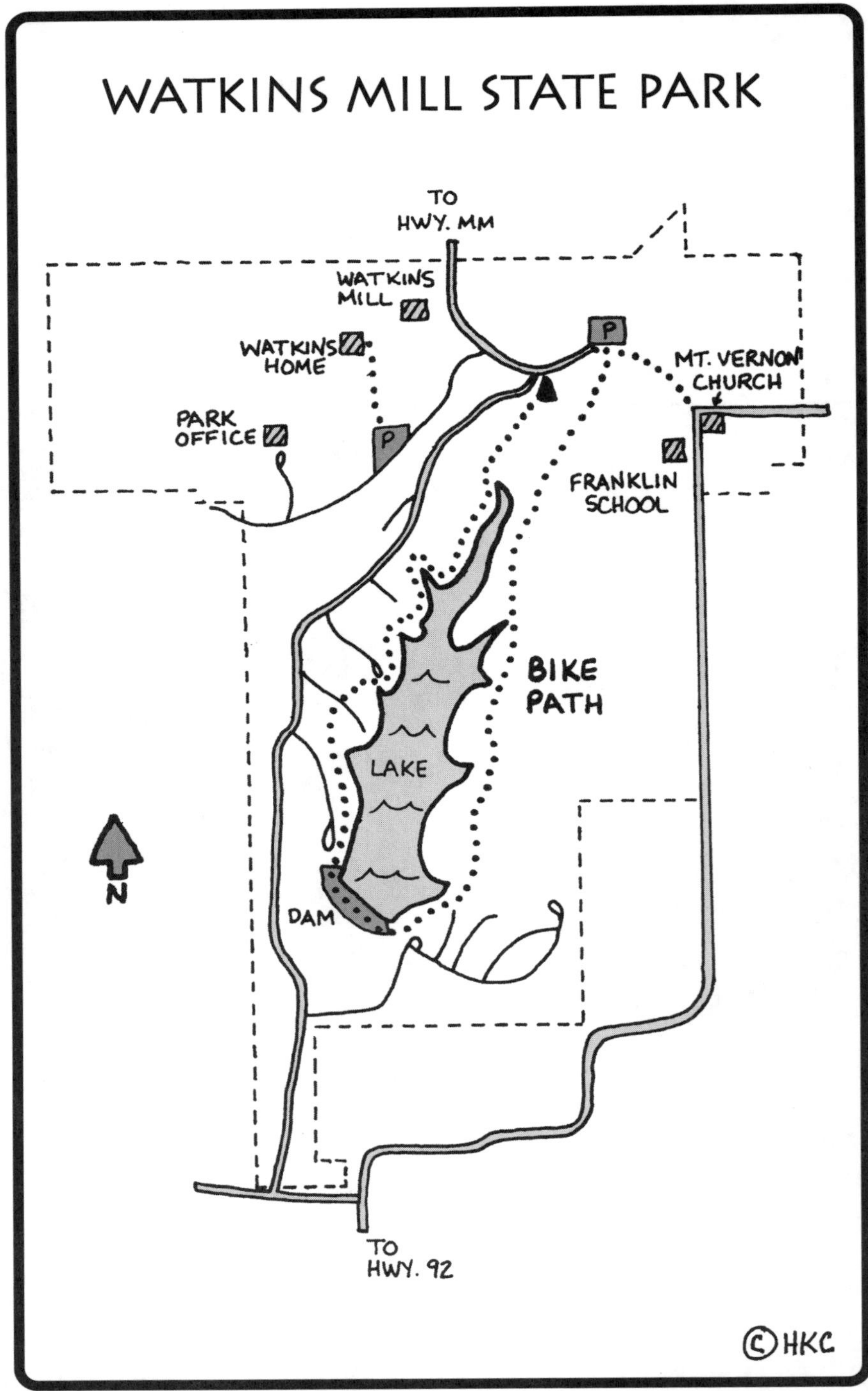
WATKINS MILL STATE PARK
TO
HWY. MM
WATKINS
MILL
WATKINS
HOME
P
MT. VERNON
CHURCH
PARK
OFFICE
P
FRANKLIN
SCHOOL
BIKE
PATH
LAKE
N
DAM
TO
HWY. 92
©HKC

The restored old woolen mill at Watkins Mill State Park is a National Historic Landmark. Its original machinery is still intact.

2
SMITHVILLE LAKE TRAIL ROUTE W TO SAILBOAT COVE (SMOKEN' DAVEY TRAILHEAD)

Clay County Department of Parks, Recreation & Historic Sites, US Army Corps of Engineers

Time: 2 Hours **Drinking Water:** Seasonally at Sailboat Cove
Distance: 4 Miles (One-way) **Accessible:** Yes
Rating: Moderate

The Smithville Lake Trail extends 20 miles (one-way) along the east shoreline of the lake. Eventually, there will be 25 miles of asphalted trail. We have divided the trail into three segments (see Trail Sites 3 and 4). This segment extends south from Route W to Sailboat Cove. Hikers will enjoy views of the large lake, native prairies and savannahs, and an abundance of birds and wilc̈s of several thousand migrating ducks and geese u̧e in the fall and spring. Bald eagle are often seen, esuring these migrations.

Directions: Drive north on U.59 and proceed 6 miles north of the intersection witri Hwy 92 to Route W. Turn right on Route W for 3 rdesignated parking area (just beyond a bridge) on youere is a sign that reads "Smoken' Davey Trailhead." is accessible from the parking lot.

Route W to Sailboat Cove Sealk south on the asphalt path. Shortly, there is an asp entering from the right. This is the winding trail show map. Take it. It will take you through rolling wooded lat gives regular views of Smithville Lake. (If you go ahead, you will be on a mile-long straight trail that ectly to the lake. If you choose this route, turn left ae and follow the winding trail for about 1.75 miles toboat Cove parking area.) On the winding trail, at aboue, there is an asphalt trail entering from the right thatownhill to an overlook of the lake. This is a very nice beware—you must walk back up the hill to continue lain winding trail.

There are several points w winding trail intersects with a straight portion (see t). These intersections give walkers an opportunity to tu the straight portion for a loop walk back to the parka or for a shorter hike to Sailboat Cove. The last oppcto make a loop walk back to the parking area is abous from the trailhead for a loop walk of less than 4 mis trail segment ends at Sailboat Cove parking area e community of Paradise. At Sailboat Cove are water, ns and a shelter.

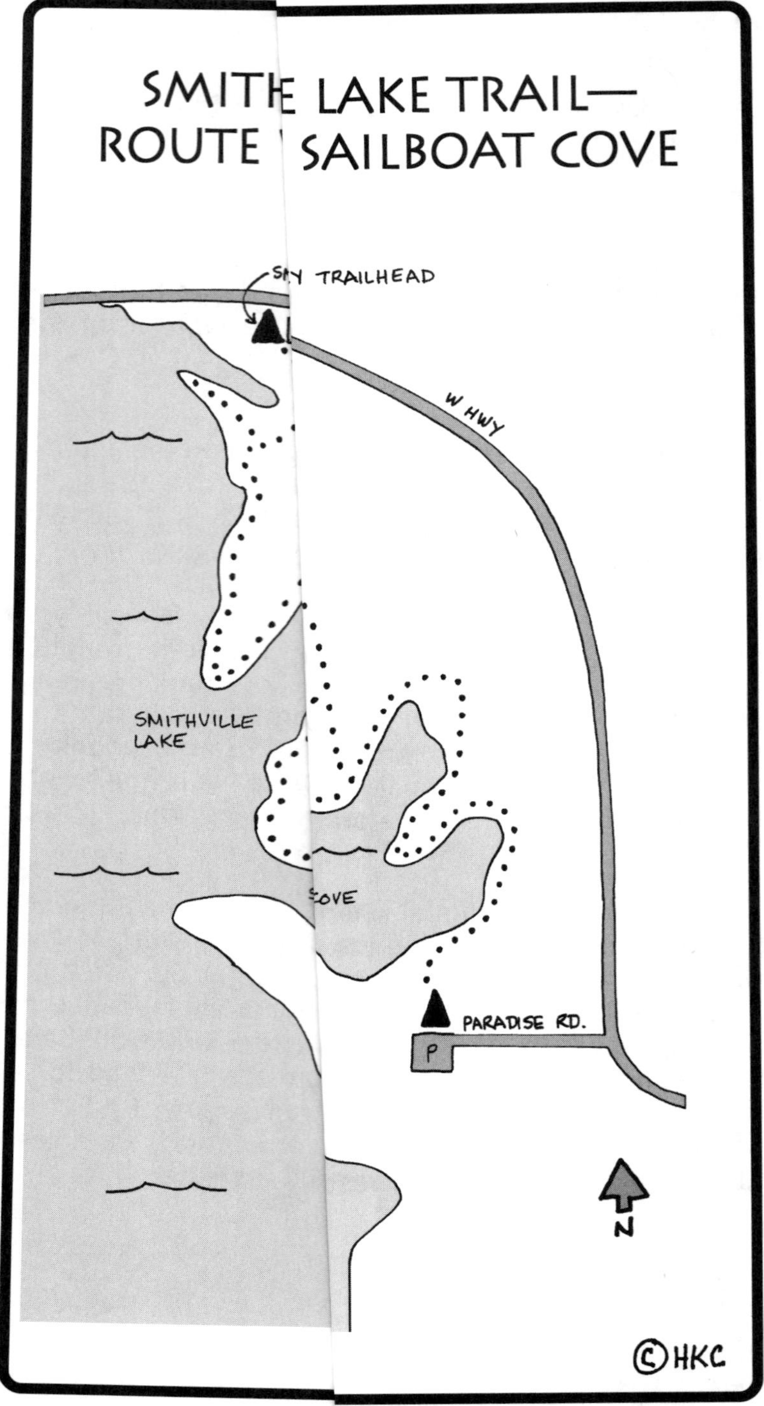
SMITH LAKE TRAIL—
ROUTE SAILBOAT COVE
TRAILHEAD
W HWY
SMITHVILLE LAKE
COVE
PARADISE RD.
P
N
©HKC

TRAIL NOTES:

3
SMITHVILLE LAKE TRAIL SAILBOAT COVE TO CAMP BRANCH PARK (BONEBENDER TRAILHEAD)

Clay County Department of Parks, Recreation & Historic Sites, US Army Corps of Engineers

Time: 2.5 to 3 Hours
Distance: 6 Miles (One-way)
Rating: Moderate
Drinking Water: Seasonally
Accessible: Yes

The Smithville Lake Trail extends 20 miles (one-way) along the east shoreline of the lake. Eventually there will be 25 miles of asphalted trail. We have divided the trail into three segments (see Trail Sites 2 and 4). This segment extends south from Sailboat Cove to Camp Branch. Hikers will enjoy views of the large lake, native prairies and savannahs, and an abundance of birds and wildlife. Flocks of several thousand migrating ducks and geese use the lake in the fall and spring. Bald eagle may be seen frequently, especially during these migrations.

Directions: The trailhead is on the east side of the lake and there are several ways to get there. One way is to drive north on U.S. 169 and proceed 6 miles north of the intersection with Missouri Hwy 92 to Route W. Turn right on Route W for 6 miles to the small settlement of Paradise where the road splits—Route W goes left and Paradise Road goes right. Turn right on Paradise Road and proceed to the Sailboat Cove parking area in about 0.5 mile. At the entrance to Sailboat Cove parking area there is a pay station. You may pay and enter the park or may find another suitable parking area.

Another way to get to the trailhead is to drive north on U.S. 169 and turn right (east) onto Hwy 92. Proceed about 6 miles to Route E. Turn left onto Route E for 3 miles to Collins Road. Turn right onto Collins Road passing Camp Branch Park and proceed about 3 miles to Paradise. Turn left on Paradise Road and proceed to the parking area for Sailboat Cove. You may choose instead to park at Camp Branch Park (there is a fee) or at the free Wildcat Holler parking area (see Trail Site 4) and walk this trail segment toward Sailboat Cove.

Several thousand migrating ducks and geese stop at Smithville Lake in the spring and fall, making encounters with wildlife a common experience.

Sailboat Cove to Camp Branch Park Trail Segment: The trailhead for this segment is at the far end of the parking lot from the pay booth. The asphalt trail heads west. At 0.1 mile, a fork enters from the left. Take it and follow it toward the lake, crossing another parking area to the south and look for the Bonebender Trailhead sign. (If you do not turn left, you proceed to a park bench and viewpoint for a round-trip walk of about 0.5 mile.) The hike has beautiful views of Smithville Lake. At 1 mile, there is a picnic table and view across the lake. The trail passes through both open and shaded areas. At about mile 4, it splits. We recommend taking the right fork that loops around the peninsula for 0.5 mile before rejoining the main trail.

When you finish the loop, you may turn right to complete the hike to Camp Branch Park or turn left to go back to Sailboat Cove for an 8.5-mile round-trip hike. To complete the hike, proceed on the trail, cross Campground Road, and hike to the end at Swim Beach. In season there are restrooms, drinking water and showers at both Sailboat Cove parking area and near the Swim Beach at Camp Branch Park. To reach the Camp Branch Park to Crows Creek Segment (Trail Site 4), you must walk to the entrance of Camp Branch Park at Collins Road and turn right across the bridge to the Wildcat Holler Trail parking area (no fee) and trailhead.

Swimmers at Smithville Lake's Ultramax Triathlon.

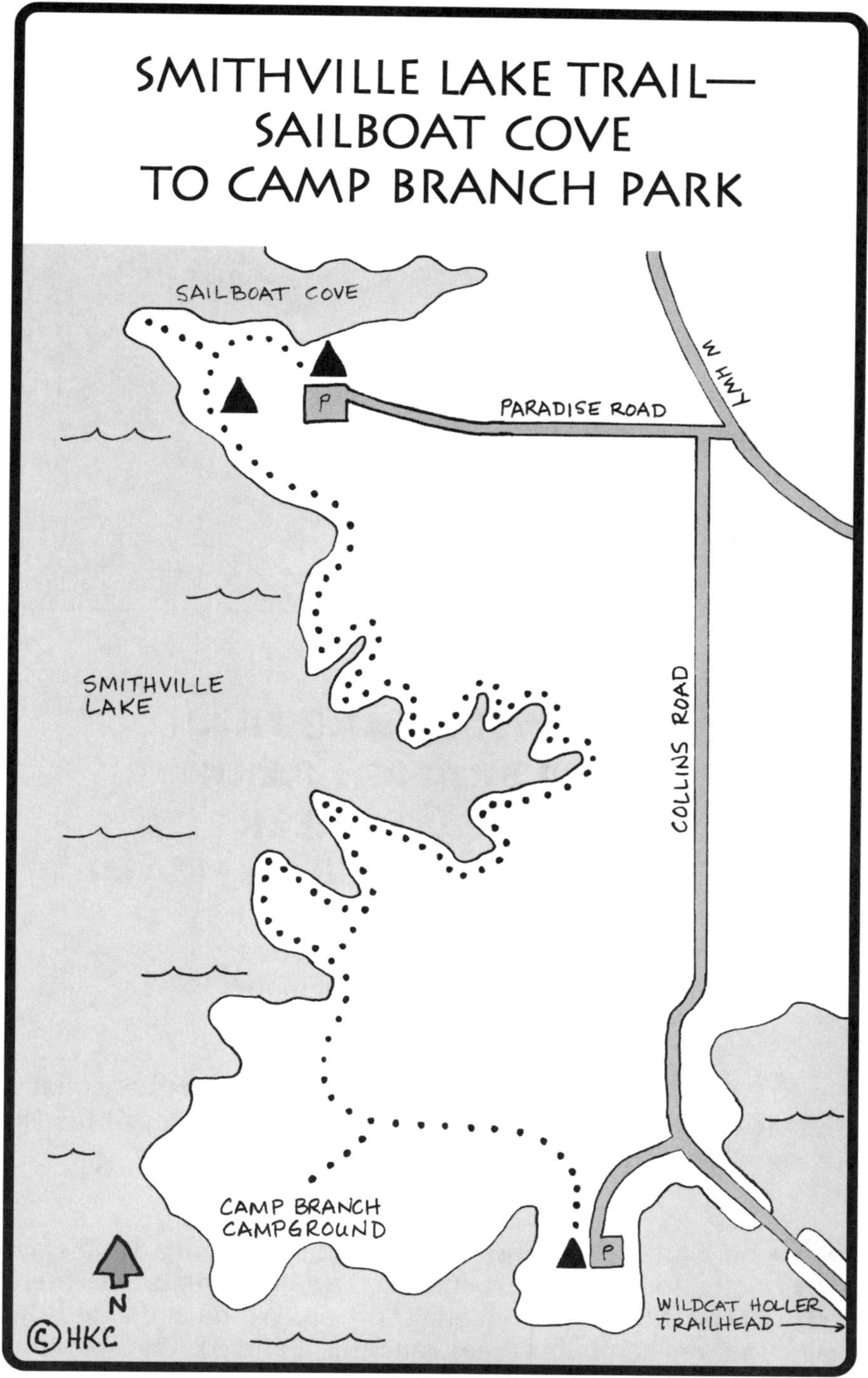
SMITHVILLE LAKE TRAIL—
SAILBOAT COVE
TO CAMP BRANCH PARK
SAILBOAT COVE
W HWY
P
PARADISE ROAD
SMITHVILLE
LAKE
COLLINS ROAD
CAMP BRANCH
CAMPGROUND
P
N
WILDCAT HOLLER
TRAILHEAD
©HKC

4
SMITHVILLE LAKE TRAIL CAMP BRANCH PARK TO CROWS CREEK (WILDCAT HOLLER TRAILHEAD)

Clay County Department of Parks, Recreation & Historic Sites, US Army Corps of Engineers

Time: 3 to 4 Hours (One-way)
Distance: 8 Miles (One-way)
Rating: Moderate
Drinking Water: Seasonally
Accessible: No

The Smithville Lake Trail extends 20 miles (one-way) along the east shoreline of the lake. Eventually, there will be 25 miles of asphalted trail. We have divided the trail into three segments (see Trail Sites 2 and 3). This segment extends south from near Camp Branch through Crows Creek Park to Access 25 (a small parking area at the end of 160th Street). Hikers will enjoy views of the large lake, native prairies and savannahs, and an abundance of birds and wildlife. Flocks of several thousand migrating ducks and geese use the lake in the fall and spring. Bald eagle are seen frequently, especially during these migrations. The Corps of Engineers' Litton Visitors Center south of the Smithville Dam is worth a visit.

Directions: The trailhead for this segment is on the southeast side of the lake. Drive north on U.S. 169 and turn right (east) onto Hwy 92. Proceed about 6 miles to Route E. Turn left onto Route E (which becomes 164th Street) for 3 miles to Collins Road. Turn right on Collins Road for 1.2 miles to a sign for Wildcat Holler Trail. This is the entrance to the parking lot and trailhead. It is the last drive on your left before crossing over the bridge. If you reach the bridge or the entrance to Camp Branch Park, you've gone too far. Park in the lot (no fee).

Camp Branch Park to Crows Creek Segment (Wildcat Holler Trail): The trailhead for this asphalt trail is at the northwest edge of the parking area. Walk south (left) on the trail. The hike provides a beautiful 8-mile (one-way) walk along the shoreline of Smithville Lake. You will walk through wooded areas, prairies and near campgrounds that have restrooms and shelters. A horseback riding trail intersects the walking trail in a few places. At Crows Creek Campground is the Cabin Fever Trailhead to this trail.

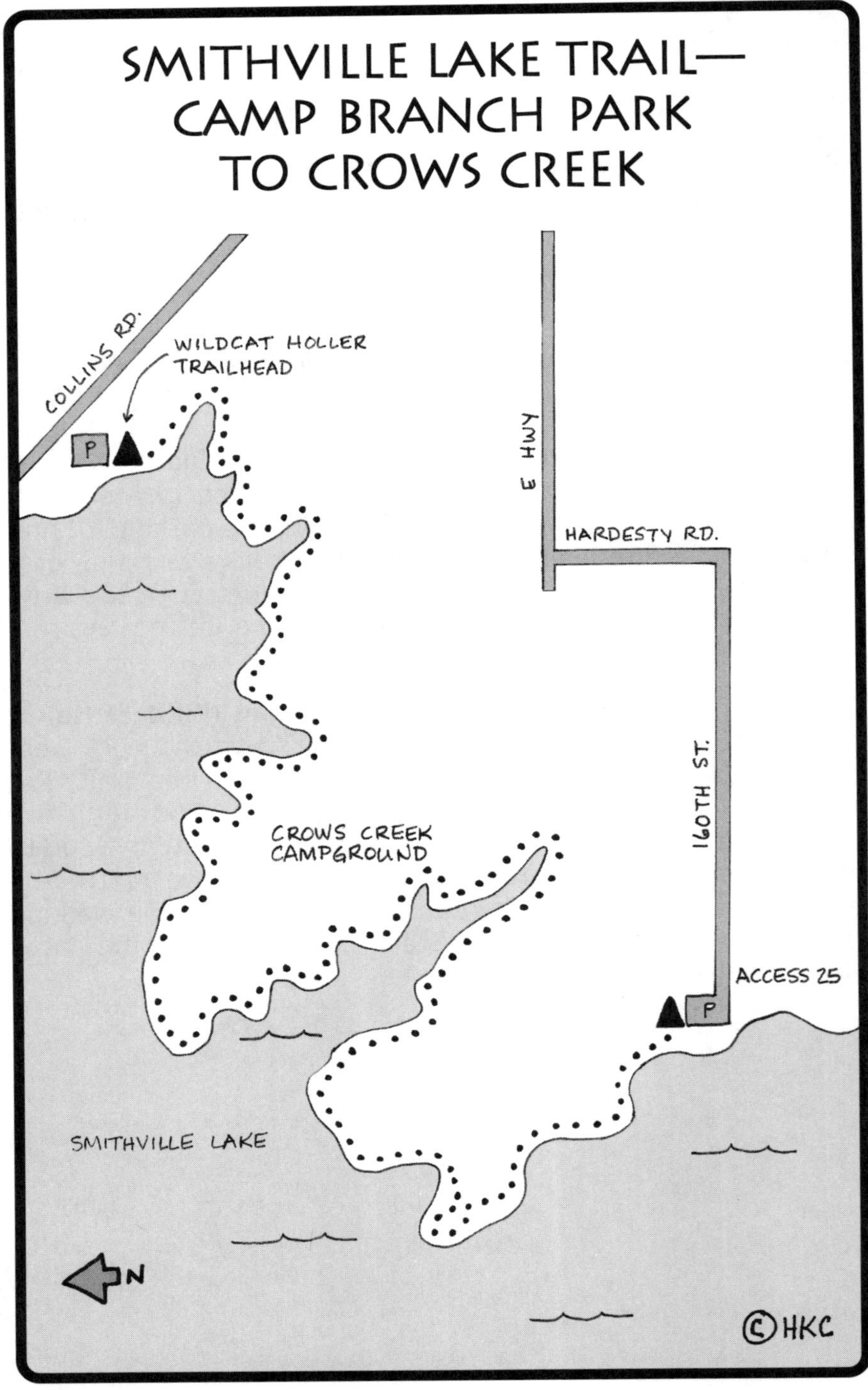
SMITHVILLE LAKE TRAIL—
CAMP BRANCH PARK
TO CROWS CREEK
COLLINS RD.
WILDCAT HOLLER
TRAILHEAD
P
E HWY
HARDESTY RD.
160TH ST.
CROWS CREEK
CAMPGROUND
ACCESS 25
P
SMITHVILLE LAKE
N
©HKC

You may find yourself sharing the trail with some hard-headed lolly gaggers.

5
WALKS IN THE NORTHLAND

New trails are being developed in the Kansas City Metropolitan Area almost faster than your authors can keep up with them. Here are some of the opportunities for pleasant walks "north of the river."

Hodge Park: Shoal Creek Living History Museum in Hodge Park is owned by Kansas City Parks, Recreation and Boulevards and operated by the Shoal Creek Association—a volunteer organization. It offers a worthwhile series of mowed pathways that traverse native grasslands and upland forests away from the city. Bobcats, deer, wild turkey, bluebirds and many other critters inhabit the area. Also, you can explore a cluster of 19th Century historic buildings assembled to interpret Missouri's early history. From I-435 north of the Missouri River turn east on Missouri Hwy 152, and in 1.2 miles turn left (north) on North Shoal Creek Parkway, and then in 0.1 mile turn left on N.E. Barry Road. Hodge Park is 0.7 mile ahead. Follow the road into the park until it ends at a parking lot. Here you will see previews of the Living History Museum, including a covered wagon. Park and walk up the gravel pathway for 0.3 mile to the old village. Check at the brick mansion or one of the other shops for a map of the trails, which begin just to the left of the mansion and wander for about 2 miles. There is no shade on much of the route. It is best to call ahead: (816) 792-2655. Events and celebrations, such as the annual Wilderness Run in November, may cause the trail system to be closed to walkers.

Excelsior Springs Walking Paths: In Excelsior Springs, the Fishing River runs at the foot of a large hill called Siloam Mountain. On either side of the river there are walking paths of approximately 1 mile each way. The Fishing River Linear Park contains a paved walkway that follows the north side under Isley Boulevard and into downtown Excelsior Springs. It passes recreation areas and the Hall of Waters, an attraction from the days when Excelsior Springs was a famous spa.

The Elms Hotel–Airport Trail begins in a park on the south side of the river and makes its way south and west above East Valley Road. The north-facing slope of Siloam Mountain is Isley Park and within the park is a 15-acre State Natural Area that is the home of many wildflowers, birds and animals. The trail is a pleasant, tree-shaded walkway that is paved until it winds its way around the west end of Siloam Mountain and becomes a natural-surface path in more dense foliage. It ascends to a grassy picnic area at the top of the hill—a rigorous but fairly short climb with occasional steps to assist. There are plans to connect it with Garland Avenue on the south side of the hill where it is within easy walking distance of the Elms Hotel. (For more information about Isley Park Woods Natural Area, read *Kansas City WildLands* by Larry Rizzo, published by the Missouri Department of Conservation.)

Directions: To reach these Excelsior Springs trails, drive north of Kansas City, Missouri on U.S. Hwy 69. At the exit for Missouri Hwy 10, turn east, drive into Excelsior Springs, and follow Hwy 10 (Isley Boulevard) through town, past the Elms Hotel to Golf Street (which is named Calhoun Street, north of Isley Boulevard). Turn south on Golf Drive and drive to the sign for the Fishing River Linear Park. Across the river is the access to the other trail.

Happy Rock Park: Owned by the City of Gladstone and located at 7601 N.E. Antioch Road, this multi-use park contains an asphalt walking path around the perimeter of athletic fields and through woods. Take I-35 north and turn off at Exit 8C onto Antioch Road. Stay on Antioch Road north for about 4.5 miles until you come to the park. Turn in and park in one of the lots. The trail circling the complex can be accessed at any convenient point for a walk of over 1 mile.

Anita B. Gorman Park: Located at the southeast corner of the intersection of Vivion Road and North Oak Trafficway, this park provides about a mile of walking along two pathways leading east from the Park. The Recreation Trail from the southeast corner of the park leads eastward along a narrow road and through woods to a YMCA complex. The Vivion Road trail departs from the northeast corner of the park and travels eastward along Vivion Road. A street from the YMCA to Vivion Road provides a way to connect the two trails.

Oak Grove Park: This pleasant suburban park at N.E. 76th Street and North Troost, a few blocks east of North Oak Trafficway, offers a walking path of about a mile around the perimeter. It is heavily used by those in the neighborhood.

Macken Park: This attractive multi-use park in North Kansas City provides a lighted 1-mile asphalt walking path around the perimeter. From Armour Road (between I-35 and Burlington in downtown North Kansas City), take Howell north for 7 blocks.

The sun setting behind prairie grass in Kansas City's northland.

TRAIL NOTES:

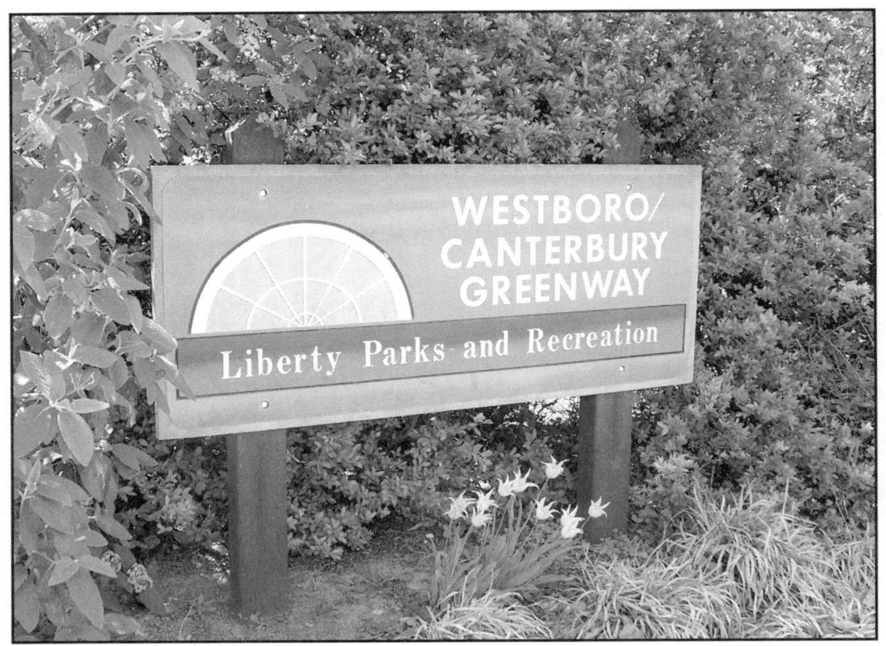

6
LIBERTY PARKS & GREENWAYS TRAILS

The City of Liberty, Missouri is building walking paths in its parks. Some are wood-chipped dirt paths and some are paved routes along streets and highways. We've highlighted some of the longer ones.

Ruth Stockdale Park: A series of footpaths meanders through this 112-acre park and adjacent Walnut Woods Natural History Area in eastern Liberty. Take Richfield Road east from Leonard Street (Hwy 33) in downtown Liberty and turn south on LaFrenz Road. The road bends left and then right and in about a mile arrives at the park on the left side. Park in the parking area and walk east to the playground. An asphalt trail leads into the woods where it connects with several natural-surface loop paths for a total of 1.5 miles. You will enjoy pleasant walking through thick woods and open prairie.

Westboro Canterbury Greenway: This is a 42-acre greenway along two creeks. Approximately 0.8 mile south of the intersection of Hwys 152 and 291, turn south off Hwy 291 onto Liberty Drive and turn immediately onto Fullerton Street. Go south on Fullerton for 0.3 mile until you spot signs and parking space for the Greenway on the right. An asphalt path leads southwest, and presently, there is a spur along a creek that goes north. This area provides 2 miles (one-way) of enjoyable, all-weather walking.

Liberty, Missouri is just a short drive from Kansas City. Hikers going there will be rewarded with nice paths through historic neighborhoods.

Cates Creek Greenway: This asphalt path parallels Hwy 291 for 2 miles. It can be accessed from several intersections, including Magnolia Avenue and Missouri Street. The pathway is largely without shade and is suited to jogging and bicycling.

Fountain Bluff Walkways: In the Fountain Bluff Sports Complex in southeast Liberty, paved walks connect and circle the many athletic fields for a total of 2.25 miles—a good spot for early morning or evening strolls. The complex is about a mile east of Hwy 291 on Old Missouri Hwy 210/Seven Hills Road.

Enjoy the picturesque creek crossings on the Westboro Canterbury Greenway.

OSAGE TRAIL NAMES IN JACKSON COUNTY PARKS

Some of the trails in Jackson County Parks are named after the Osage. The names and their meanings are listed here and are also found on trailhead signs.

Pa-Huska Nature Trail, Sailboat Cove, "Head Osage Indian Chief"

Clermont Nature Trail, Missouri Town Trail, "Soldier of Oaks" Arkansas Band Osage Chief

Shin-Ga-Wa-Sa Nature Trail, Longview Lake Campground, "Beautiful Bird" Warrior who signed 1885 treaty

Tchong-Tas-Sab-Bee Nature Trail, Landahl Park Trails, Truman Road, "Black Dog" Chief of the Upland Forest Group

Washingsabba Nature Trail, Landahl Park, Argo Road Trails, "Black Spirit"

Wa-Cesh-Uk Nature Trail, Blue and Gray Campground 0.5 mile loop, "War"

Mar-Chark-Ita-Toon-Hah Nature Trail, Monkey Mountain Nature Trail, "Walking Newspaper" Big Soldier

Wa-Mash-Ed-Sheek Fitness Trail, Sports Complex, "He Who Takes Away" (not featured in this book)

Mun-Ni-Pus-Kee, Hoofed Animal Enclosure, Lake Jacomo, "He Who is Not Afraid"

Note: The Jackson County Parks and Recreation Department has an "Adopt A Trail" Program. Individuals or organizations may have their names placed on a sign at the trailhead by agreeing to provide inspection and maintenance for one of the county's trails. Call (816) 229-8980 for more information.

7
HIDDEN VALLEY NATURAL AREA
Kansas City Parks & Recreation Department

Time: 1 Hour
Distance: 1.4 Miles
Rating: Moderate

Drinking Water: No
Accessible: No

An interesting walk in a rugged and densely wooded park with old-growth maple, oak and sycamore trees can be found here. Designated a natural area by the Missouri Department of Conservation, this site features a reward at the end of the trail.

Directions: Just north of the Missouri River on I-35, turn east on Hwy 210 (Armour Road) and go 1.7 miles. Turn north on Searcy Creek Parkway. In 1 mile, turn east on Russell Road. Follow it 0.5 mile to a parking area on top of the hill, on the north side of the road.

Hidden Valley Trail: This walk begins on the south side of Russell Road across from the parking area. Follow a wood-chipped path through a large meadow to a path into the woods at the southeast corner. The trail passes through two densely wooded valleys and two open hilltops.

On the second hilltop, at about 0.4 mile, the path intersects a narrow dirt road. Follow this road to the right for about 0.1 mile to where it ends at a large log platform that looks out over a deep ravine. If you sit quietly, you will see and hear birds and other wildlife. This is a good place for a picnic. South of this platform lies Hidden Valley—an area with wooded hills and ravines. Several paths wander through the area. To explore this area, walk south from the platform following the edge of the field for 0.25 mile until you come to a pathway on the right that leads into the woods. Improvements for the Hidden Valley Natural Area began in 2006. Grants from Kansas City's Public Improvements Advisory Committee (PIAC) are providing funds for a comprehensive plan for protection and restoration of the area and the development of a trail system.

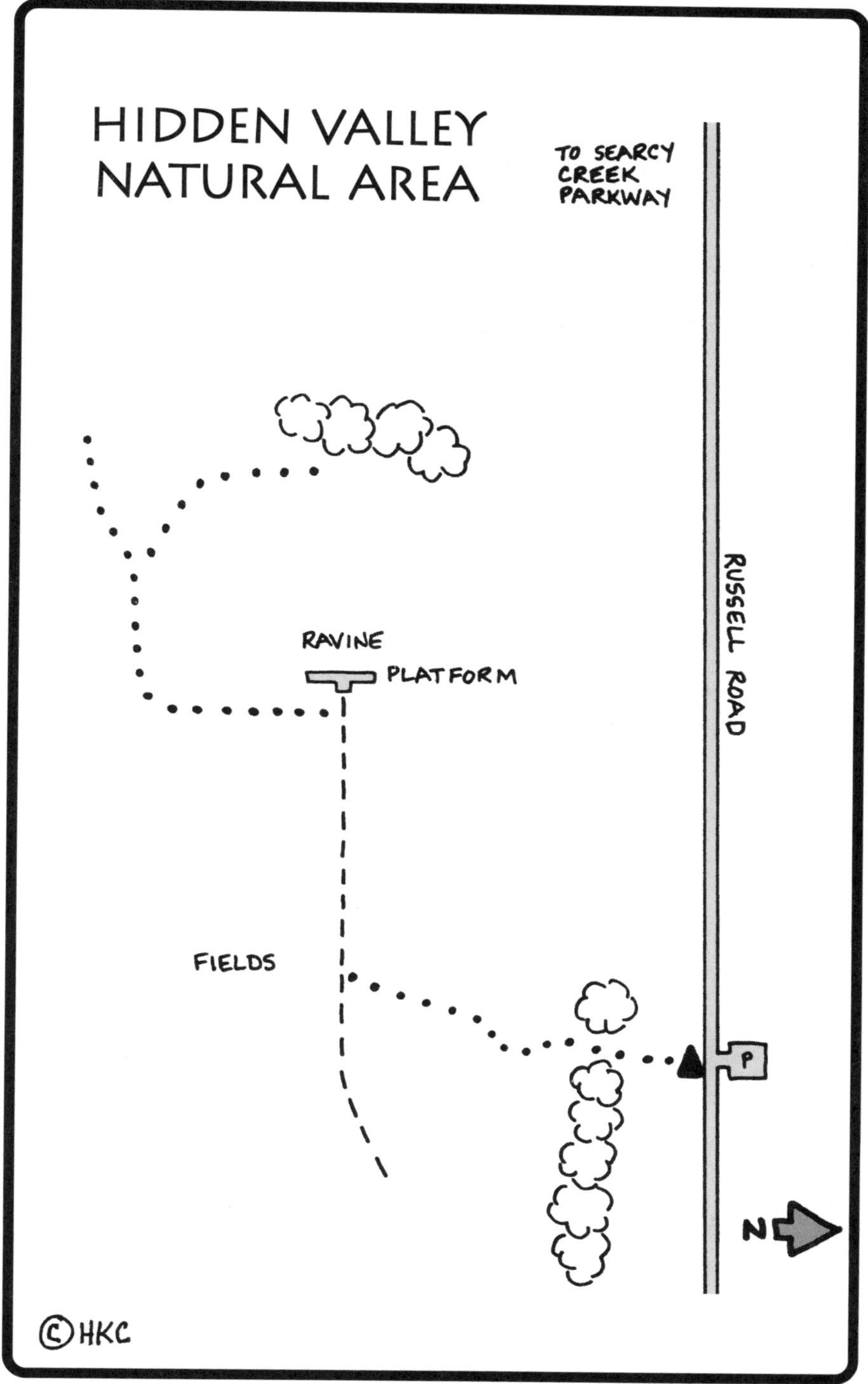
HIDDEN VALLEY
NATURAL AREA
TO SEARCY
CREEK
PARKWAY
RUSSELL ROAD
RAVINE
PLATFORM
FIELDS
P
N
©HKC

Tawnee Dufur explores the nature sanctuary's winding trails.

8
MARTHA LAFITE THOMPSON NATURE SANCTUARY

Time: 1 to 2 Hours
Distance: 3.5 Miles
Rating: Easy

Drinking Water: Yes
Accessible: Portions

This nature sanctuary, located on the eastern edge of Liberty, Missouri, is a nature lover's prize. It is a private, non-profit oasis with a series of carefully maintained, attractive short loop trails.

Directions: The sanctuary is relatively close to the William Jewell campus. Drive north on I-35 to the Liberty Exit for Hwy 152 east. Continue on 152 (Kansas Street) through the downtown square to Lightburne Street. Turn right and go 1 block. At the traffic light, turn left onto Mill Street/Hwy H. Continue on Mill Street for 2 blocks, and at the light, follow Mill to the right. Go over railroad tracks and a bridge. The first left is LaFrenz Road, 0.5 mile from the bridge. Turn left on LaFrenz and go 0.25 mile to the nature sanctuary entrance.

Turn right into the drive. Parking is available by the picnic shelter and the nature center, where maps and other information is available. Trails are open every day from 8:30 a.m. until sunset. There is an outdoor water fountain at the nature center entrance. Bikes and pets are not permitted on the trails.

Woodland Trail begins on the north side of the road across from the picnic shelter. It loops through woods, past a pond and along Rush Creek, before returning to its beginning point.

Rush Creek Trail begins at the picnic shelter. This trail is paved from the picnic shelter to the creek overlook and has an accessible grade. It is 0.5 mile each way. The trail continues, unpaved, crossing the creek twice and looping back to connect to the paved portion.

Wornall Trail begins just behind the nature center. It is an all-weather asphalt trail, providing easy access for strollers but is too steep for wheelchairs.

Prairie Trail and South Meadow Trail are southeast of the shelter. They can be reached from the Rush Creek or Wornall Trails. They form a series of three short loops for a walk of about a mile.

Bridge Spur Trail begins at the Rush Creek overlook, accessible by taking the Rush Creek Trail. The short spur follows Rush Creek through a wooded bottom and ends with a nice view of an interurban railroad bridge built in 1927.

Be sure to allow time to visit the nature center, library and great gift shop.

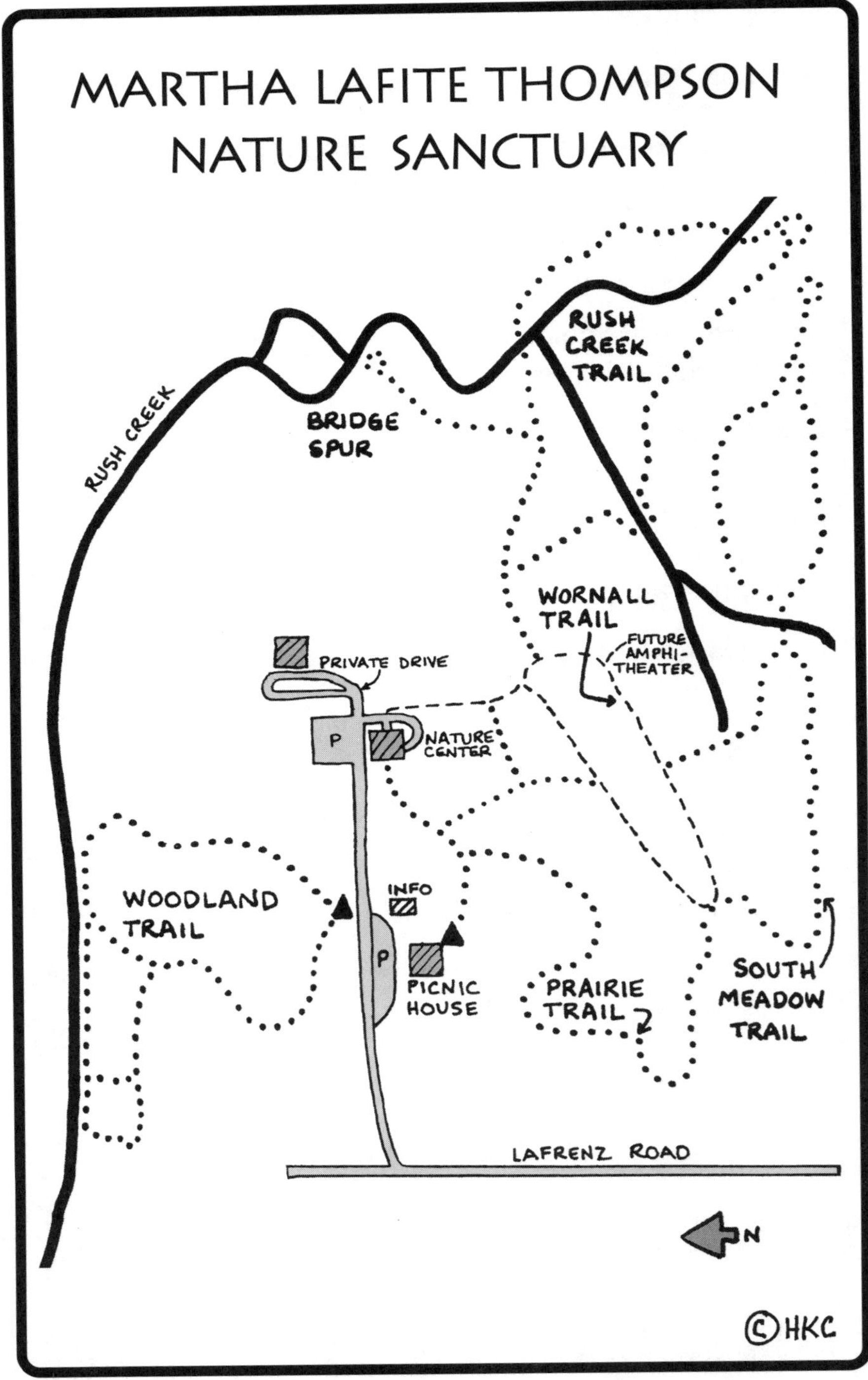
MARTHA LAFITE THOMPSON
NATURE SANCTUARY
RUSH CREEK
BRIDGE SPUR
RUSH CREEK TRAIL
WORNALL TRAIL
FUTURE AMPHI-THEATER
PRIVATE DRIVE
P
NATURE CENTER
WOODLAND TRAIL
INFO
P
PICNIC HOUSE
PRAIRIE TRAIL
SOUTH MEADOW TRAIL
LAFRENZ ROAD
N
©HKC

Follow the Bridge Spur Trail along Rush Creek through a wooded bottom to a nice view of a railroad bridge built in 1927.

9
MAPLE WOODS NATURE PRESERVE

Missouri Department of Conservation, the Nature Conservancy & City of Gladstone

Time: 0.5 Hour
Distance: 1.4 Miles
Rating: Easy

Drinking Water: No
Accessible: No

This 40-acre tract is a joint project of the Missouri Department of Conservation, the Nature Conservancy and the City of Gladstone. It preserves one of the largest stands of old-growth maple trees in the Midwest.

Directions: The preserve can be reached by driving north on North Oak Trafficway, then east on 76th Street to what would be Prospect if the street ran through. Once on 76th Street, go approximately 1.5 miles to reach the parking area. Or, from eastern Kansas City, Missouri, take I-435 north to Hwy 152. Turn west on Hwy 152 and travel 1.5 miles to Hwy 1. Go south on Hwy 1 for 0.5 mile to Maple Woods Parkway, which enters from the right and follow it south (it becomes 76th Street) 0.7 mile to the parking lot on the left just before a hill.

Maple Woods Trail: Leave your car in the parking area south of 76th Street, cross the footbridge and take the trail to the right. It will take you around the perimeter of the park if you take the right fork at each opportunity. Several interior trails bisect the loop and allow for a hike of 1.4 miles. As you walk this trail, keep an eye out for the large old-growth maple trees. They are rare in our area. This is a good autumn walk.

Maple Woods allows hikers to enjoy rare, old-growth maple.

10
RIVER BLUFF NATURE RESERVE
Jackson County Parks & Recreation Department

Time: 2 Hours
Distance: 2.6 Miles
Rating: Difficult
Drinking Water: No
Accessible: No

This primitive loop trail through the bluffs south of the Missouri River provides a challenging, but rewarding, hike through dense woods, along steep hillsides and beside limestone cliffs.

Directions: Drive east on either Hwy 24 or I-70 to Hwy 291. From I-70, turn north (or from Hwy 24 turn south) on 291 to Courtney Road, which is the first road south of Liberty Bridge over the Missouri River. Turn east on Courtney Road for 0.7 mile, then turn abruptly left on Courtney-Atherton Road for 0.9 mile to a parking area and trailhead on the left side.

River Bluff Nature Trail: From the parking area, the trail descends to the north, crosses a creek and turns left along the edge of a field. It then enters deep woods and follows a twisting route up and down steep hills and across small streams. The trail then crosses a meadow and returns to woods along the top of a limestone bluff. At the west end of the ridge, one must climb down a rock ledge to find the trail that heads back east on the north side of the bluffs. In about 0.5 mile, the path turns uphill (south) and rejoins the trail on the ridge. You can then return to the trailhead by retracing the route through the woods. Or, about 0.25 mile east of the trail junction, there is a dirt road that skirts private property and leads back to Courtney-Atherton Road about 0.2 mile west of the trailhead. We recommend good hiking boots, long pants, insect repellent and drinking water for this hike.

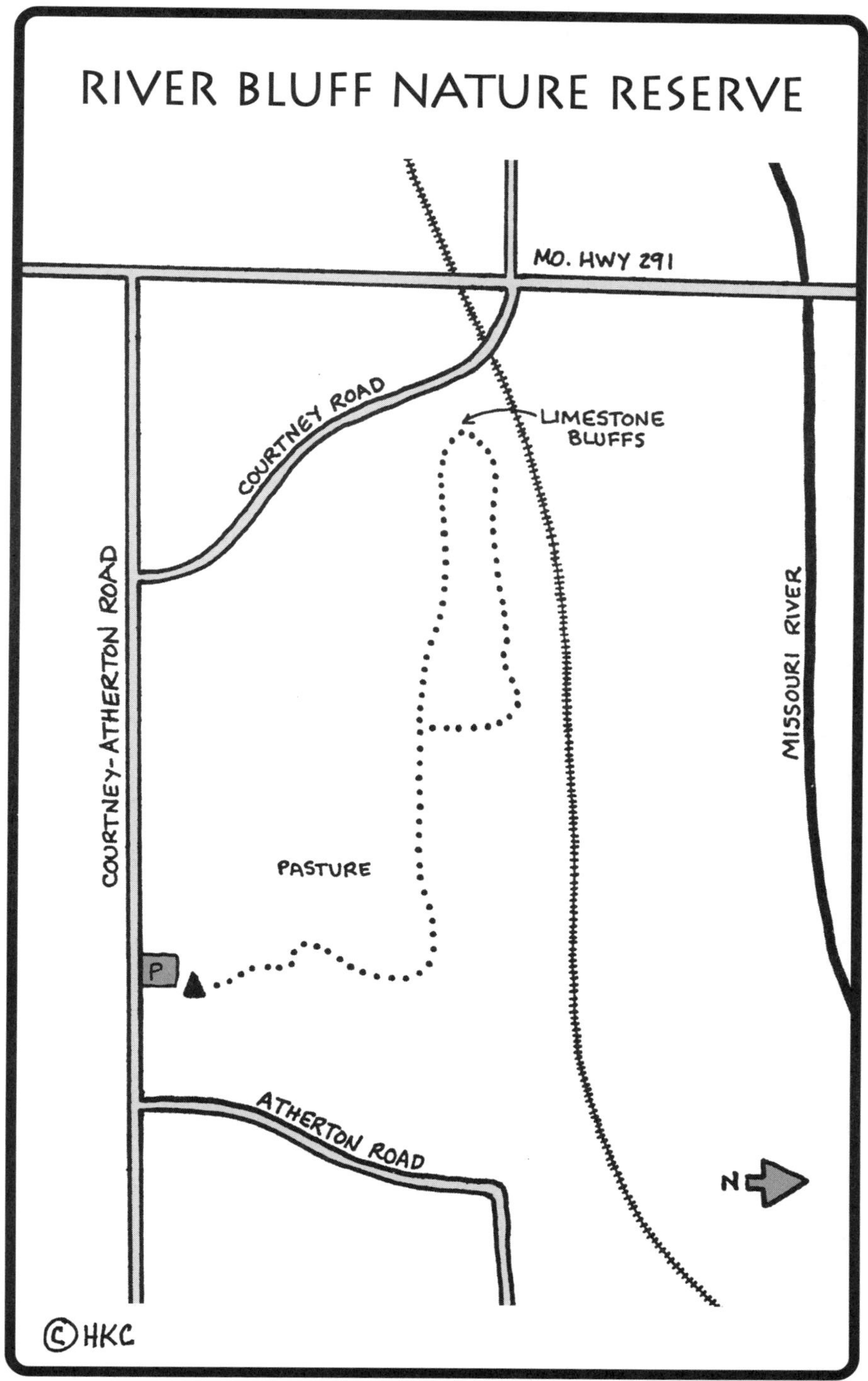
RIVER BLUFF NATURE RESERVE
MO. HWY 291
COURTNEY ROAD
LIMESTONE BLUFFS
COURTNEY-ATHERTON ROAD
MISSOURI RIVER
PASTURE
P
ATHERTON ROAD
N
©HKC

11
LaBENITE PARK
Sugar Creek, Missouri

Time: 1.5 Hours
Distance: 3.4 (Round-trip)
Rating: Easy

Drinking Water: No
Accessible: No

This park borders the south bank of the Missouri River. The trail parallels the river while proceeding through thick woods and meadows.

Directions: The park is on Missouri Hwy 291 just south of the Liberty Bridge over the Missouri River. Route 291 can be reached from I-70 or Missouri Hwy 210.

The LaBenite Trail: As you drive into the park, go to the right to the east end of the parking lot. The trail starts there. The path is wide and mulched—an advantage in summer when ticks are clinging to grass and weeds. There are occasional informational signs. The trail parallels the Missouri River for 1.7 miles, providing many good views. Once you've gone far enough to enjoy the solitude the river provides, it is easy to be reminded of Lewis and Clark's early Missouri. Plans are in the works to extend this trail.

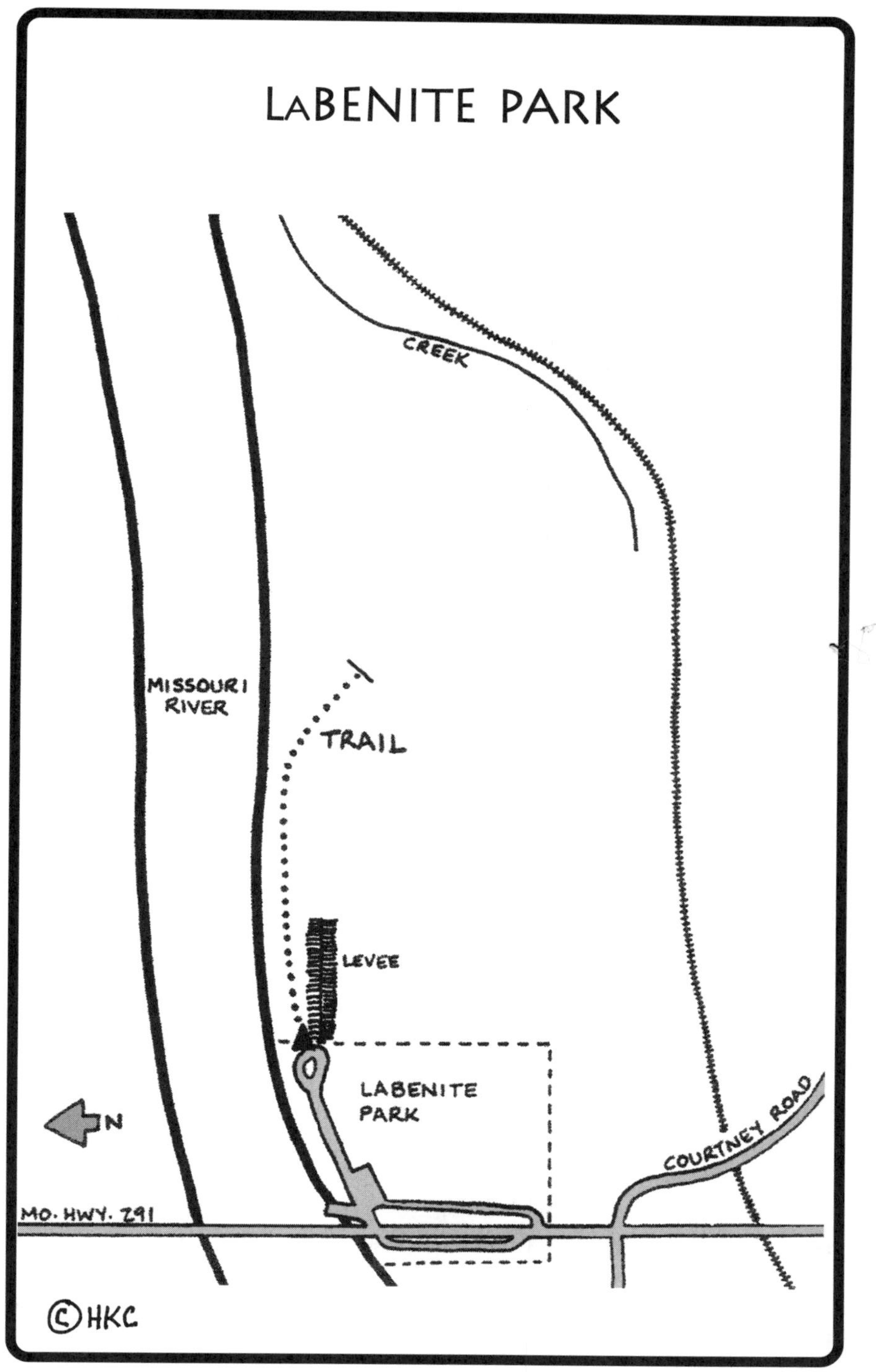
LaBENITE PARK
CREEK
MISSOURI
RIVER
TRAIL
LEVEE
LABENITE
PARK
N
COURTNEY ROAD
MO. HWY. 291
©HKC

12
LITTLE BLUE TRACE
Jackson County Parks & Recreation Department

Time: 4 to 5.5 Hours
Distance: 10 Miles One-way (20 Round-trip)
Rating: Easy
Drinking Water: No
Accessible: Yes

This is an all-weather hiking and biking trail, which follows the Little Blue River in northeastern Jackson County. It is well laid out and features shelter houses and restrooms about every 2 miles. The trail passes through open valleys, meadows and heavily wooded areas. On hot sunny days, hike the trail in the early morning, because much of it has no shade from the midday sun. For those who want to see the entire trail, but do not wish to walk for 20 miles, a second car can be left at one of the parking areas along the route so you can drive back to the beginning point. Small children will enjoy this easy trail.

Directions: There are several access points, as indicated on the map. The south trailhead is just north of I-70 at a large parking area on the east side of South Little Blue Parkway. Use Exit 17. All the other access points can be reached from Hwy 291 north of I-70 as shown on the map. Our trail description begins in about the middle of the trail. To reach the trailhead shown on the map, take Hwy 291 north to Hwy 78. Follow Hwy 78 east for 4.6 miles to Fisher Road, which is opposite the park entrance where the trail begins. (Fisher Road is 1.5 miles from the intersection of Hwy 78 and Truman Road, a 4-way stop, and about 0.2 mile beyond the bridge over the Little Blue River.) At Fisher Road, turn north and park near the shelter house. The trail, a wide gravel path, heads north just to the east of the shelter and is marked as a bicycle trail. If you wish to walk south, head west from the parking area.

The Little Blue Trace Trail: The route north from the trailhead at Hwy 78 proceeds through meadows and woods, across a footbridge and along the edge of farm fields in the Little Blue Valley. At about 2 miles the trail goes under Bundschu Road. At 3.5 miles there is another shelter and, in the southeast corner of the parking lot, a Civil War monument (not well-marked) describing the battle that took place in the area on October 21, 1864. The trail then passes under Hwy 24 and ends at 4.5 miles at a shelter on Blue Mills Road. Blue Mill was an early day landing on the Missouri River. None of the shelters have running water. Return the way you came for a round trip of about 9 miles. Including snack stops, it will take about 4 hours.

Heading south from the trailhead at Hwy 78, follow the path west from the parking area, cross the highway and walk 0.1 mile west across the bridge. Then turn south on the trail. The path follows the river through meadows and woods with nice vistas. The trail goes under Truman Road and at 2.2 miles, crosses a footbridge. Continue 1.3 miles to the parking lot at Necessary Road. From there, it is 2 miles more to the parking area on Little Blue Parkway for a one-way hike of 5.5 miles, 11 round trip. It is possible to extend your walk 1.5 miles by walking south on the sidewalk along Little Blue Parkway, across the bridge and then turning left and walking the paved path. It ends in 0.75 mile at I-70.

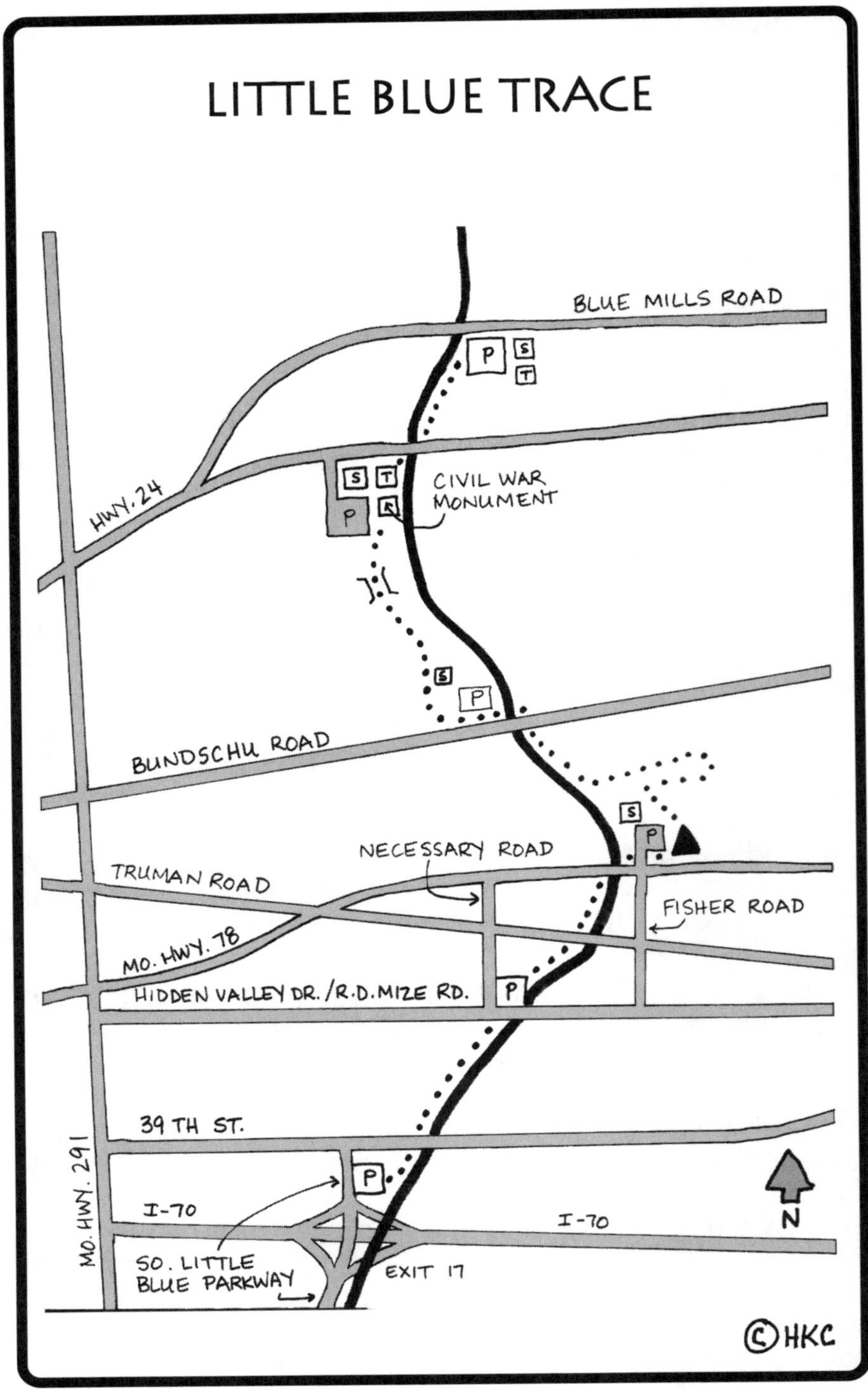
LITTLE BLUE TRACE
BLUE MILLS ROAD
HWY. 24
CIVIL WAR MONUMENT
BUNDSCHU ROAD
NECESSARY ROAD
TRUMAN ROAD
FISHER ROAD
MO. HWY. 78
HIDDEN VALLEY DR. /R.D. MIZE RD.
39 TH ST.
MO. HWY. 291
I-70
I-70
SO. LITTLE BLUE PARKWAY
EXIT 17
N
©HKC

A Civil War battle took place in this area in October of 1864.

Winners of the Fat Tire Mountain Bike Race show off their trophies.

13
LANDAHL PARK – NORTH TRAIL
Jackson County Parks & Recreation Department

Time: 2 Hours
Distance: 3.6 Miles
Rating: Moderate to Difficult
Drinking Water: No
Accessible: No

Landahl Park (formerly Lake City Park) is named for the late Bill Landahl, who was for many years Director of Parks in Jackson County, Missouri. It is a fitting tribute to the man whose vision led to the acquisition of much of the acreage that forms the beautiful Jackson County Park system. Three loop trails of 0.6, 1.3 and 3.6 miles in this park provide very pleasant hikes through a variety of terrain and offer several vistas of the surrounding countryside. There is also a system of trails developed by mountain bikers. Links to maps can be found at www.earthriders.org.

Directions: The park is midway between Hwy 24 on the north and I-70 on the south. Turn onto Hwy 7. At Route FF (Truman Road), turn east. A mile after passing Owens School Road, on the right is a parking area, shelter and restroom. There may be a sign, "Truman Shelter." Park here.

The Landahl Park–North Trail: Named the Tchong-Tas-Sab-Bee Nature Trail, the trailhead is a footbridge 75 yards southwest of the shelter, hidden by trees. Cross the bridge and go through a field. At the gravel road, turn right and go about 50 yards, then go left up a hill. At the first fork, bear right to the top of the sledding hill to enjoy a nice view. Follow the trail to the right until the next fork (at about 0.75 mile). Take the left fork up the hill to a field. You will find a sign indicating you can walk 1.3 miles straight ahead to get back to the trailhead, or you can go right (south) for 3 miles. The trail may be indicated by vertical markers. Regardless, walk south until you come to a grass trail at the southeast (left) corner of the field. After having hiked for 2 miles, you come to a kiosk and, across a parking lot on Argo Road, Landahl Park—South Trail (see Trail Site 14). Follow the path east and north to the campsite, where you will come to a gravel road. Follow the road north for about 0.2 mile to the trailhead for a 2.9-mile hike. For a longer hike, instead of following the gravel road, turn left into a grassy area and walk west across the dam of a pond, into the woods and up a hill. At the top of the hill, turn right. At your first opportunity, turn right down the hill, cross a grassy field to the gravel road and retrace your route to the bridge where the trail began for a hike of about 3.6 miles.

Hikers pause to enjoy the vista from Sled Hill.

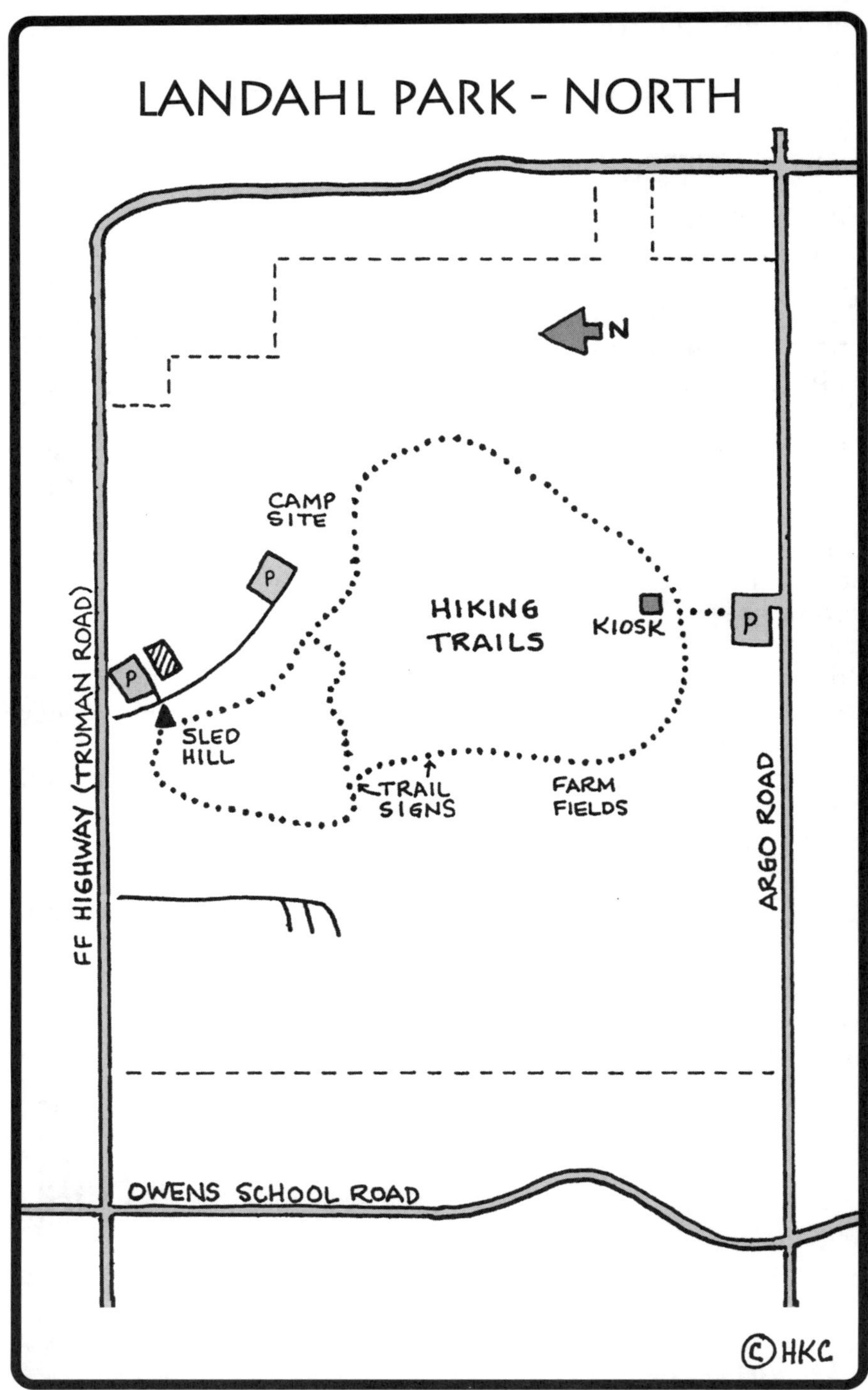
LANDAHL PARK - NORTH
N
CAMP SITE
P
HIKING TRAILS
KIOSK
P
P
FF HIGHWAY (TRUMAN ROAD)
SLED HILL
TRAIL SIGNS
FARM FIELDS
ARGO ROAD
OWENS SCHOOL ROAD
©HKC

One of the many pleasant views along the Landahl–North Trail system.

14
LANDAHL PARK – SOUTH TRAIL
Jackson County Parks & Recreation Department

Time: 2 Hours
Distance: 3.5 Miles (or 1.1 Miles)
Rating: Moderate

Drinking Water: No
Accessible: No

Directions: To locate the south trail, drive north from I-70 at Blue Springs on Hwy 7. The road passes the Lake City Training Center Shooting Range and a campground. In 2.7 miles, turn right (east) on Argo Road. There is a shelter house and open fields on the south side of the road, and a large sign indicates the park and the availability of hiking trails. Park in the parking area.

The Landahl Park–South Trail: Named Washingsabba Nature Trail, this trail is reached by walking west along a fence line adjacent to the field toward the woods where the trail begins. Shortly after you enter the woods there is a fork. Take the left path. This loop proceeds along the edge of a field, up a hill and back into the woods. In about a mile, it rejoins the original trail. Turn left (west). (A right turn would take you back to the field for a hike of 1.1 miles.) The trail proceeds west for another 0.2 mile past a pond and then divides to form another loop. You can take it in either direction, returning to this point in a little less than 2 miles. The trail leads through heavy woods, up and down hills and across open meadows. We were startled by a large flock of wild turkeys. When you have completed this loop you can return northeast back along the trail to the fields and parking area. If you feel energetic, you may wish to hike the North Trail in Landahl Park (see Trail Site 13).

Note: Since our original description, the paths have become wide, mowed swaths to accommodate horses, so this area is a lot less "woodsy" than previously described, but the paths now certainly offer better protection from poison ivy. Also, more loops have been added on the west side, but they all eventually lead back to the main trail. A firing range north of this site operates from noon to 7 p.m. Thursday through Sunday, making a morning hike desirable for those seeking tranquility.

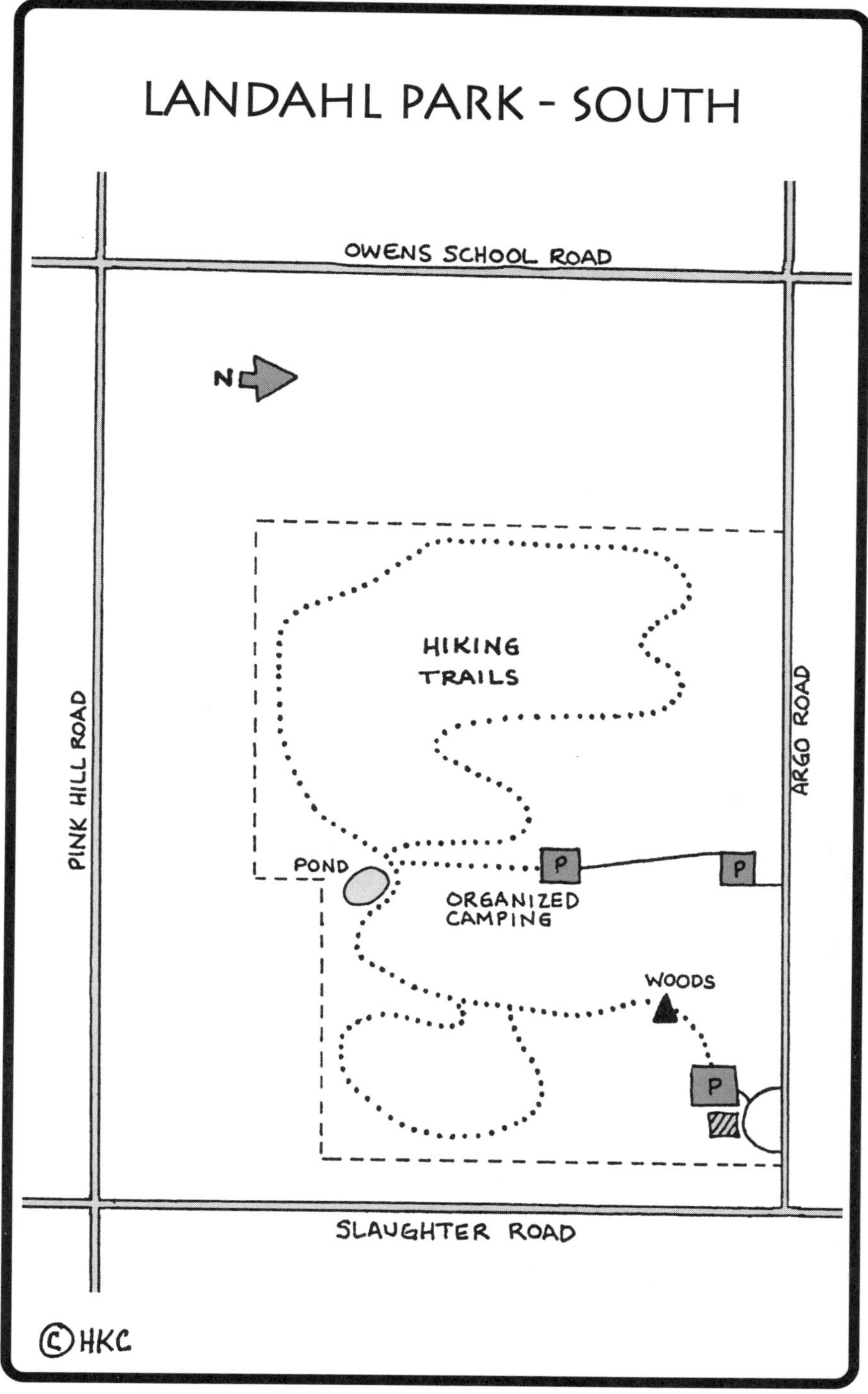
LANDAHL PARK - SOUTH
OWENS SCHOOL ROAD
N
HIKING TRAILS
PINK HILL ROAD
ARGO ROAD
POND
P
P
ORGANIZED CAMPING
WOODS
P
SLAUGHTER ROAD
©HKC

15
BURR OAK WOODS
Missouri Department of Conservation

Time: 0.5 to 1.5 Hours (Each Trail)
Distance: 0.8 to 1.6 Miles (Each Trail)
Rating: Easy to Moderate
Drinking Water: Yes
Accessible: One

Burr Oak Woods Nature Center, just 18 miles east of downtown Kansas City, is one of the finest in western Missouri. It houses excellent animal, bird, fish and plant displays. The nature center and trails are in a 1,000-acre urban forest managed by the Missouri Department of Conservation.

Directions: To reach Burr Oak Woods, drive east to Blue Springs on I-70 to Hwy 7. Take Hwy 7 north about 1 mile. There is a sign on the west side of Hwy 7 for Burr Oak Woods. Turn left from Hwy 7 onto Park Road. If you get to Pink Hill Road, you've gone too far on Hwy 7. We suggest you first visit the nature center to walk the short Discovery Trail and obtain trail guides of the Habitat, Hickory Grove, Bethany Falls and Missouri Tree Trails. Pets are not allowed on this trail.

The Wildlife Habitat Trail: The trailhead is at the southeast corner of a parking lot south of Park Road about 0.2 mile after you enter the park. This 1.5-mile loop trail passes through a glade, by a pond, through limestone outcroppings, by old fields and through a deep woods with several types of hardwoods. It is well-maintained, covered mostly with wood chips and easy to follow. There are information markers along the way that can be used with the trail guide available at the nature center. The most difficult part of the trail is a 140' rise in elevation. It is suitable for wet weather and winter hiking. Restrooms are available at the trailhead and nature center.

Hickory Grove Trail: At the northwest corner of the same parking lot that serves the Wildlife Habitat Trail is the trailhead for this trail. It is about 1.6 miles long (3.2 miles round-trip), has a wood-chipped surface and is easy to follow. The trail abounds with wildlife. You are likely to see deer, turkey and many songbirds. It emerges at the parking area for the Bethany Falls Trail. There are restrooms at the trailhead.

Bethany Falls Trail: Proceed west 0.25 mile past the nature center on the main road, which ends at a parking area. The trailhead is easy to spot on the north side. This interesting trail loops north under and through rugged escarpments of Bethany Falls limestone. There are restrooms here.

Missouri Tree Trail: The trailhead is at the southwest corner of the nature center. This 0.8-mile paved loop trail passes by eighty-one specimens of native Missouri trees. It is an easy, enjoyable walk and is accessible. Deer and turkey have been spotted from this trail.

Discovery Trail: This 0.5-mile paved (but not handicap-accessible) nature trail begins behind the nature center and leads through the finest stand of climax oak-hickory forest in the area. It features wildflowers in season, wildlife sightings and a scenic overlook.

The Landahl Park Trails can be reached by continuing north on Hwy 7 and following the directions for Trail Sites 13 & 14.

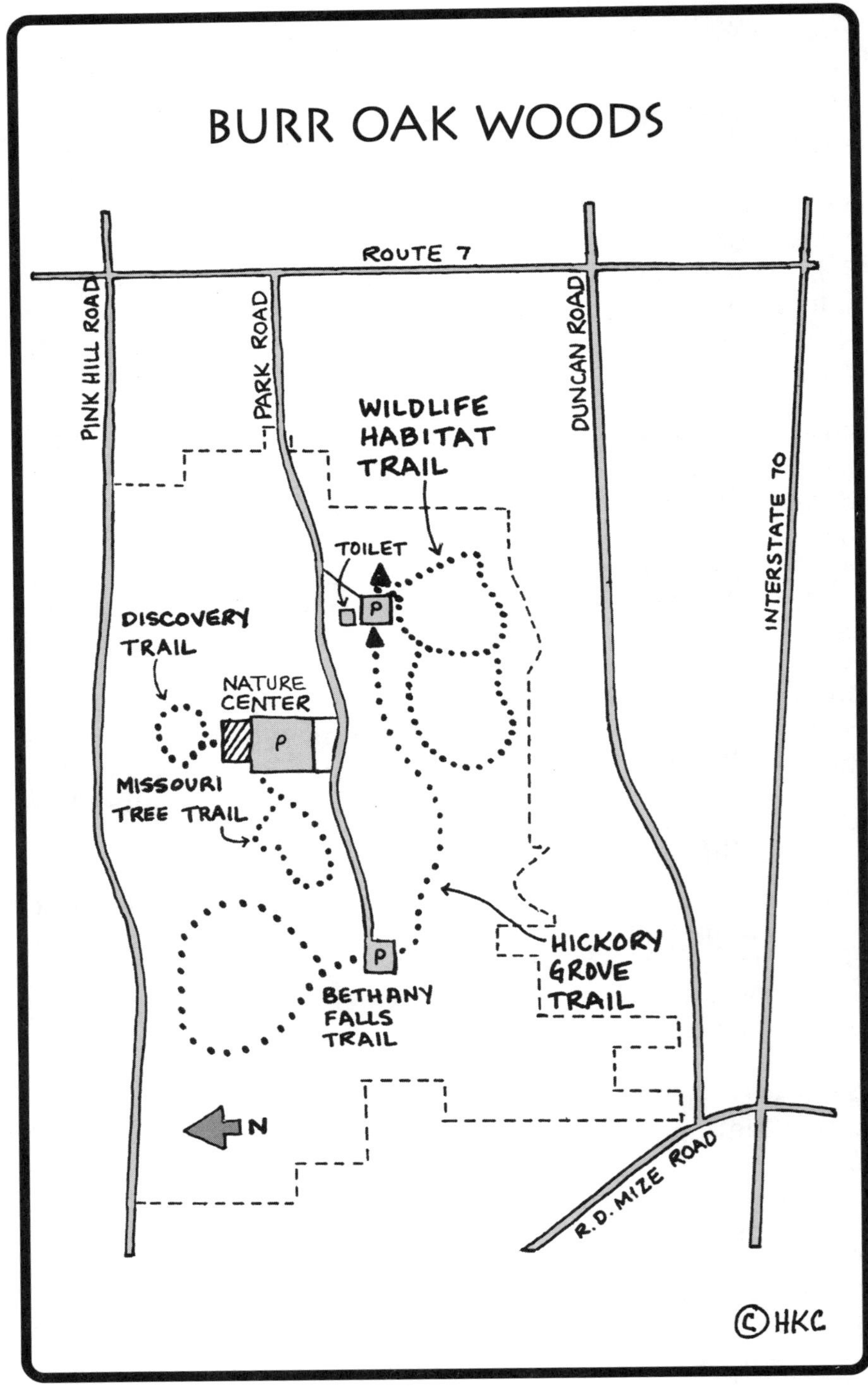
BURR OAK WOODS
ROUTE 7
PINK HILL ROAD
PARK ROAD
DUNCAN ROAD
INTERSTATE 70
WILDLIFE HABITAT TRAIL
TOILET
P
DISCOVERY TRAIL
NATURE CENTER
P
MISSOURI TREE TRAIL
HICKORY GROVE TRAIL
P
BETHANY FALLS TRAIL
N
R.D. MIZE ROAD
© HKC

The Missouri Department of Conservation operates an outstanding nature center at Burr Oak Woods. Take time for a visit.

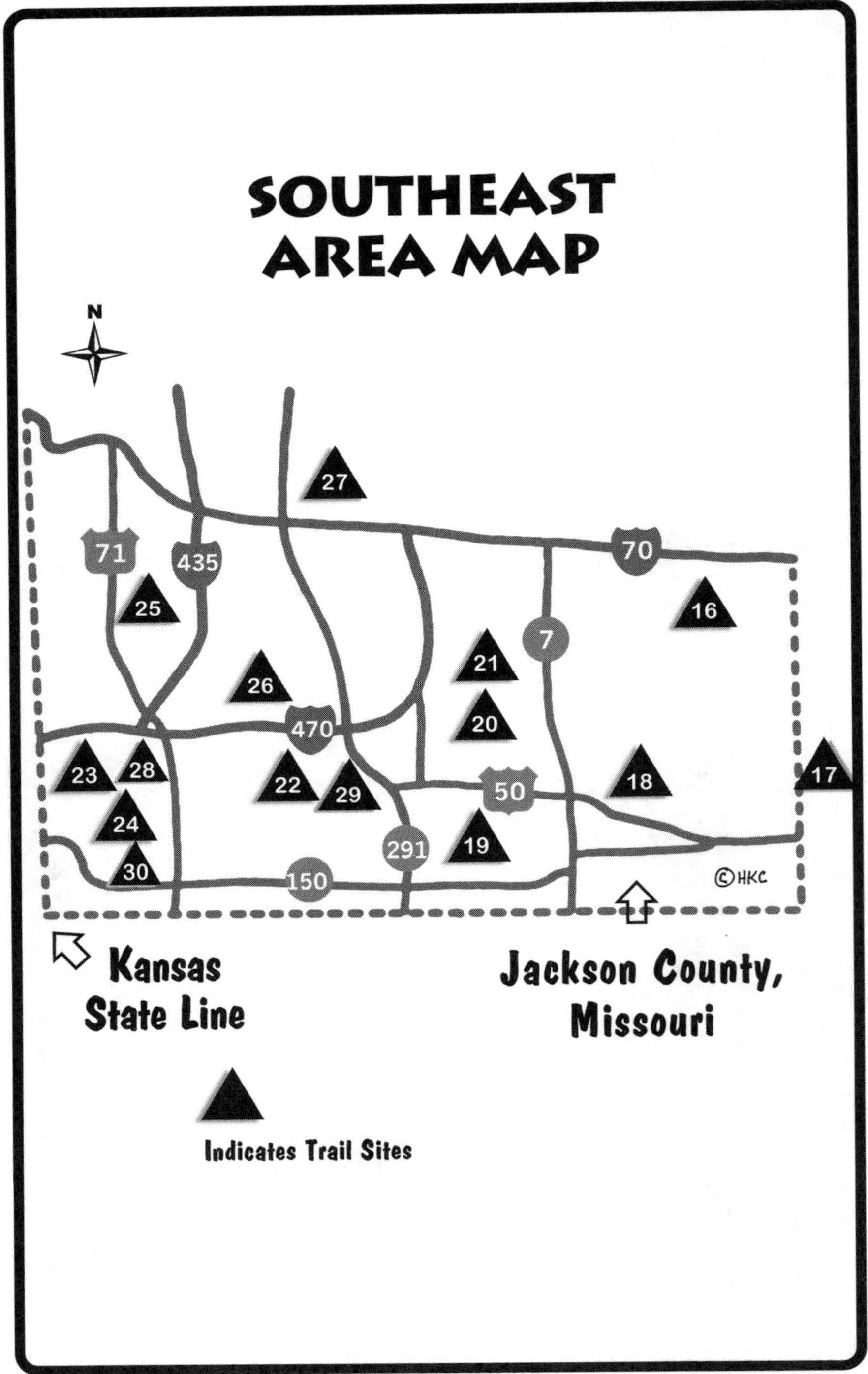
SOUTHEAST
AREA MAP
N
27
71
435
70
25
16
7
21
26
20
470
23
28
17
18
22
29
50
24
19
291
30
150
©HKC
Kansas
State Line
Jackson County,
Missouri
Indicates Trail Sites

TRAIL SITES IN SOUTHEAST AREA

Note: ( ) denotes the number of trails at that location

16
MONKEY MOUNTAIN PARK & NATURE RESERVE

Jackson County Parks & Recreation Department

Time: 1.5 Hours and 1.75 Hours
Distance: 2.5 Miles and 3.5 Miles
Rating: Moderate to Difficult
Drinking Water: No
Accessible: No

Monkey Mountain is a large, wooded hill rising up from meadows in eastern Jackson County. The trail up the mountain traverses meadows, woods and limestone outcroppings, with a beautiful view north at the summit. Winter and spring are good times to hike this trail.

Directions: Take I-70 east from Kansas City and turn south at the Grain Valley Exit. This is Route AA (also Main Street and the Buckner Tarsney Road). To get to Trail 1, go straight (south) for 2 miles to R.D. Mize Road. Drive east on R.D. Mize for 1.3 miles to a parking lot entrance on the left, where there is a sign, "Monkey Mountain Park Horse Trail." To get to Trail 2, turn left off Route AA on Old Hwy 40 as indicated below.

Trail 1: The trail begins behind an outbuilding at the north edge of the parking lot. Take the left branch (the right branch goes up a steep hill, which you will descend at the end). The trail proceeds through a grassy, lightly wooded area where we saw several bluebirds. Soon, there is a choice to go straight ahead (east) or follow a trail to the left. Go left. The trail is well-defined, although it is not marked. At 1.5 miles, the trail emerges at the north end of the park, offering a nice view. Take the path on your immediate right, which heads south and uphill. At 2 miles, the trail emerges into a grassy area and heads southeast. At 2.25 miles, the trail comes to a hedgerow and divides. Take the path on the right (west side of the hedge row). Shortly, you come to a limestone outcropping. Take the time to explore the area to your left (east), which has a fire ring, trail and a nice view. Return to the trail that proceeds straight south, down a hill to the parking lot.

Trail 2: The trailhead, which is in the north part of the park, is reached from old Hwy 40. From I-70, go south on Route AA. At the edge of town, Route AA turns right, but continue straight ahead on Main. Turn left at the next intersection. Follow the road across two bridges to the park sign. Park in the parking area and walk south, downhill to the trailhead sign. The trail passes through fields and woods, and at 1.4 miles crosses an old wooden fence and comes out in a meadow. Follow the edge of the meadow west and south until you come to a marker at the tree line. Cross into another meadow and bear left until you come to a dirt road. Follow it west almost to the crest of the hill. There is a marker to the north at the edge of the woods. The trail leads north below the crest of Monkey Mountain. At the north end of the hill, take the trail down and to the right to the valley, across the footbridge and uphill to the trailhead.

Note: The trail system is currently being redeveloped to accommodate hikers and horseback riders. The trail descriptions may become inaccurate.

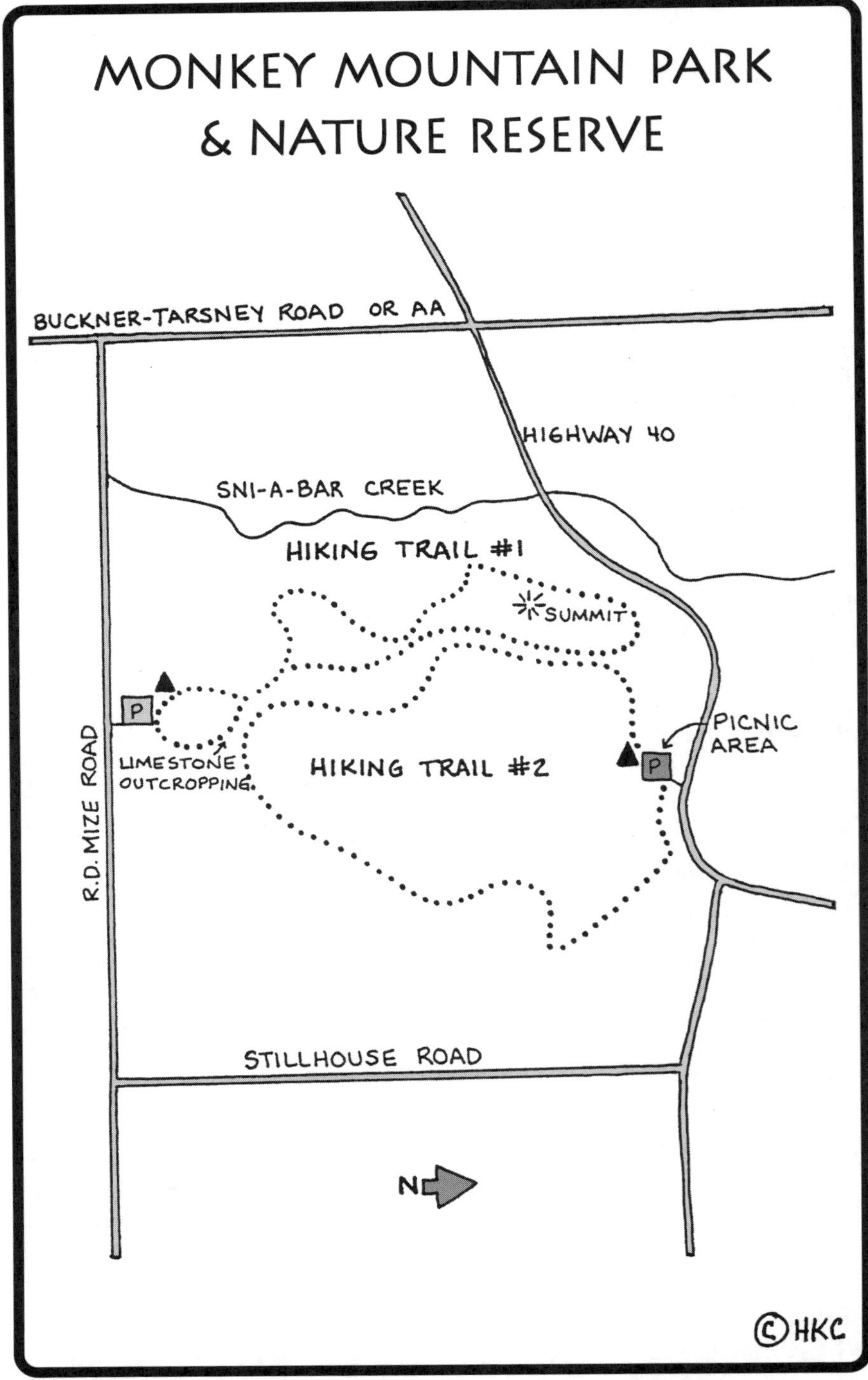
MONKEY MOUNTAIN PARK
& NATURE RESERVE
BUCKNER-TARSNEY ROAD OR AA
HIGHWAY 40
SNI-A-BAR CREEK
HIKING TRAIL #1
SUMMIT
P
LIMESTONE
OUTCROPPING
HIKING TRAIL #2
PICNIC
AREA
P
R.D. MIZE ROAD
STILLHOUSE ROAD
N
©HKC

WELCOME
TO
MONKEY
MOUNTAIN
GUIDE
MONKEY
MTN.
GUIDE

With four major gardens, a wildflower meadow, a conservatory and a chapel, Powell Gardens offers something for everyone.

17
POWELL GARDENS BYRON SHUTZ NATURE TRAIL
Powell Family Foundation & Shutz Foundation

Time: 2 Hours
Distance: 3.25 Miles (Loop)
Rating: Moderate
Drinking Water: Visitors Center
Accessible: No

Powell Gardens is a 915-acre botanical garden and natural area that provides a wonderful opportunity to enjoy horticulture and nature. In addition to a nature trail and short beaver trail, this interesting and attractive preserve offers a visitors center that sells refreshments and Best of Missouri's Hands art and crafts. Also, there are ornamental gardens, vegetable gardens and other horticulture displays. Many special events are held throughout the year. There is an admission fee.

Directions: Drive southeast of Kansas City on Hwy 50. At the east edge of Lee's Summit, you pass the Hwy 291 interchange. Stay on Hwy 50 for about 18.5 miles. You will see signs for Powell Gardens, which is located a mile north of the highway. Stop at the visitors center for a map and directions to trails.

Nature Trail: Through the generosity of Mr. Shutz, Powell Gardens has built an interesting and educational 3.25-mile nature trail. The trail begins at a kiosk about 200 yards from the visitors center. Ask for directions and a detailed map. The thoughtfully developed trail exposes the hiker to woodlands, wetlands, prairies, ridges and hilltops, ponds and remnants of earlier inhabitants. Interpretive signs and a brochure point out opportunities to learn even more about trees, animals and the impact of civilization. The trail ends across the lake from the visitors center, but paths to the center either across or around the lake are obvious. Boots, long pants and insect repellant are recommended in summer months to help ward off ticks and chiggers.

Before or after your hike, visit the many gardens and horticultural displays on this 915-acre site.

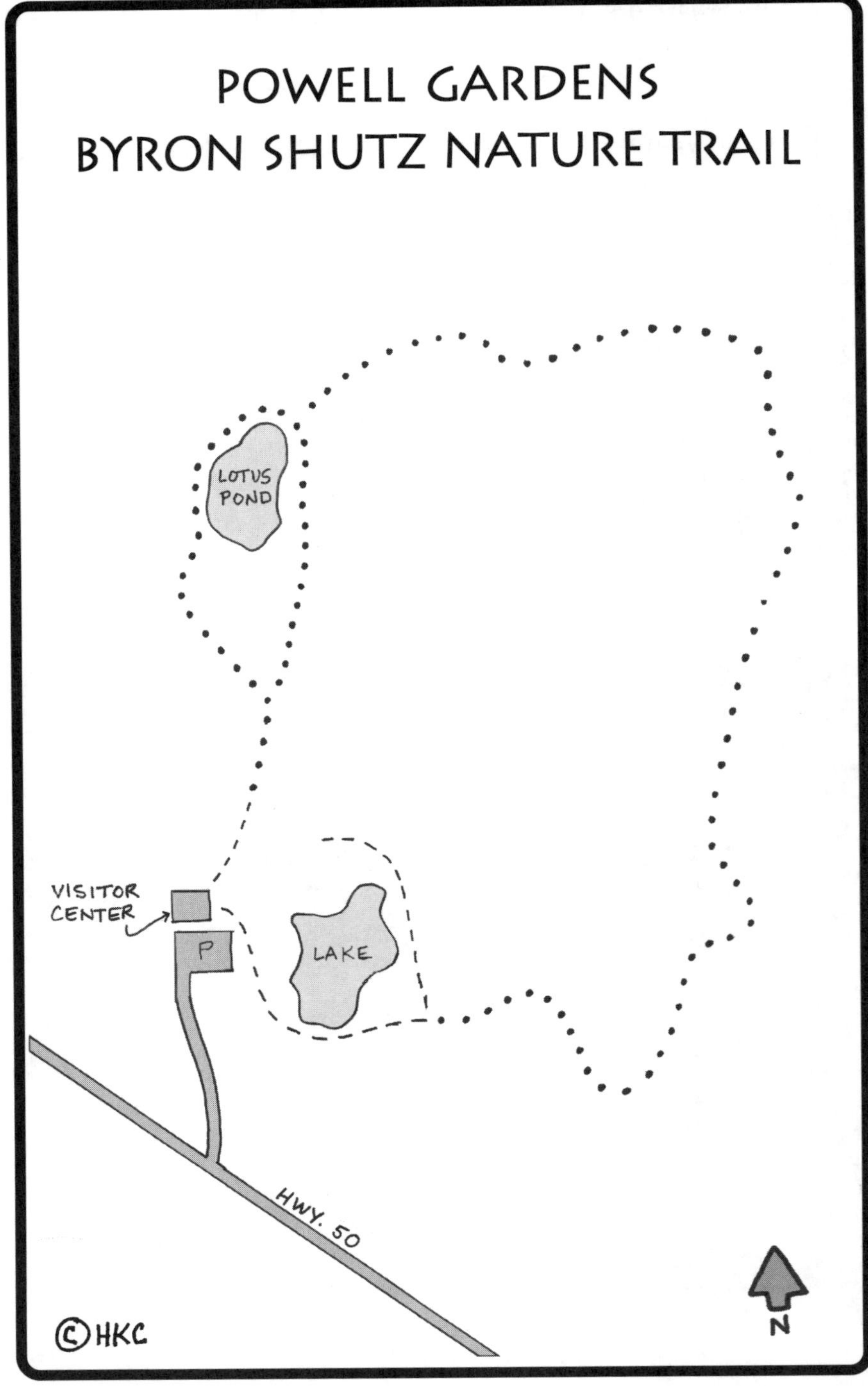
POWELL GARDENS
BYRON SHUTZ NATURE TRAIL
LOTUS
POND
VISITOR
CENTER
P
LAKE
HWY. 50
N
©HKC

TRAIL NOTES:

18
BLUE & GRAY PARK
Jackson County Parks & Recreation Department

Time: 2 Hours
Distance: 4 Miles (Circuit)
Rating: Moderate

Drinking Water: No
Accessible: No

This 2,000-acre, heavily wooded area in southeastern Jackson County is largely undeveloped and provides some of the most isolated hiking anywhere in Kansas City. The area is covered with horseback riding and foot paths, some of which are blazed (paint spots on trees). Some care needs to be taken to observe the instructions and the blaze colors indicated for the hike we describe. The Lone Jack Civil War Trail, a route that follows backroads from Missouri Town 1855 at Lake Jacomo to the Civil War Museum in Lone Jack, traverses the park and forms a part of our trail route.

Directions: Drive southeast on Hwy 50. About 7 miles east of Lee's Summit is Buckner-Tarsney Road, where you turn north. If you reach Lone Jack on Hwy 50, you've gone too far east. You will see a sign, gate and parking for the organized camping area 1.5 miles north of Hwy 50. The route begins here.

Blue and Gray Park Trails: Walk east from the gate along a gravel road to a hilltop camping area. The Jackson County Sheriff's Posse maintains the segment of the Lone Jack Civil War Trail that runs from northwest to southeast in the park. The main route follows this horse trail, which sometimes takes a different route than described in earlier printings of this book. Look for trail signs on the east side of the camping area. The route meanders generally southeast through some surprisingly rugged and isolated terrain, crosses several creeks and ends at the south end of the park near Lone Jack. Retrace your steps to return to your car.

The Lone Jack Civil War Trail intersects a number of side trails that are used mostly by horses. Watch for signs to keep you on the main trail, which is not easy, especially on the return. If you decide to explore the side trails, keep track of your directions by compass or the sun, remembering that the parking area is on the park's western boundary. Long pants are recommended due to poison ivy.

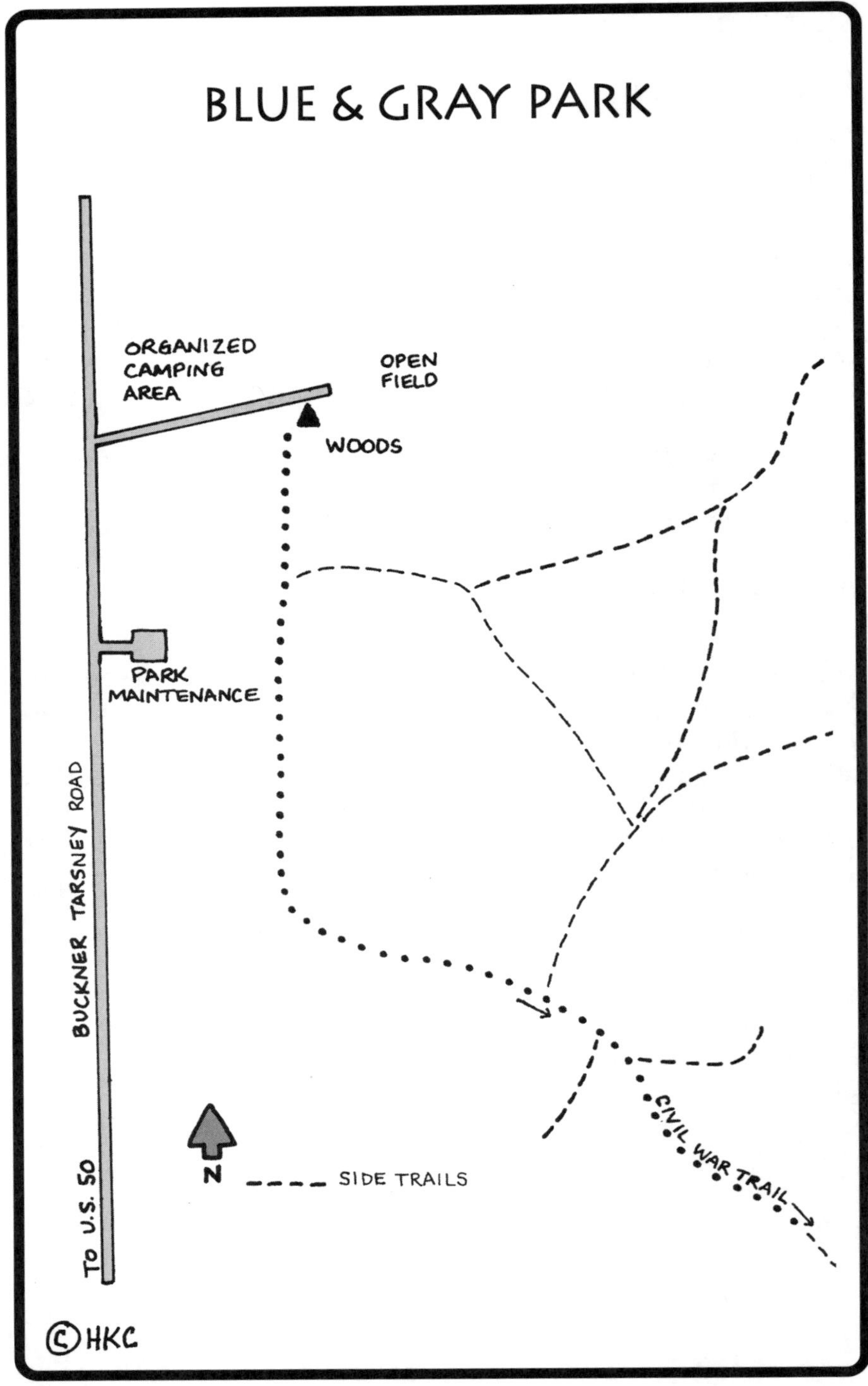
BLUE & GRAY PARK
ORGANIZED CAMPING AREA
OPEN FIELD
WOODS
PARK MAINTENANCE
BUCKNER TARSNEY ROAD
TO U.S. 50
N
SIDE TRAILS
CIVIL WAR TRAIL
©HKC

Author Bill Eddy out enjoying one of Blue & Gray Park's woodland trails.

19
JAMES A. REED WILDLIFE AREA
Missouri Department of Conservation

Time: 1.5 Hours
Distance: 3 Miles (Series of Loops)
Rating: Moderate
Drinking Water: Yes
Accessible: No

The James A. Reed Wildlife Area southeast of Kansas City is an interesting, multiple-use park. In addition to the Shawnee Trace Trail system, there is small game hunting, fishing and horseback riding. In the spring and fall, you can see migrating waterfowl. We suggest checking at the administration building to see if it is hunting season before venturing out on the trails.

Directions: Drive east on Hwy 50 from Lee's Summit. About 2 miles past the Hwy 291 intersection, turn right off Hwy 50 onto S.E. Ranson Road (a sign points to the Wildlife Area). The entrance is a mile south of Hwy 50, on the left side of Ranson Road. Follow the drive a short distance to the administration building, where a trail map is available.

Bodarc Lake Trail: Drive southeast from the administration building on the main gravel road, following the signs to the parking area and trailhead at the north edge of Bodarc Lake dam. The trail begins at the edge of the woods, 50 feet southeast of the parking area. There is a system of trails from which a hike of about 3 miles can be put together. There are also small boats here that you can rent for a small fee. Life jackets and paddles are provided at the self-serve station.

Shawnee Trace Nature Trails: Follow the trail southeast from the trailhead through the woods, across a small stream and along the west side of Big Creek. At 0.3 mile, the trail divides. Take the right branch and continue along the creek. In another 0.2 mile, the trail divides again. Take the right branch. (Do not cross the bridge on your left unless you wish to take the alternate trail.) The trail crosses the creek and then crosses it twice more at the base of limestone cliffs. It then leads steeply uphill away from the creek.

After 1 mile, the trail divides, with the left branch looping back toward its beginning. Take the right fork and follow it northeast and then back west through upland fields. The trail crosses other trail segments, but do not follow them. Continue west on the trail until you come to an intersecting trail. Take the trail to the right and follow it north to a gravel road that leads around the west side of a waterfowl marsh and then directly west and back to the parking area.

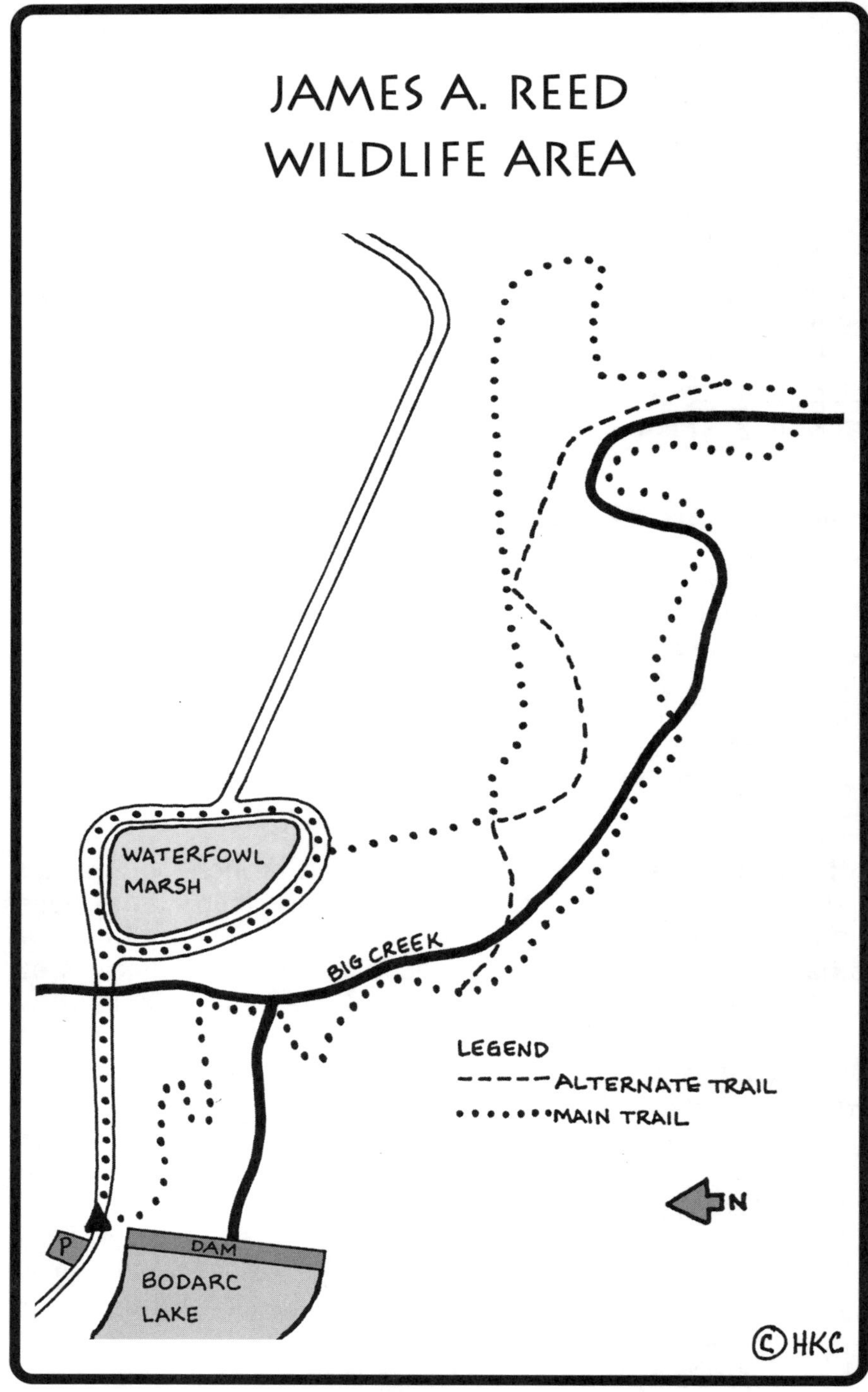
JAMES A. REED
WILDLIFE AREA
WATERFOWL
MARSH
BIG CREEK
LEGEND
ALTERNATE TRAIL
MAIN TRAIL
N
P
DAM
BODARC
LAKE
©HKC

This area is named after James A. Reed, former Kansas City mayor and U.S. senator. It is a multi-use area shared with hunters and fishermen.

20
FLEMING PARK – LAKE JACOMO
Jackson County Parks & Recreation Department

Time: 1 to 4 Hours
Distance: Up to 10 Miles
Rating: Moderate
Drinking Water: Yes
Accessible: No

Seven attractive trails in Fleming Park at Lake Jacomo provide pleasant walking through varied terrain. It is necessary to drive from one trail to the next. A map is available at the ranger's station on Woods Chapel Road. To locate the numbered trailheads, see page 73.

Directions: To get to Lake Jacomo, proceed east out of Kansas City, Missouri on I-70 and turn south on I-470. (Or, alternatively, go east on I-470 from south Kansas City.) Get off I-470 on Woods Chapel Road and travel east a short distance to Fleming Park. Just past the Fleming Meeting Hall, you will see the ranger's station on the south side of the road.

1) The Rock Ledges Nature Trail is a 1.5-mile loop on the southwest side of the lake. Take West Park Road south until you see a road leading to Shelter 14. There is a large, open organized camping area. Park along the gravel drive. The trail begins on the north side of the shelter house and goes north into the woods. This side of the loop takes you through upland rocky areas and then down to the lake. The trail then turns back to the right (south) along the edge of the lake and to a point where you go up a steep hill and into the organized camping area east of the shelter.

2) The Prickly Pear Cactus Glade Trail can be reached from Colbern and Beach Roads. Look for the trail in the northwest corner of that intersection. You will see a trailhead sign and markers. Follow markers to the top of the bluff. The view of Prairie Lee Lake from that point is beautiful. The trail proceeds north toward a campground for a total of almost 1 mile round-trip. Prickly Pear Cactus may be found along the trail.

3) The Clermont Trail is on the east side of the lake adjacent to Missouri Town 1855. Park in the designated area and walk north on the pathway through the old town. Hours are 8 a.m. to 5 p.m. Wednesday through Sunday. An admission fee is required. Register at the gift shop. At the north end of this path, turn left (west) at the law office and follow the path for a few hundred feet to the northwest to a sign that directs you into the woods. The trail loops through interesting rock formations and provides nice views of the lake. It ends at Missouri Town for a walk of about 0.75 mile, which is in addition to the approximately 0.5-mile round-trip to the parking area.

4) The Tcha-To-Ga Nature Trail begins near a pond across the road (west) from the hoofed-animal enclosure on East Park Road and loops 1.2 miles to a lake overlook.

5) The Pa-Hu-Ska Nature Trail is reached by going to East Park Road and proceeding north to Sailboat Cove, about 0.25 mile. There is a bridge across the end of the cove and a parking area on the east side. The trail leads south along a creek, which it eventually crosses on a bridge, and then uphill through woods and back to the cove for a 1.2-mile loop.

6) Mun-Ni-Pus-Kee Trail is a 2-mile loop around the hoofed animal enclosure. You can see bison, elk and white-tail deer. Park at the southwest corner of the enclosure.

7) Larry Mattonen Memorial Trail is a 3.3-mile trail. Exit Colburn Road north on Cyclone School Road and drive for 1 mile to a yellow gate and well-marked trailhead. The trail follows an abandoned road for 0.2 mile, turns south for 0.4 mile, loops left (northeast) for a couple of hundred yards and then heads downhill and southwest to Colburn Road. Return by the same route.

For more hiking in this area, see the Blue Springs Lake Trails (Trail Site 21).

The Pa-Hu-Ska Nature Trail is a moderate to steep, well shaded, 1.2-mile loop trail—perfect for sunny days. Look for the trailhead and parking area across from Sailboat Cove.

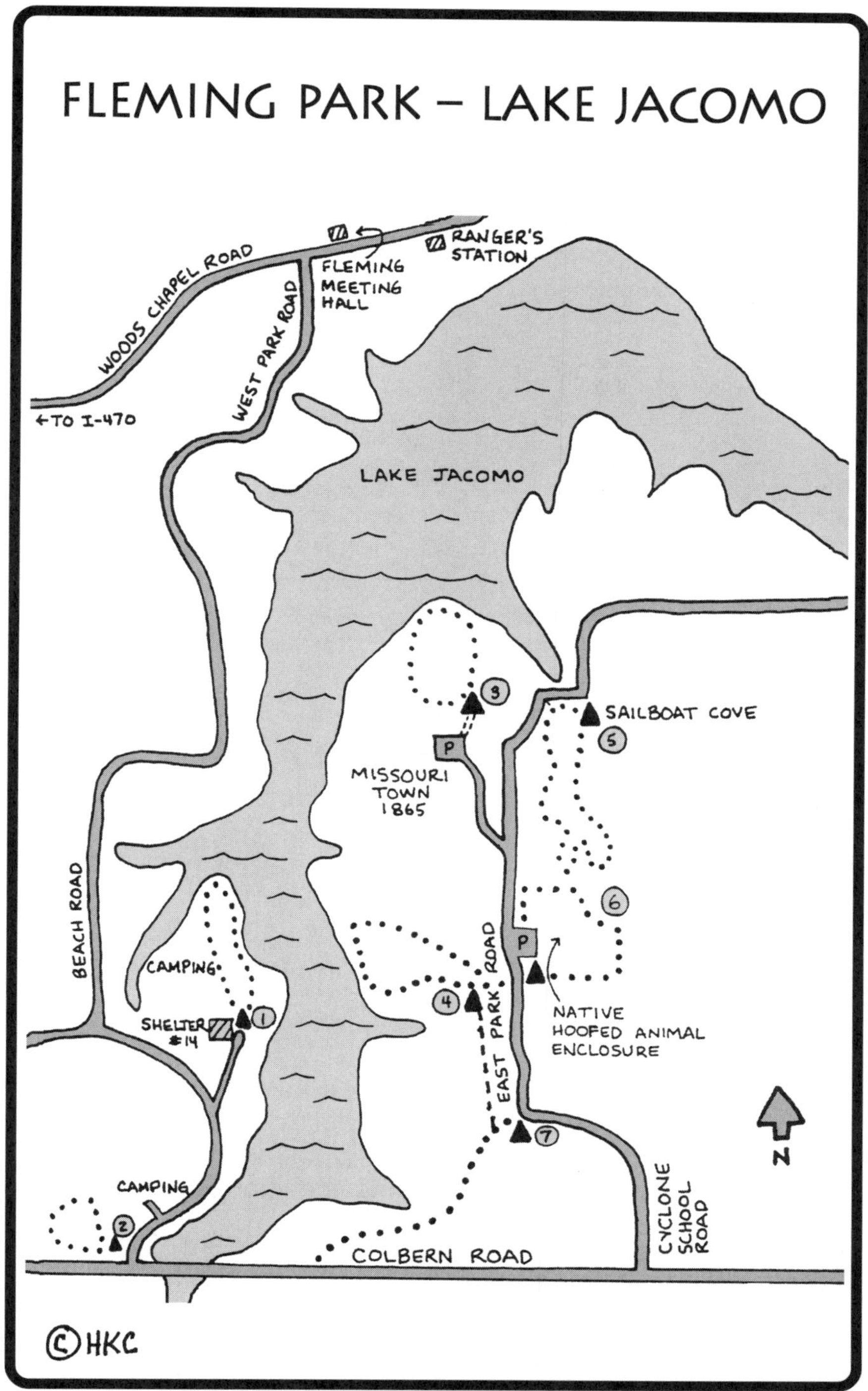

FLEMING PARK – LAKE JACOMO
RANGER'S STATION
FLEMING MEETING HALL
WOODS CHAPEL ROAD
WEST PARK ROAD
←TO I-470
LAKE JACOMO
SAILBOAT COVE
MISSOURI TOWN 1865
BEACH ROAD
CAMPING
SHELTER #14
EAST PARK ROAD
NATIVE HOOFED ANIMAL ENCLOSURE
N
CYCLONE SCHOOL ROAD
CAMPING
COLBERN ROAD
©HKC

The two trails at Blue Springs Lake offer a total of 4.7 miles of fairly level walking along the shoreline.

21
BLUE SPRINGS LAKE
Jackson County Parks & Recreation Department

Time: 2 to 4 Hours
Distance: 1.7 Miles and 3 Miles (One-way)
Rating: Easy to Moderate
Drinking Water: At Picnic Shelters (Summer)
Accessible: Partially Gravel-surface

Blue Springs Lake is a multi-use lake built on the east fork of the Little Blue River, north of Lake Jacomo in Fleming Park. It has two trails for a total of 4.7 miles (one-way) of fairly level walking along the shoreline.

Directions: The lake is south of Blue Springs, just south of Hwy 40. Traveling east from Kansas City on I-70, exit at the Hwy 291 interchange, going south. Immediately exit Hwy 291 onto Hwy 40 and proceed east for 3 miles to Woods Chapel

Road. Turn south on Woods Chapel Road into Fleming Park, passing an access road on the right (west) that leads to picnic facilities. Both trails begin at different trailheads adjacent to Woods Chapel Road.

North Shore Trail: This trail begins 0.5 mile south of Hwy 40 on Woods Chapel Road. Park on the right (west) side of the road, just before a bridge. There is no designated parking area, but there is room on the shoulder to leave a car. North Shore Trail, often used by fishermen, stays close to the shoreline for about half its length and then moves slightly inland and ends where a small tributary enters the lake at about 1.7 miles. Return by the same route. Side trails lead uphill to two picnic areas. Plans call for this trail to be extended along the north shore of the lake to the observation platform adjacent to the dam. This would nearly double the trail's length.

Blue Springs Trail: Access to this trail is on the east side of Woods Chapel Road, 0.3 mile south of the Fleming Park entrance on Hwy 40. Turn left at your only opportunity before the bridge and drive up a hill about 150 yards to a parking area. The gravel trail meanders southeast, following the contour of the land above the lake—a very worthwhile round-trip hike of 6 miles.

A 0.75-mile extension to Blue Springs Trail is planned. It will connect to Liggett Road, Woods Chapel Road and the bridge on the south end for a loop of 5 miles back to the beginning point. The last one-third will be on roadways.

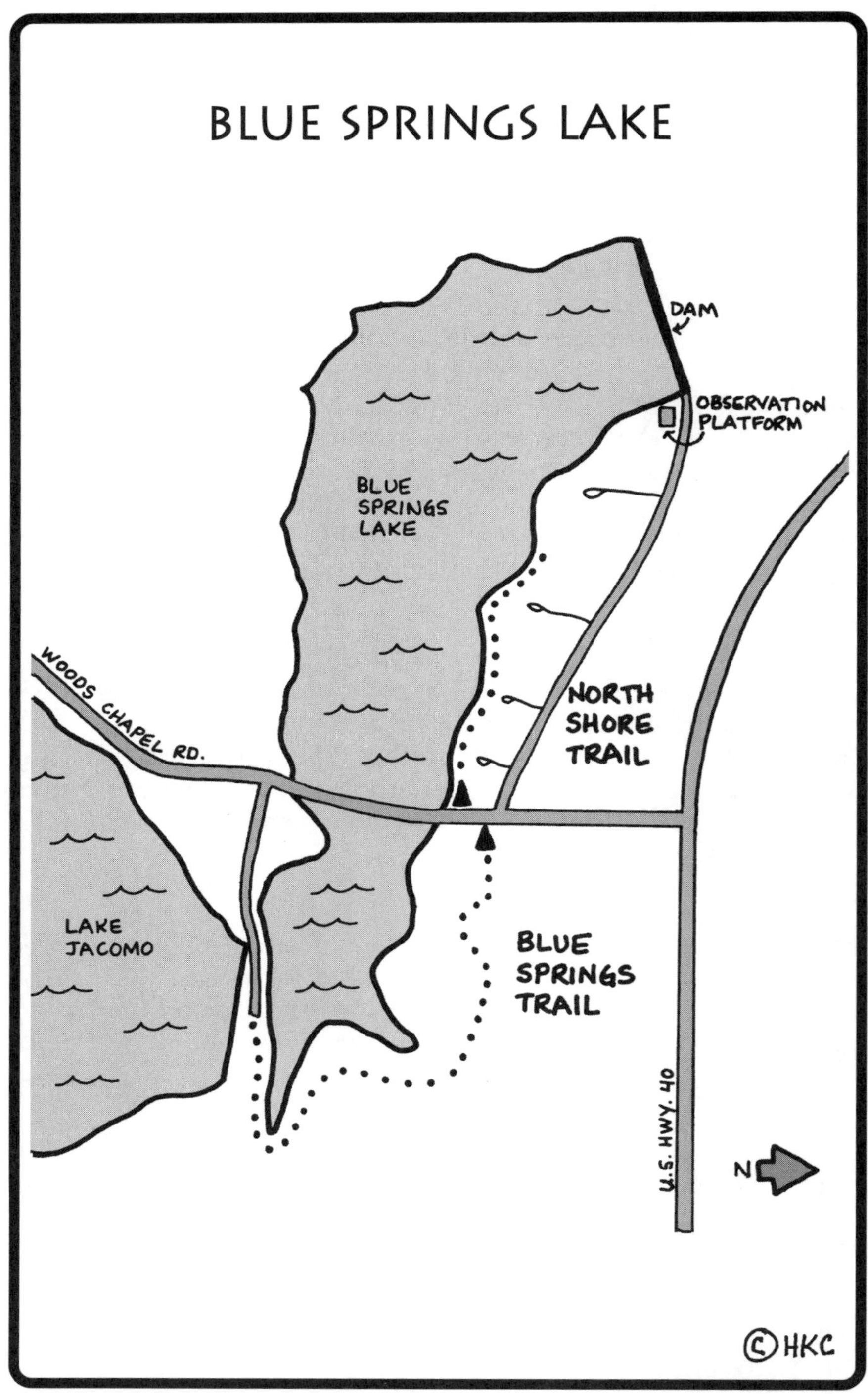
BLUE SPRINGS LAKE
DAM
OBSERVATION PLATFORM
BLUE SPRINGS LAKE
WOODS CHAPEL RD.
NORTH SHORE TRAIL
LAKE JACOMO
BLUE SPRINGS TRAIL
U.S. HWY. 40
N
©HKC

The trails at Blue Springs Lake offer a variety of scenery. Along tributaries to the lake, busy beavers fell trees for food and dam-building.

22
LONGVIEW LAKE
Jackson County Parks & Recreation Department

Time: 1 to 3.5 Hours
Distance: 1.2 Miles, 3 Miles, 7 Miles (One-way)
Rating: Moderate to Difficult
Drinking Water: Yes
Accessible: Yes

Longview Lake is a large U.S. Army Corps of Engineers lake in southeast Jackson County on the site of the former Longview Farm. Jackson County maintains it as a multi-use facility, with marinas, playing fields and shelter houses. The hiking trail is adjacent to an organized camping area in the south end of the park. There is also a 7-mile asphalt jogging, walking and bicycle path, and a horse trail.

Directions: Drive east out of south Kansas City, Missouri on I-470 (or west on I-470 from Lee's Summit) to the Raytown Road exit. Go south on Raytown Road a couple of miles to High Grove Road. Turn left (east) onto High Grove and drive for about 0.25 mile to a sign on the south side of the road for

"Organized Camping." If the gate is closed, park off the road where you don't block the entrance and walk south along the asphalt road for 0.2 mile to the parking area. (If the gate is open, you can drive to the parking area.)

The Longview Lake Hiking Trail is named the Shin-Ga-Wa-Sa Nature Trail. On the south side of the parking area, there is a yellow gate at the edge of the woods. The trailhead is about 50 yards east (downhill). The trail, which is not always well-marked except at crucial points, progresses past a pond and crosses a powerline clearing. On the other side of the clearing it again goes into the woods where it follows old roads and cuts across the corner of an open field. At about 0.6 mile, the trail loops back along the edge of Lumpkin Fork Creek for a 1.2-mile circuit, or continue ahead to complete the 3-mile loop. The trail heads downhill, across a marshy area, uphill past the pond and a campground, and back to the yellow gate.

Bicycle and Hiking Trail is reached by taking Raytown Road south from I-470. Turn left on Longview Road and go to Shelter 14 where the trail begins. This asphalt, accessible trail wanders southwesterly along the edge of the lake for about 7 miles, ending at another shelter house.

Loop Trail is a nice 1-mile loop trail. It begins at the trailhead at the west end of the Shelter 9 parking area. The trail crosses a creek and proceeds through woods and along a meadow, where a variety of birds and wildlife are likely to be seen. Bear to your left at each intersection to return to the start.

Blue River Trail is a southwest extension of the Bicycle and Hiking Trail. It proceeds for about 1 mile to the corner of 137th and Winchester in Grandview, where there is a trailhead.

The Horseback Riding Trail is on Sampson Road, south of High Grove/Scherer Road. Turn south for about a mile to a trailhead parking lot on the west side. The trail, which is quite suitable for hiking, wanders northwest through woods and open uplands, along the west side of the Mouse Creek Arm of Longview Lake for 3 miles.

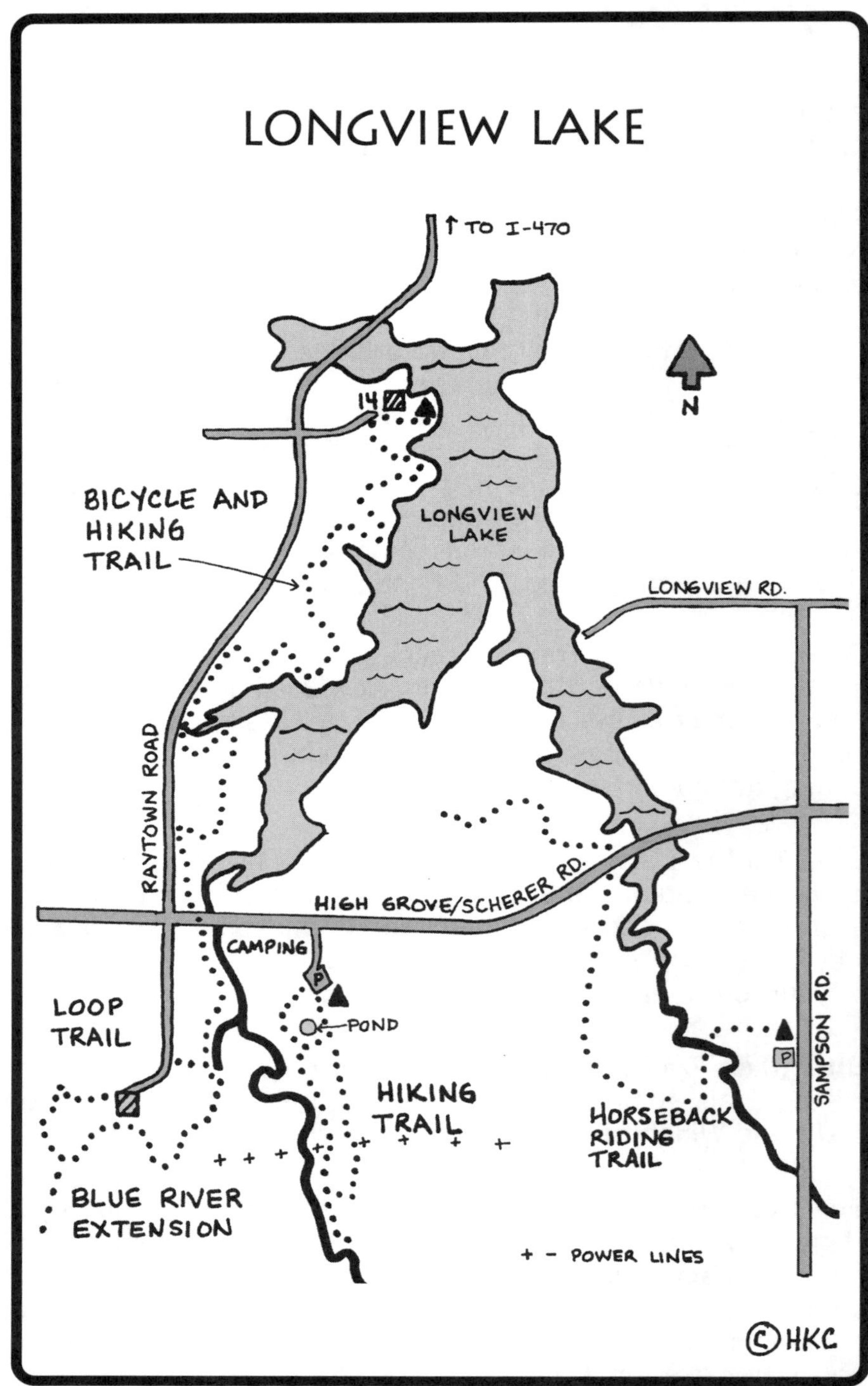
LONGVIEW LAKE
↑ TO I-470
N
14
BICYCLE AND HIKING TRAIL
LONGVIEW LAKE
LONGVIEW RD.
RAYTOWN ROAD
HIGH GROVE/SCHERER RD.
CAMPING
P
POND
LOOP TRAIL
HIKING TRAIL
HORSEBACK RIDING TRAIL
SAMPSON RD.
P
BLUE RIVER EXTENSION
+ - POWER LINES
©HKC

Longview Lake's Bicycle and Hiking Trail begins at Shelter 14. This asphalt, accessible trail wanders along the edge of the lake (shown above) for about 7 miles, ending at another shelter house.

23
BLUE RIVER PARKWAY – NORTH TRAIL

Jackson County Parks & Recreation Department

Time: 1.5 to 2 Hours
Distance: 3.5 Miles Round-trip
Rating: Easy

Drinking Water: No
Accessible: No

A forest footpath along an abandoned railroad right-of-way paralleling the Blue River makes this a pleasant trail. It offers deep woods, limestone formations and several vistas of the Blue River from high bluffs. It is one of our favorites. Although the trail is in a designated mountain bike area, it is wide and not heavily used, so it can be enjoyed by all users.

Directions: The trailhead can be reached from the end of 118th Street about 0.2 mile east of Troost. Drive on Holmes Road to 117th Terrace and turn east to Troost. Take Troost to 118th Street and drive east to where the street dead-ends. There is a parking area beyond the yellow gate.

The Blue River Parkway North Trail is reached by walking south from the gate 0.1 mile and then east 0.1 mile on old roadways. When the roadway intersects the trail, turn right (south). The trail follows an abandoned rail bed through deep woods atop high bluffs overlooking the Blue River. There are also several low places and a shallow stream to ford, or cross, so the trail could be difficult to hike in wet weather or after a rainy period. The trail ends at the railroad tracks. Future plans call for this trail to be connected to the Blue River Parkway South Trail (see Trail Site 24). The mountain bike community has developed several miles of trails within Blue River Parkway south of Blue Ridge Road on both sides of the river. Links to maps can be found online at www.earthriders.org.

Hikers will see tributaries of the Blue River while exploring the Parkway's North Trail.

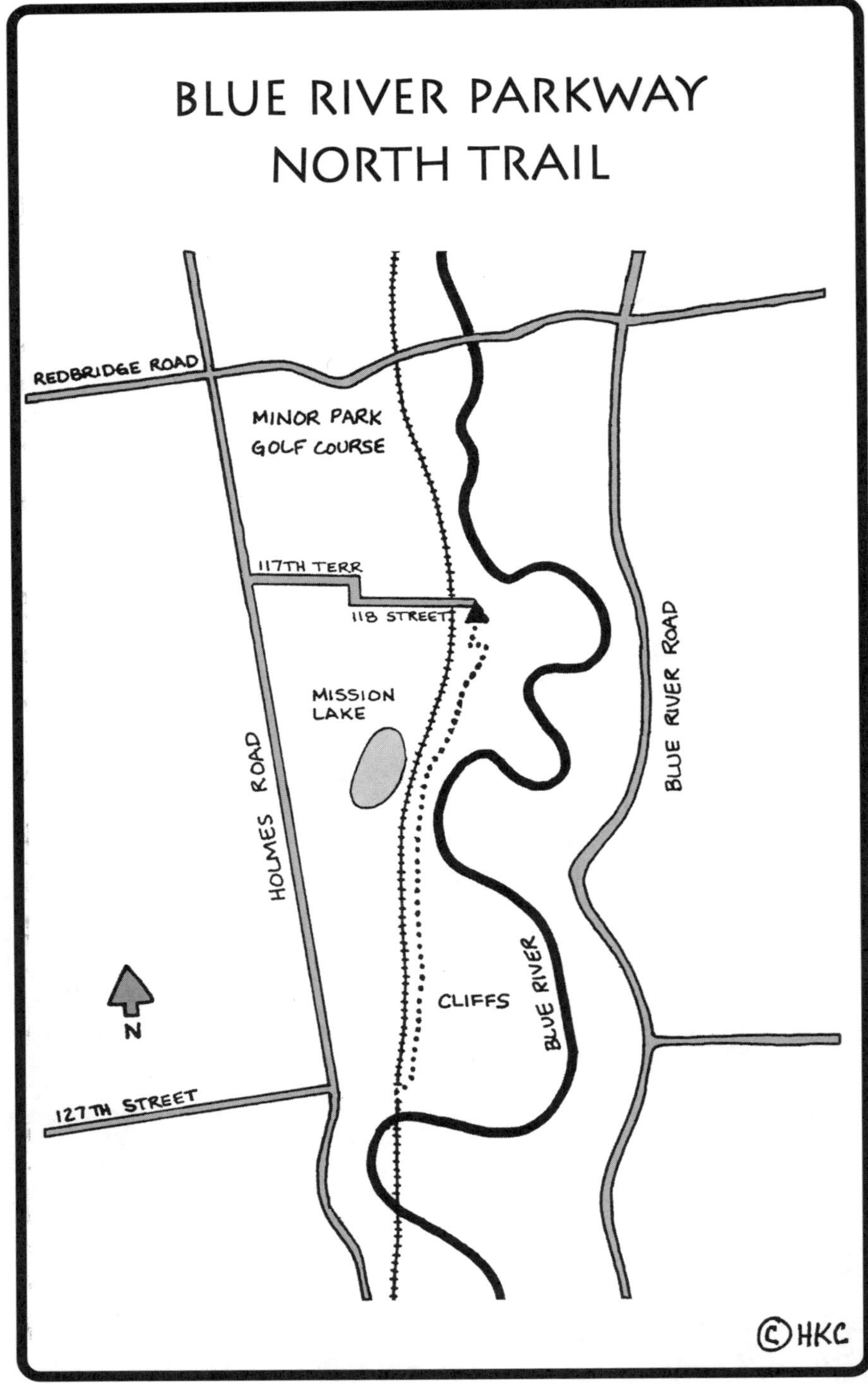
BLUE RIVER PARKWAY
NORTH TRAIL
REDBRIDGE ROAD
MINOR PARK
GOLF COURSE
117TH TERR
118 STREET
MISSION
LAKE
HOLMES ROAD
BLUE RIVER ROAD
BLUE RIVER
CLIFFS
N
127TH STREET
©HKC

PERSPECTIVE

24
BLUE RIVER PARKWAY – SOUTH TRAIL
Jackson County Parks & Recreation Department

Time: 2 Hours
Distance: 4 Miles
Rating: Easy

Drinking Water: Yes
Accessible: No

This secluded trail follows the Blue River through Jackson County's Blue River Parkway from the south end of the parkway off Kenneth Road to 140th Street and Holmes. It runs about 2 miles each way through heavy woods and open meadows. Designated a horse trail, it is easy to follow. It provides a pleasant walk close to the city—especially for those living in the south part of the metropolitan area. We saw bluebirds, cardinals, killdeer and deer.

Directions: To pick up the trail at the south end, drive south on Holmes Road from Martin City. About 3 miles south of Martin City, take Kenneth Road west for about 1.2 miles, where you come to a sign, "Blue River Parkway Kenneth Road Recreation Facility." (If you reach a one-lane bridge over the Blue River, you've gone too far.) Turn north into the recreation area and park in the gravel parking lot.

The Blue River Parkway South Trail is reached by walking north of the parking lot up a short road to the polo field. Directly across the field, on the north edge, is an opening where the trail begins. The trail offers interesting views of the river, fields, thick woods and a footbridge. Since it follows the river valley, it is level and easy to walk. There are side trails that lead back to the main trail or to the east park boundary. Currently, the trail is bisected near the middle by the re-routing of Hwy 150. Water in the river may require you to turn back. There are plans for a bridge crossing. At the north end of the trail is Holmes Playing Fields Complex. The trail enters the southeast corner of the area at a gravel parking lot. From here, the parkway switches to the east side of the Holmes where the bridge crosses the Blue River. (The Blue River—North Trail follows the river northward to 118th Street, but the two segments are not yet connected.)

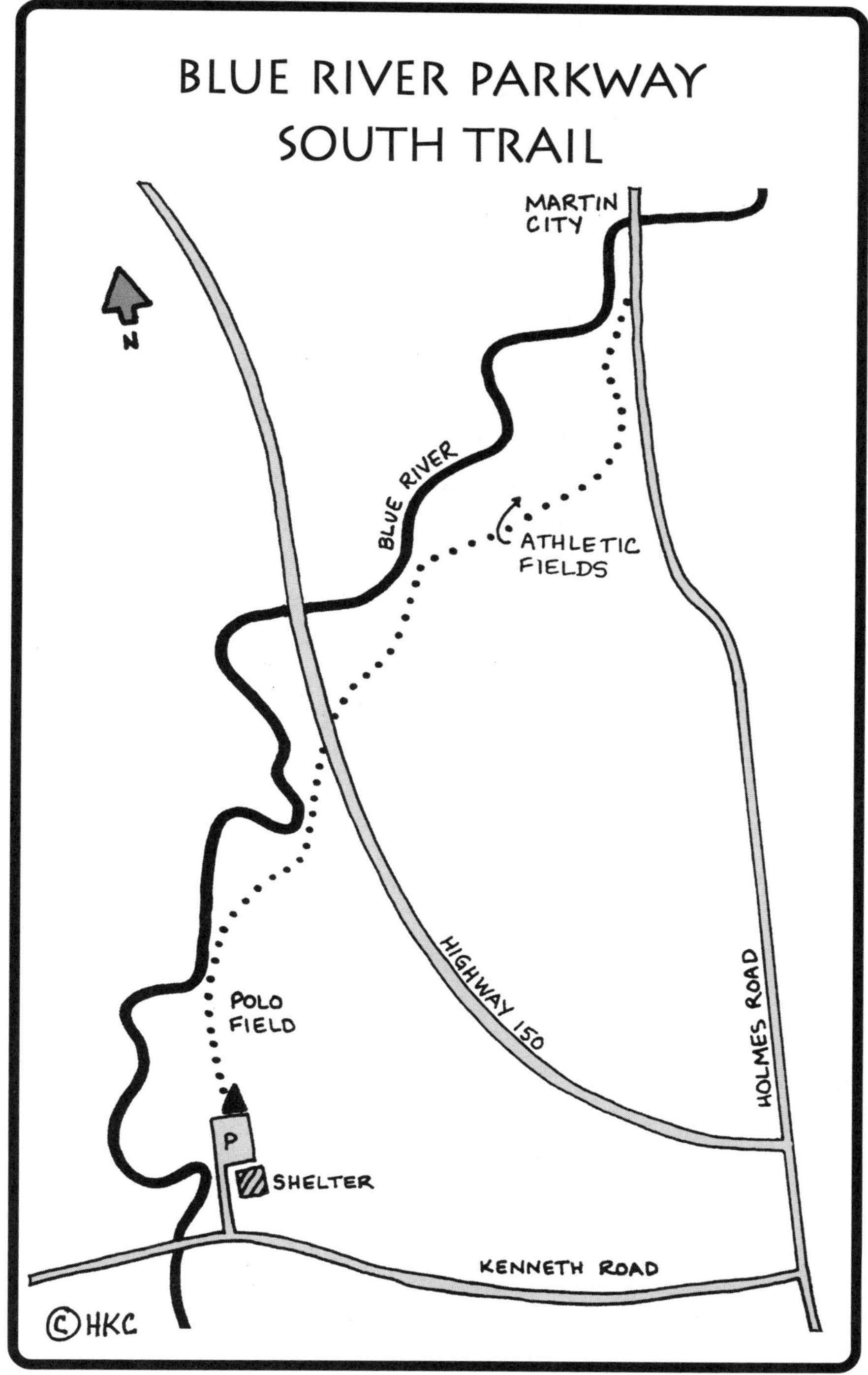
BLUE RIVER PARKWAY
SOUTH TRAIL
MARTIN CITY
N
BLUE RIVER
ATHLETIC FIELDS
HIGHWAY 150
HOLMES ROAD
POLO FIELD
P
SHELTER
KENNETH ROAD
©HKC

Authors Richard Ballentine, at left, and William Eddy.

25
EDDY - BALLENTINE & BLUE RIVER GLADES TRAILS

Jackson County Parks & Recreation Department

Time: 1.5 Hours
Distance: 2.5 Miles
Rating: Difficult

Drinking Water: No
Accessible: No

Rugged is the way to describe these trails in the northern portion of the Blue River Parkway. It's an overlooked county park with deep woods, streams and bluffs. The "difficult" rating is due to steep hillsides, stream crossings and uneven trail surfaces. Hikers should wear sturdy shoes and walk only when visibility is good. Please don't walk alone. In 1999, this trail was named the Eddy-Ballentine Trail to recognize the authors' contributions to the Kansas City area hiking community.

Directions: The trail begins at Blue River Road, 0.5 mile south of the Swope Park Blue River Golf Course. Connect with Blue River Road on the north from Oldham Road or from 87th or 95th Streets on the south. The trailhead is on the east side of the road. Look for a clearing separated from the road by large rocks and a sign. Park along the shoulder.

Eddy-Ballentine & Blue River Glades Trails: Walk directly east from the parking area for about 50 feet. On the right (south), you will see a dirt road. Start up the road, and in about 25 feet, the trail diverges on the left side, marked by orange blazes. The trail progresses east, cuts uphill, swings east again and follows the contour of the hillside above a valley with limestone bluffs. In about 0.5 mile, the trail turns uphill and emerges at the edge of a meadow. Be on the lookout for bluebirds. Turn immediately left and follow the trail along the edge of the open area for about 50 feet. It then drops back into the woods and leads up the valley, where it swings left (east), crosses a stream and starts back down the valley (north). The trail runs through thick woods and along a rock crevice, then crosses the stream and follows it on the west side. There are spots where footing is loose and rough. Continue on the trail and follow the blazes through a flat valley area, staying off the private property beyond the fence.

The trail crosses a larger stream, swings left and then right and begins to ascend the bluffs. There are spots that are steep, rough or loose. The trail meanders to the east, staying below the bluffs, switches north between large rocks and leads up to a flat, nearly treeless grassy area—the third glade. It then heads west across the glade, dips into a ravine and climbs into the first and second glades. Then it descends steeply between rocky ledges and arrives at Blue River Road. Follow the road south (left) to your car.

Through a land swap, Jackson County has acquired the third (east) glade. This trade may require the rerouting of the southern portion of the trail. A trail leading up to the third glade is being developed from where 83rd Street dead-ends on the east side of the park land. Another loop trail, indicated by the broken line on the map, is being developed north of the glades.

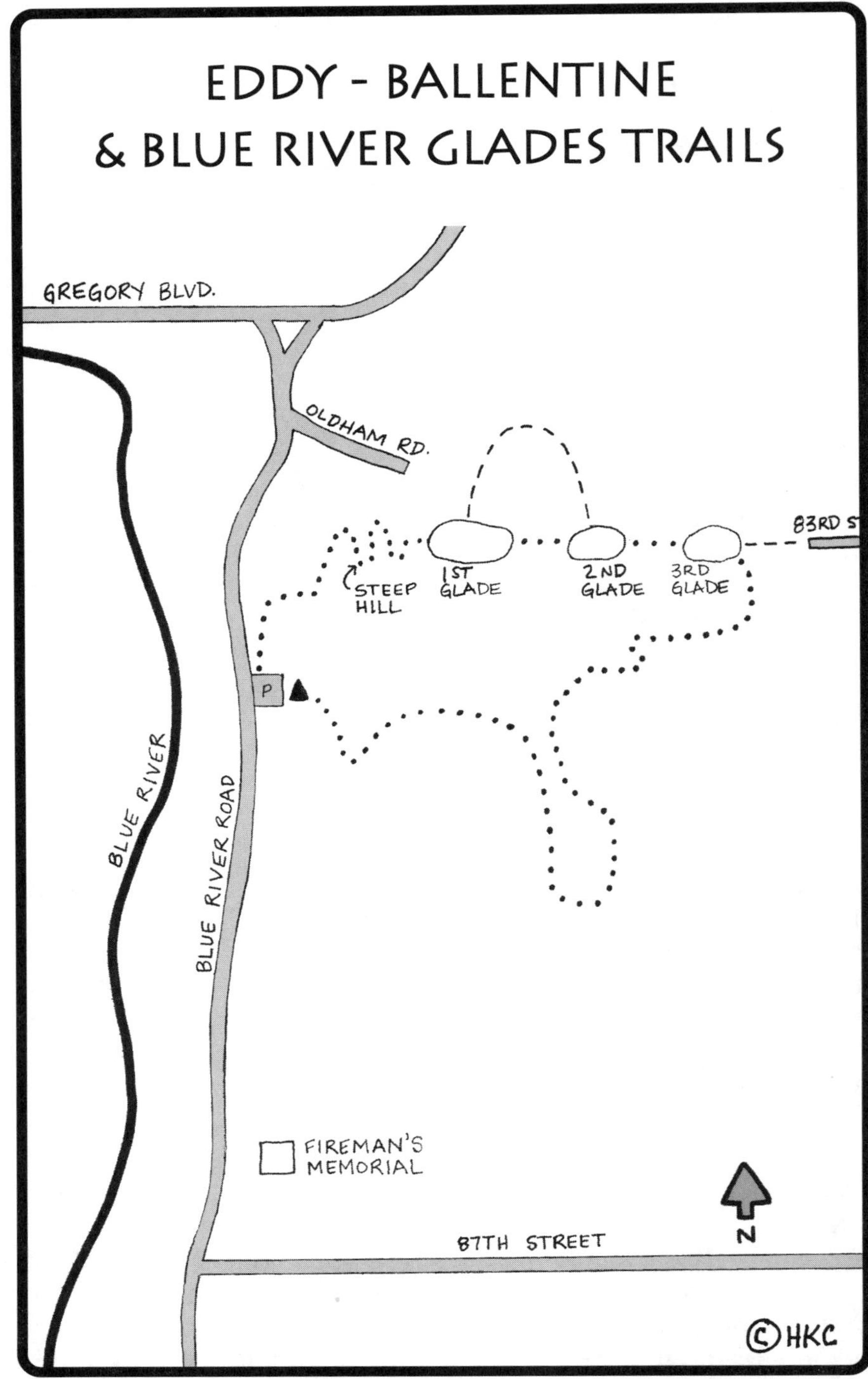
EDDY - BALLENTINE
& BLUE RIVER GLADES TRAILS
GREGORY BLVD.
OLDHAM RD.
83RD ST
STEEP HILL
1ST GLADE
2ND GLADE
3RD GLADE
P
BLUE RIVER
BLUE RIVER ROAD
FIREMAN'S MEMORIAL
N
87TH STREET
©HKC

The trails in the northern portion of the Blue River Parkway pass through thick woods and along a rock crevice, then cross a stream and follow it on the west side. There are spots where footing is loose and rough, so be sure to wear sturdy shoes or hiking boots.

26
KLEIN PARK – CAVE SPRING

Jackson County Parks & Recreation Department, Cave Spring Association, Inc.

Time: 1 Hour or Less
Distance: 1.5-Mile Loop System
Rating: Easy
Drinking Water: Yes
Accessible: Portion

This historic spot is easy to reach and provides about 2 miles of interesting walking. Although short, the path is sometimes steep, and the woods are surprisingly deep for an area in the midst of the city. Much of the trail system is wood-chipped. This area is on the route of the old Santa Fe Trail. Travelers are said to have stopped at the spring at the end of their first half-day of traveling from Independence.

Directions: Drive 1.1 miles east of I-435 on Gregory Boulevard, east of Swope Park. Just before reaching Blue Ridge Boulevard (the route of the Santa Fe Trail), turn south into the parking area. When the nature center is open, stop for a trail map and directions to the trailhead. (Open all week, sunrise to sundown.)

Cave Spring Trail: At the west side of the parking area, about 50 yards south of the park entrance, an opening in a wooden fence points the way to the trailhead. Follow the path west and south into the woods. Stay to the right at the first branch of the trail. Very soon, the trail branches again. Take the left branch, which leads to the old spring. If you continue on past the spring, you will come to a road that leads back to the nature center, for a very short hike of perhaps 0.25 mile. Our suggestion is that you turn around at the spring and rejoin the main trail to continue the circuit. Your route will take you through woods, along a dam, across wooden bridges built by Boy Scouts, past limestone chimneys from old cabins, near a pond and back to the nature center for a very pleasant walk. If you wish, you can follow some of the side paths that lead off from the main trail. These return to the trail or to one of the dirt roads through the park. The park area is fairly small, some 40 acres, so one really can't become lost.

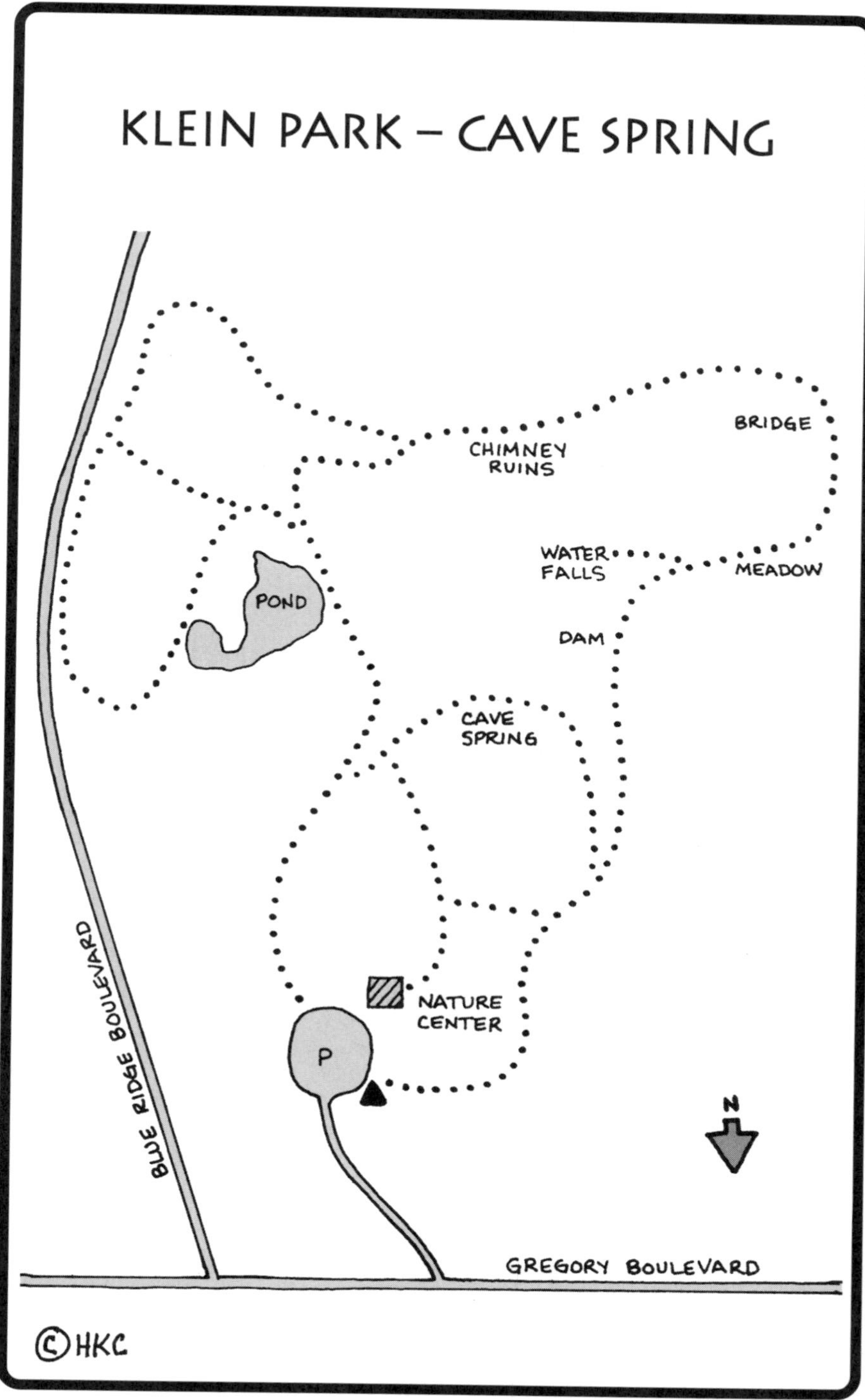
KLEIN PARK – CAVE SPRING
BRIDGE
CHIMNEY RUINS
WATER FALLS
MEADOW
POND
DAM
CAVE SPRING
NATURE CENTER
P
N
BLUE RIDGE BOULEVARD
GREGORY BOULEVARD
©HKC

27
GEORGE OWENS NATURE PARK

Department of Parks & Recreation
Independence, Missouri

Time: 2 Hours **Drinking Water:** Yes (At Nature Center)
Distance: 4 Miles of Loop Trails **Accessible:** No
Rating: Moderate

This 80-acre nature park, located in the northwest part of Independence, is an attractive and well maintained multi-use area that was donated to the city by Mr. Owens. In addition to fishing ponds, shelter houses and a campground, it features a series of well laid out loop trails through upland rock formations, deep woods, valleys and clearings.

Directions: From I-70 in Independence, go north on Hwy 291 to 23rd Street (Hwy 78), or go south on 291 from Hwy 24. At 23rd Street, drive east to Speck Road, just beyond a school. Turn north on Speck Road for less than a mile. The entrance to the nature park is obvious. Park in the parking lot and go to the park office to obtain a map of the trails.

Trails: Six interconnected loop trails are located around the park. All are named and marked with their own colors. However, since all intersections are not well-marked, it is sometimes difficult to find your location on the map. The trails are well traveled and easy to see. A couple of very pleasant hours can be spent exploring this system.

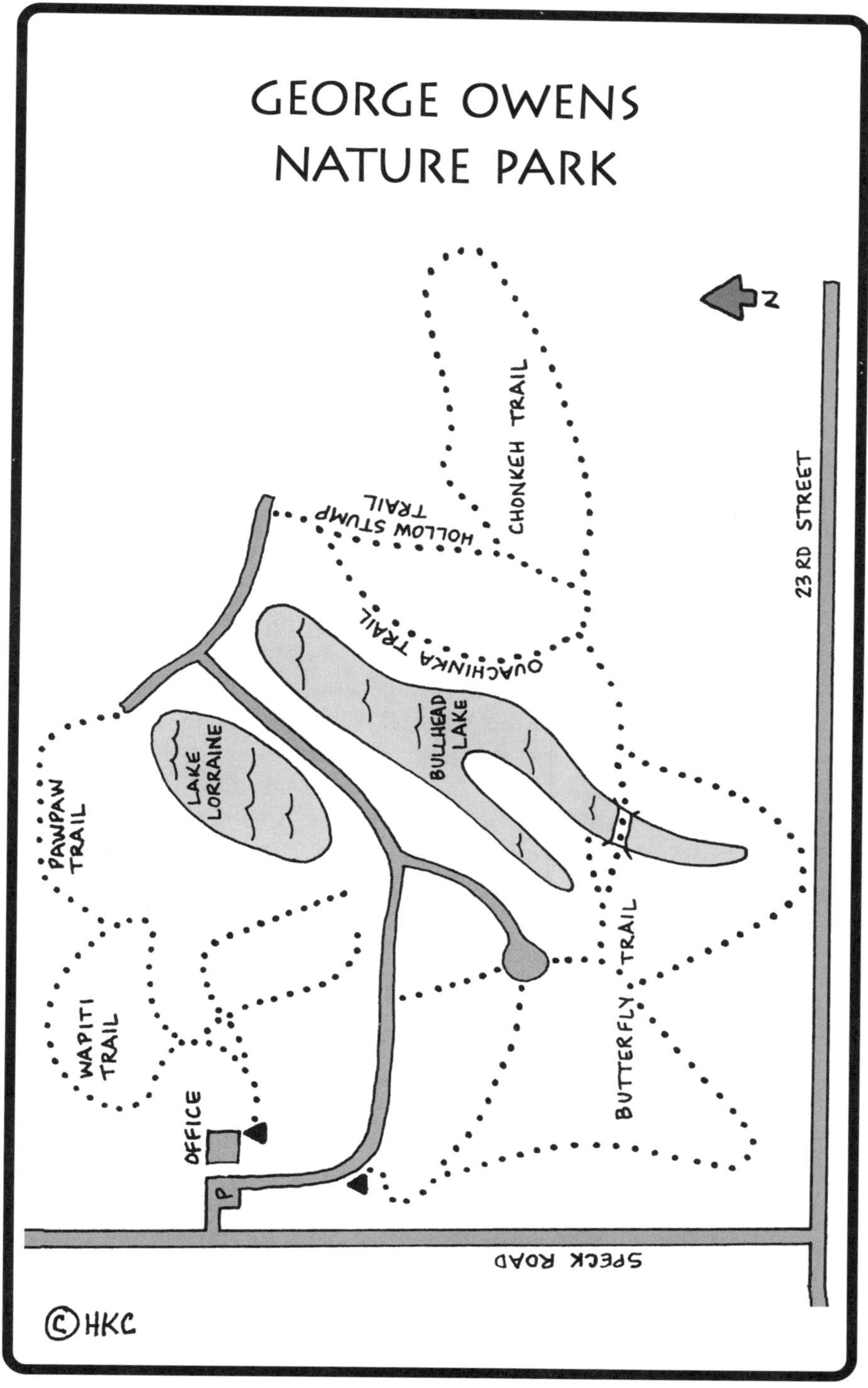
GEORGE OWENS
NATURE PARK
N
CHONKEH TRAIL
HOLLOW STUMP TRAIL
OUACHINKA TRAIL
23 RD STREET
BULLHEAD LAKE
LAKE LORRAINE
PAWPAW TRAIL
WAPITI TRAIL
BUTTERFLY TRAIL
OFFICE
P
SPECK ROAD
© HKC

28
SWOPE PARK WALKS
Kansas City, Missouri Parks & Recreation

Swope Park, the second largest urban park in the nation, is a preserve of varied terrain with forests, wetlands, bluffs and glades. Restoration activities are returning some of the sites to their original condition. The park contains many opportunities for walks. Four opportunities are listed below.

Fox Hollow Trail, Lakeside Nature Center: This interesting, 2-mile horseshoe loop trail traces it way south and west across glades, below rugged limestone bluffs and along a stream. Upland forests of oak and other native trees contrast with grassy, treeless glades. Enter an opening in the wing wall just east of the Lakeside Nature Center, 4701 East Gregory, to access a gravel pathway. Take that path to the left and follow the signs to a wood-chipped trail that leads into the forest. This is the main entrance to the trail. You can return to the nature center at two midway points via the gravel trail, or you can complete the entire 2-mile loop ending in a grassy area west of the nature center. The trail was developed under the leadership of volunteers Ken Hightower and Gordon Havens, with the help of many other volunteers, including 14 Scouts who obtained their Eagle Scout badges for trail work. Pick up a brochure and map at the nature center for more information. Note: The gravel nature trail is an option for a short walk.

Marsh Trail: A marsh is located behind a small limestone building at the intersection of Gregory Boulevard and Oldham Road, near the Lake of the Woods. This loop trail begins behind the building and leads down into the wetlands adjacent to the Blue River. (If you encounter flooding or deep mud, it is best to reschedule the hike for a drier time.) This marsh trail of approximately 1 mile provides a unique opportunity to see native vegetation and animals that inhabit the wetlands. Stop at the Lakeside Nature Center on Gregory Road, about 0.5 mile west of this location, for a brochure that will help you identify plants, birds and animal tracks.

Camp Lake of the Woods Limestone Glade Trail: On a hilltop above the Lake of the Woods is a rugged area that was once used for residential camps and is now devoted to day camps and organized outdoor activities. A south-facing glade just below the camp buildings is the site of major restoration efforts. Invasive plants and shrubs are being removed to allow native grasses and wildflowers to return. A 0.75-mile trail leads south from the road down into the glade, across it, into an area that has yet to be restored and back to the road—giving the walker a clear picture of the changes that have been made. The camp is located on Oakwood Drive. However, permission is required to enter this area. Check in at Lakeside Nature Center for information about how to access the trail.

The Kansas City Zoo: There are many miles of walking paths in the zoo at Swope Park. Of particular interest are walks around the wild animal habitats and opportunities to see many birds and native vegetation. There is a modest admission charge to enter the zoo.

There are many miles of walking paths at the Kansas City Zoo in Swope Park. See animals from places as diverse as Alaska to Zimbabwe on one walk.

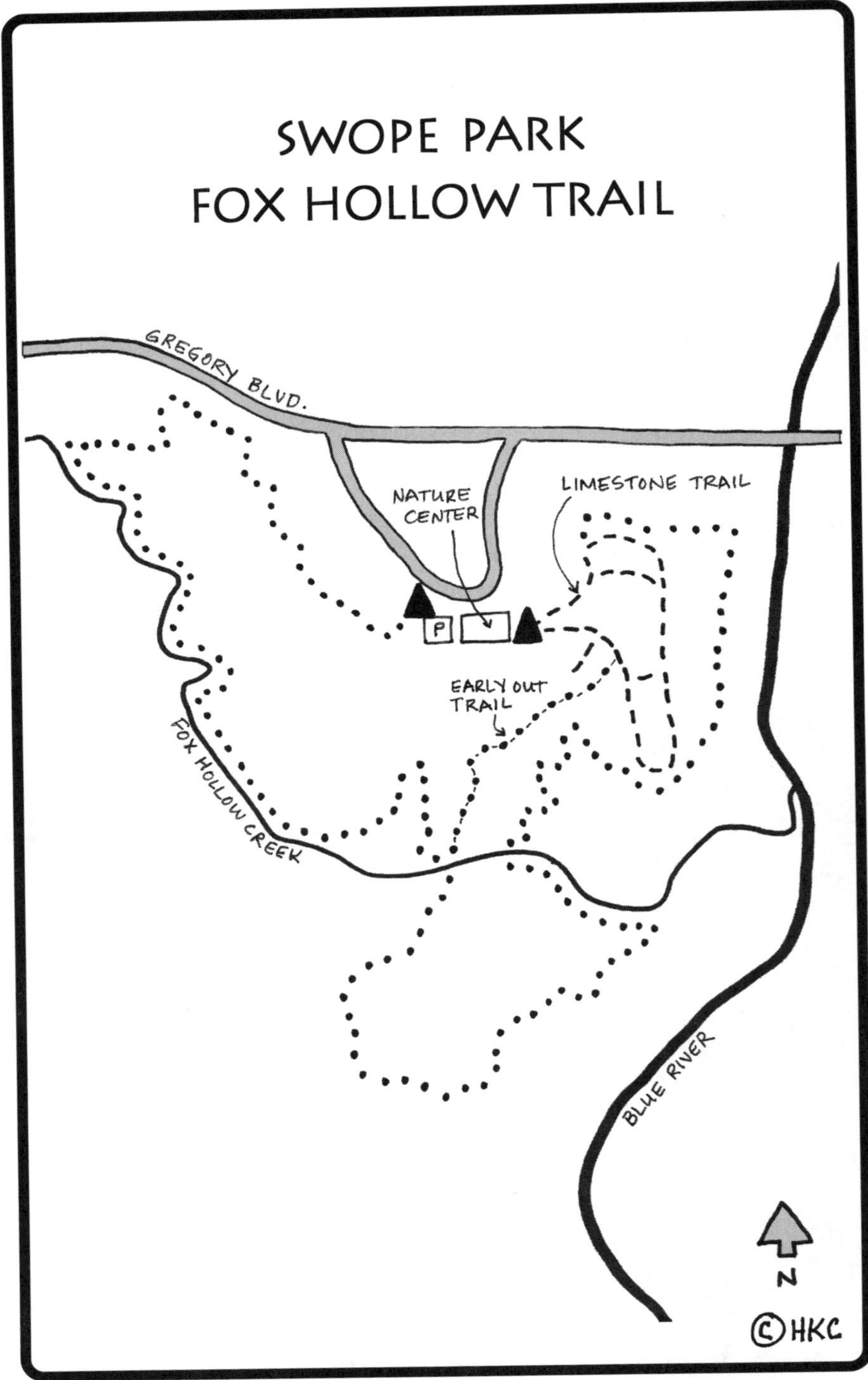
SWOPE PARK
FOX HOLLOW TRAIL
GREGORY BLVD.
NATURE CENTER
LIMESTONE TRAIL
P
EARLY OUT TRAIL
FOX HOLLOW CREEK
BLUE RIVER
N
©HKC

Swope Park's winter trails, draped in snow drifts, provide a breathtaking, but challenging, walk.

29
UNITY VILLAGE TRAIL SYSTEM
Unity Village, Missouri

Time: 1 to 2 Hours
Distance: 2.2 Miles (Little Cedar Creek)
Rating: Moderate
Drinking Water: No
Accessible: Parts

Unity Village, a separately incorporated municipality between Raytown and Lee's Summit, Missouri, has opened its 1,275-acre grounds to hikers. At present, one loop hiking trail with several branches is open. Others will be added. There is also an exercise trail and a labyrinth. Visitors are welcome to walk the streets and roadways within the village. Please respect the privacy of employees and guests on Unity Village grounds.

Directions: To reach Unity Village from central Kansas City, drive southeast from Raytown on Hwy 350, or drive east on Bannister Road. From the intersection of Bannister (which becomes Colburn Road) and Hwy 350, travel 0.1 mile east on Colburn to a flashing signal. Turn left (north) into the Unity grounds. (Travelers from the south will turn right on Colburn.) From the entrance, proceed straight ahead for 2 blocks until you come to Mockingbird Lane. Turn right on Mockingbird Lane and go for about a block to where it intersects with Quail Drive. The trail begins here. For a hike of several miles, you can walk the main trail, its branches and the Exercise Trail. Park in any of the nearby parking lots, but do not park on roadways. Large groups should request permission by calling the Unity Village Facilities Department Monday through Thursday at (816) 251-3569.

Little Cedar Creek Trail: This attractive trail leads under a railroad bridge into a preserve of forest, grasslands and a few crop fields. It follows gravel and dirt tracks that provide maintenance access. Wildlife is abundant, and there is a wildlife feeding station just off the trail. Features include two lakes, deep woods with old growth trees and upland prairie—some of which is being restored to its natural state. Signs at trail intersections provide directions to the main trail and the several branches, as well as information about the preserve.

Exercise Trail: A branch of the exercise trail leads to a natural bridge, one of the historic natural sites of Missouri. The trailhead for this 1-mile trail is on Mockingbird Lane. Please do not walk on the railroad tracks or on the immediately adjacent railroad right-of-way. Trains come through this area going very fast with little or no advance warning.

Note: Several miles of multi-use hiking trails are scheduled to open soon in Legacy Park. This 700-acre Lee's Summit park is 5 miles east of Hwy 350 on Colburn Road.

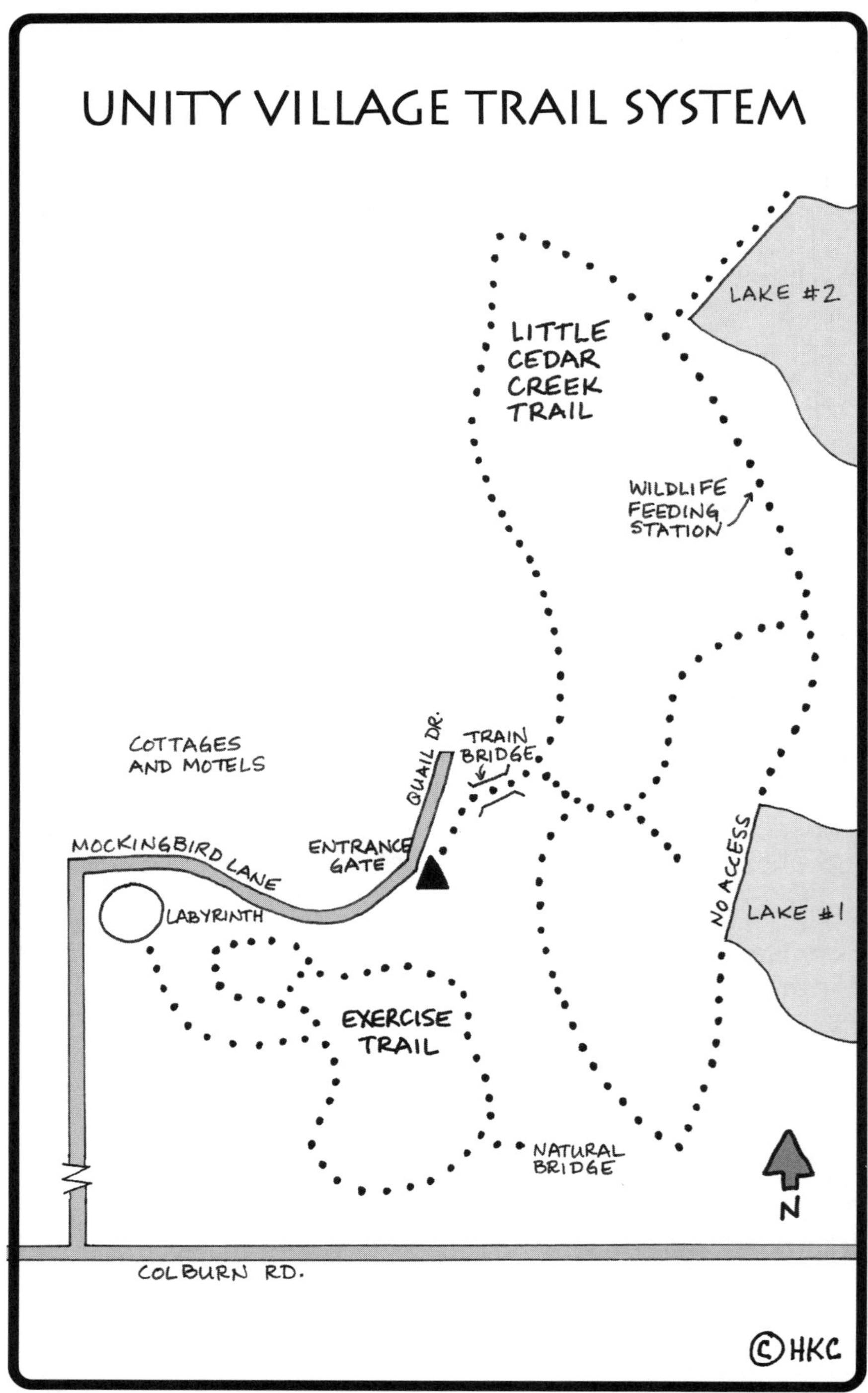
UNITY VILLAGE TRAIL SYSTEM
LAKE #2
LITTLE CEDAR CREEK TRAIL
WILDLIFE FEEDING STATION
COTTAGES AND MOTELS
QUAIL DR.
TRAIN BRIDGE
MOCKINGBIRD LANE
ENTRANCE GATE
NO ACCESS
LAKE #1
LABYRINTH
EXERCISE TRAIL
NATURAL BRIDGE
N
COLBURN RD.
©HKC

TRAIL NOTES:

30
JERRY SMITH PARK TRAIL

Kansas City, Missouri Parks & Recreation, Missouri Department of Conservation

Time: 1 Hour
Distance: 2.5 Mile Loop
Rating: Moderately Easy

Drinking Water: No
Accessible: No

Jerry Smith Park and the adjacent Saeger Woods Conservation Area contain remnants of native prairie lands that are being restored to their original state. As the land is cleared of invasive brush and plants and controlled burns are carried out, a profusion of native plants and wildflowers emerge. Big bluestem, blazing stars, the imperiled-eared false foxglove, purple cornflower and willow-leafed sunflower are among the many varieties. Bird populations include the American woodcock and the dickcissel. Restoration is being conducted by the Missouri Department of Conservation and Kansas City, Missouri Parks and Recreation, with the assistance of Kansas City WildLands, a coalition of some twenty conservation organizations dedicated to the protection and restoration of remnant native sites.

Directions: Take Holmes Road south of Martin City. Immediately after the Blue River Bridge, turn east on 139th Street. The Park entrance is approximately 0.75 mile on the left. Follow a gravel road 0.3 mile from the entrance to a designated parking area.

Trail System: The 2.5-mile double loop trail heads north from the parking area. The south loop of 1.5 miles is joined by a 1-mile north loop. The surface is wood-chipped, and there are segments that are moderately steep. Each season offers a unique opportunity to view prairie wildflowers and wildlife.

Note: For more information on native sites being restored by the Kansas City WildLands partnership, see *Kansas City WildLands,* written by Larry Rizzo and published by the Missouri Department of Conservation. Online at www.kcwildlands.org.

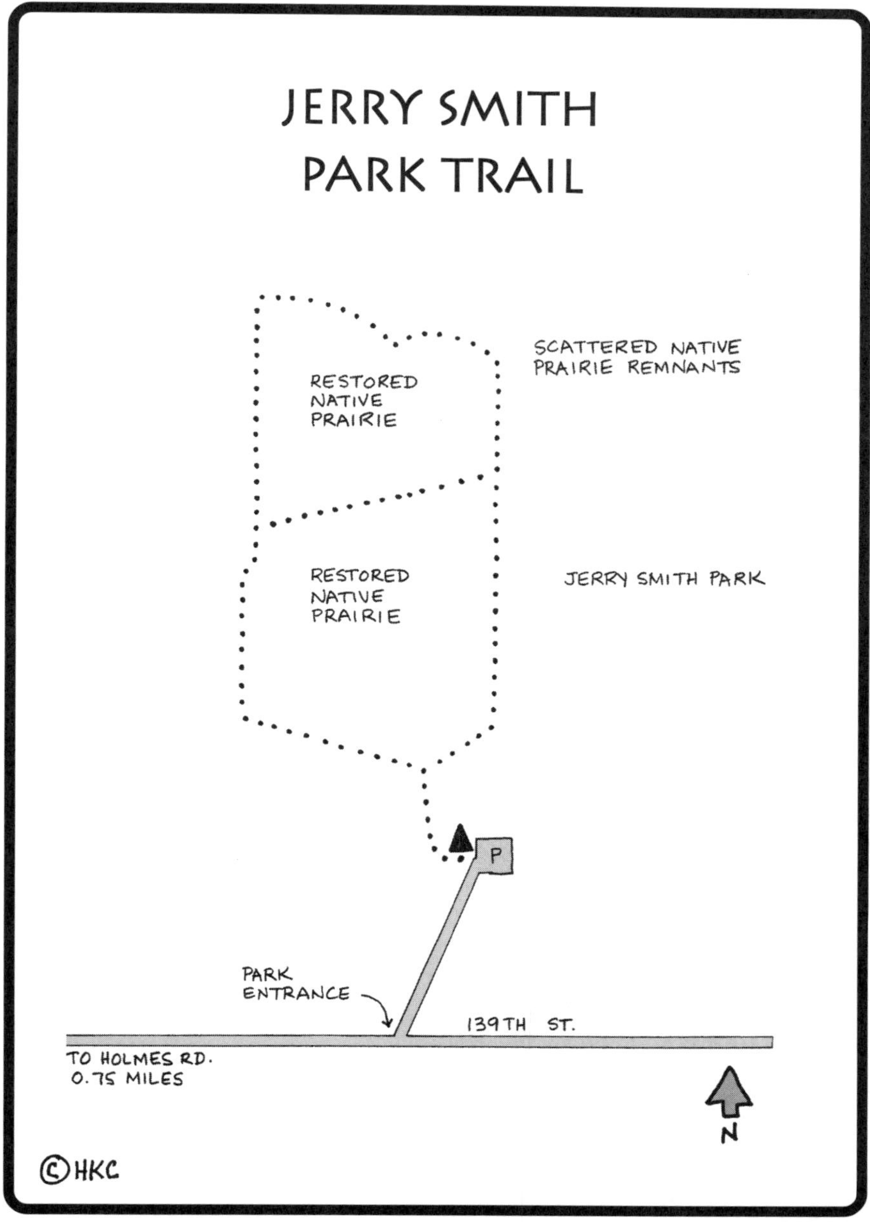

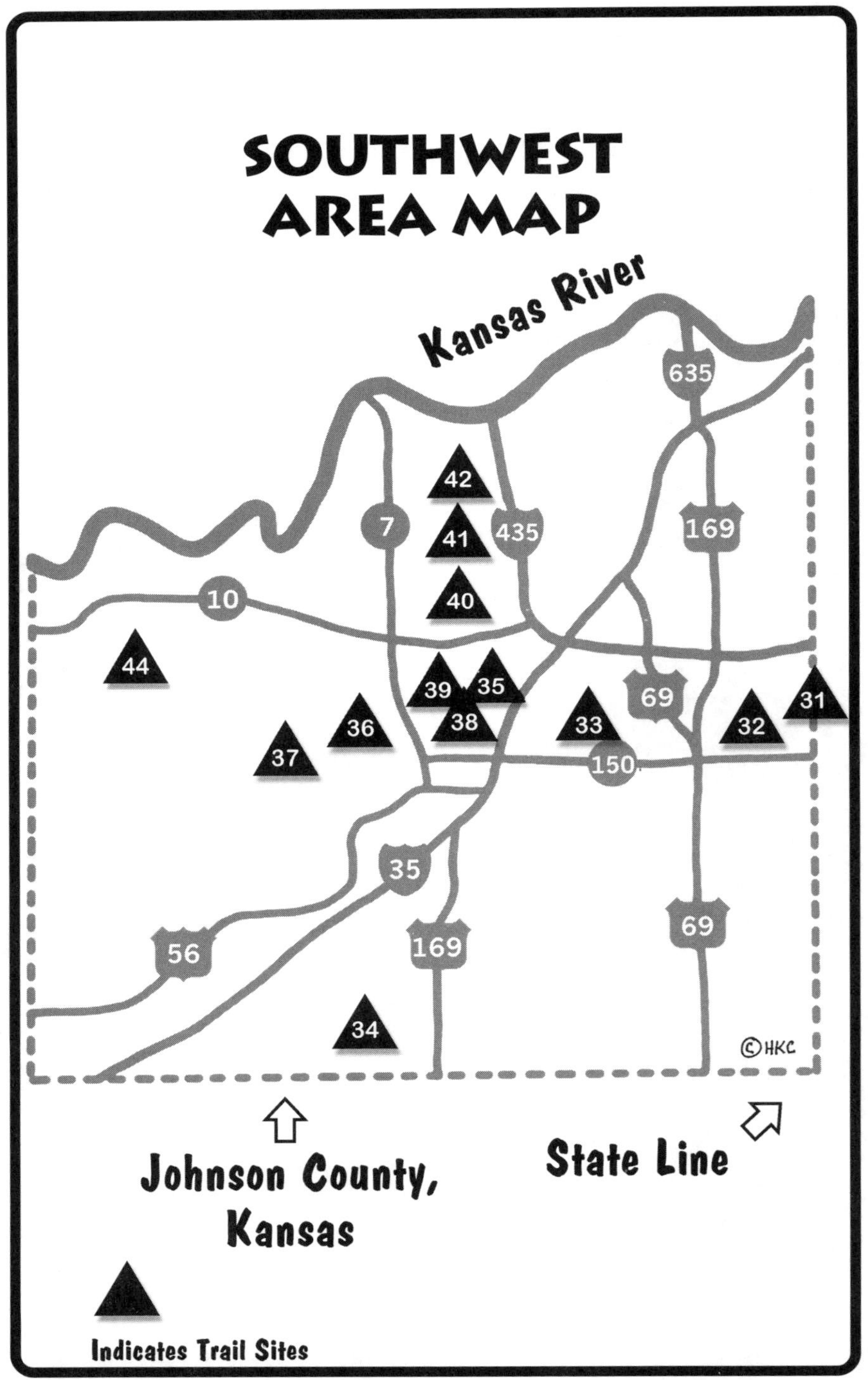
SOUTHWEST
AREA MAP
Kansas River
635
42
7
41
435
169
10
40
44
39
35
69
31
36
38
33
32
37
150
35
56
169
69
34
©HKC
Johnson County,
Kansas
State Line
Indicates Trail Sites

TRAIL SITES IN THE SOUTHWEST AREA

Note: ( ) denotes the number of trails at that location

31
TOMAHAWK CREEK GREENWAY
City of Leawood, Kansas Parks & Greenway

Time: 2 Hours (One-way)
Distance: 4.75 Miles (One-way)
Rating: Easy to Moderate
Drinking Water: Yes
Accessible: Portions

Woods and native prairie grasses wind alongside this asphalt trail beside Tomahawk Creek between I-435 on the north and beyond 127th Street on the south. Plans are to extend it to near 139th Street and Antioch Road. It is a fine urban trail out of sight and sound from local traffic. Birds and other evidence of wildlife are abundant. This trail connects to the eastern terminus of Overland Park's Indian Creek Bike & Hike Trail (see Trail Site 32) and the Indian Creek Greenway Trail in Kansas City, Missouri.

Directions: You may begin hiking the trail at one of the four trailheads, two north and two south. The first north trailhead is in Overland Park's Foxhill Park, which may be reached as described under the description of Trail Site 32. The second north trailhead is in Leawood City Park at the south end of

Lee Boulevard (located between State Line and Mission Road). Signs clearly indicate the trailhead. There are two south trailheads. One is south of 119th Street west of Mission Road. The other is on Nall Avenue just north of 127th Street in Leawood's I-Lan Park.

The Tomahawk Creek Greenway Trail: The trail is well-used by walkers, hikers, joggers and cyclists. Stay on the right side of the trail to permit cyclists to pass. Most are polite enough to warn you of their approach by calling, "passing on your left." There are mile markers at half-mile intervals and, at several places, benches to rest with a view of Tomahawk Creek. Trees along the trail include burr oak, maple, sycamore, elm and shagbark hickory. Look for signs of beaver. Water is available at the trailhead in the Leawood City Park and at I-Lan Park. Restrooms are available there and at the park near 119th Street.

The best access for people with disabilities is at 119th Street near Mission Road. From Leawood Park south to 119th Street is 2 miles (one-way), and from 119th Street to I-Lan Park is 1.75 miles (one-way). From Leawood Park east to State Line Road is 1 mile (one-way). From I-Lan Park, walkers can proceed south on the sidewalk to 127th Street and then west along 127th for about 0.25 mile, where the paved trail continues under a bridge north and south. Going south and west, the path runs along a golf course for about 1 mile (one-way) to Metcalf Avenue. Plans are to extend the trail under Metcalf Road, Route 69 and 135th Street. Going north at the bridge on 127th Street puts walkers on a paved path through Nottingham Park for about 1 mile (one-way) to 123rd Street. Both walks offer pleasant views. This trail extends east to 103rd and State Line Road. From there, Kansas City Parks and Recreation has continued the trail east along Indian Creek to 99th Street just east of Holmes Road.

Plans call for this trail to be extended east to the Blue River and north to 85th Street to the Harry Wiggins Trolley Track Trail (see Trail Site 49), linking Kansas and Missouri county trail systems. Possible links to the Katy Trail State Park are also being considered.

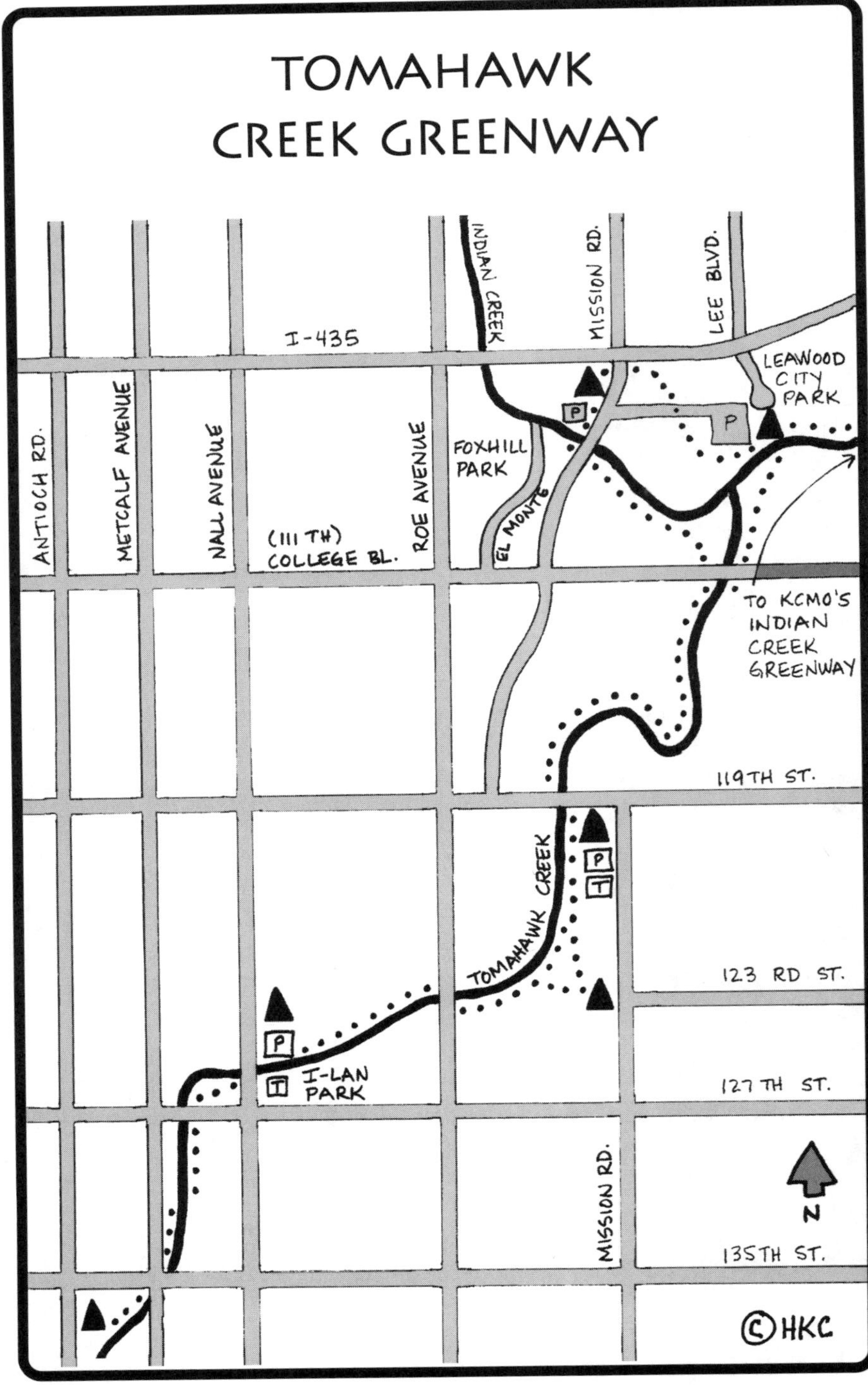
TOMAHAWK
CREEK GREENWAY
INDIAN CREEK
MISSION RD.
LEE BLVD.
I-435
LEAWOOD
CITY
PARK
FOXHILL
PARK
EL MONTE
ANTIOCH RD.
METCALF AVENUE
NALL AVENUE
ROE AVENUE
(111 TH)
COLLEGE BL.
TO KCMO'S
INDIAN
CREEK
GREENWAY
119TH ST.
TOMAHAWK CREEK
123 RD ST.
I-LAN
PARK
127 TH ST.
MISSION RD.
N
135TH ST.
©HKC

Waterfowl and small mammals, including beavers, frequent Indian Creek (see trail description on the next page).

32
INDIAN CREEK BIKE & HIKE TRAIL
Overland Park, Kansas Parks & Recreation

Time: 5 to 5.5 Hours (One-way)
Distance: 10.5 Miles (One-way)
Rating: Easy
Drinking Water: Yes
Accessible: Portions

This asphalt trail runs east to west along Indian Creek in the general vicinity of 103rd Street between Mission Road on the east and Pflumm Road on the west. At the east end, it connects with Leawood's Tomahawk Creek Greenway, which heads east to State Line Road where it connects to the Kansas City Indian Creek Greenway (see Trail Site 31). The Tomahawk Creek Greenway also heads south and west 4 miles to I-Lan Park on Roe Avenue near 127th Street and will eventually go to 139th Street near Antioch Road. On the west end, the trail connects with Olathe's Indian Creek Greenway and Trail (see Trail Site 33). The combined Olathe (8.8), Overland Park (10.5), Leawood (2) and Kansas City (2) Indian Creek trails extend for 23.5 miles. The trail is used by hikers, bikers and joggers. On some days and in some sections, this trail may seem crowded.

Directions: You can pick up the trail at several points and walk parts of it as your time and energy allow. See the map for starting points. A parking lot at the east end of the trail in Foxhill Park may be reached by driving south on Roe Avenue to College Boulevard (111th Street) and turning left on 111th Street to El Monte. Turn left on El Monte to the parking lot. The obvious start of the trail is about 20 yards north of the parking lot, near a posted trail map. From there, you may hike the Indian Creek Trail to the west or the Tomahawk Creek Trail to the east or south.The best parking lot near the west end of the trail is at Quivira Park, just south of 119th Street. From the park, walk north toward 119th Street to enter the trail.

The Indian Creek Trail follows the creek through wooded areas and park land. Underpasses allow you to hike the entire trail without crossing any major streets. Most of the trail is away from the sight and noise of traffic, except for a 1-mile stretch along the Brookridge Golf Club, which parallels I-435. The only commercial area adjacent to the trail is at Roe Avenue near 107th Street. You may wish to stop here for refreshment. Rock outcroppings and nice vistas of Indian Creek appear at various points. Indian Creek often floods during heavy rains, making the trail impassable or muddy, so plan accordingly.

A sure cure for "cabin fever" is a winter hike. Dress appropriately.

The trail proceeds south just beyond Antioch Road and traverses the Corporate Woods parks. About 2.7 miles south of Corporate Woods, it goes under Quivira Road and then proceeds through thick woods to Pflumm Road near 127th Street, where it connects with Olathe's Indian Creek Greenway and Trail. Many parts of the trail are flat, although the underpasses are too steep to be negotiated by most wheelchair users. However, the section between Mission Road and Roe Avenue would be a good one to try.

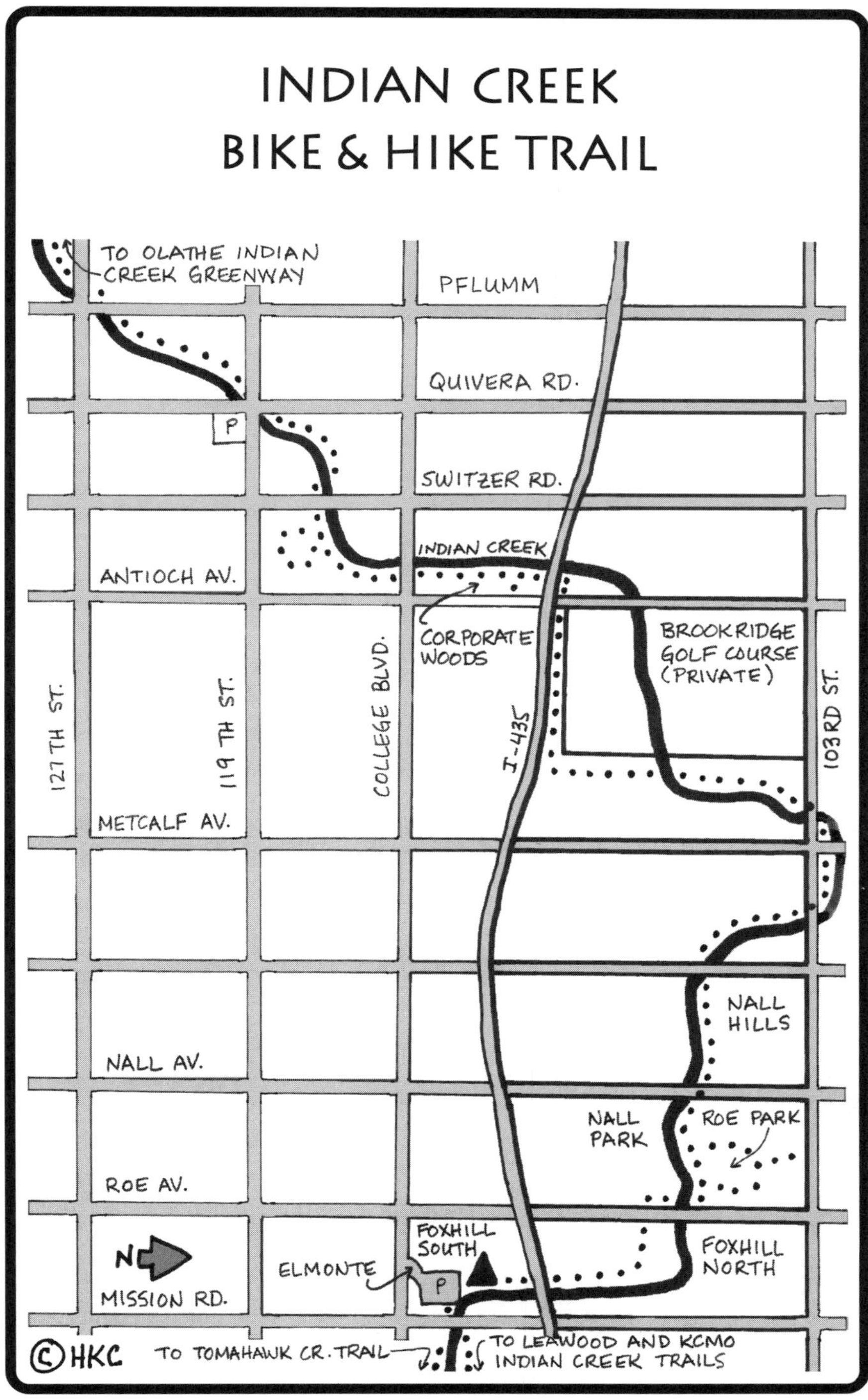
INDIAN CREEK
BIKE & HIKE TRAIL
TO OLATHE INDIAN CREEK GREENWAY
PFLUMM
QUIVERA RD.
P
SWITZER RD.
INDIAN CREEK
ANTIOCH AV.
CORPORATE WOODS
BROOKRIDGE GOLF COURSE (PRIVATE)
127 TH ST.
119 TH ST.
COLLEGE BLVD.
I-435
103RD ST.
METCALF AV.
NALL HILLS
NALL AV.
NALL PARK
ROE PARK
ROE AV.
FOXHILL SOUTH
FOXHILL NORTH
N
ELMONTE
P
MISSION RD.
©HKC
TO TOMAHAWK CR. TRAIL
TO LEAWOOD AND KCMO INDIAN CREEK TRAILS

33
INDIAN CREEK GREENWAY & TRAIL
Olathe Parks & Recreation

Time: 4.4 Hours
Distance: 8.8 Miles
Rating: Easy

Drinking Water: No
Accessible: Yes

This 10'-wide asphalt trail extends from Pflumm Road just north of 127th Street to 153rd Terrace west of Mur-len Road in Olathe. It is designed for accessibility with no grade greater than five percent. Completely off the road, the trail follows Indian Creek through woods and open, grassy areas. On the east, it connects with Overland Park's Indian Creek Bike and Hike Trail (see Trail Site 32). Trailheads with parking are on the east side of Blackbob Road, just south of 127th Street; on the north side of 143rd Street, west of Mur-len Road (park at Havencroft School); north of 151st Street in Arrowhead Park near Heritage School; and at Southdowne Park. Mur-len and Blackbob Roads intersect Kansas Hwy 150 (Santa Fe) east of I-35.

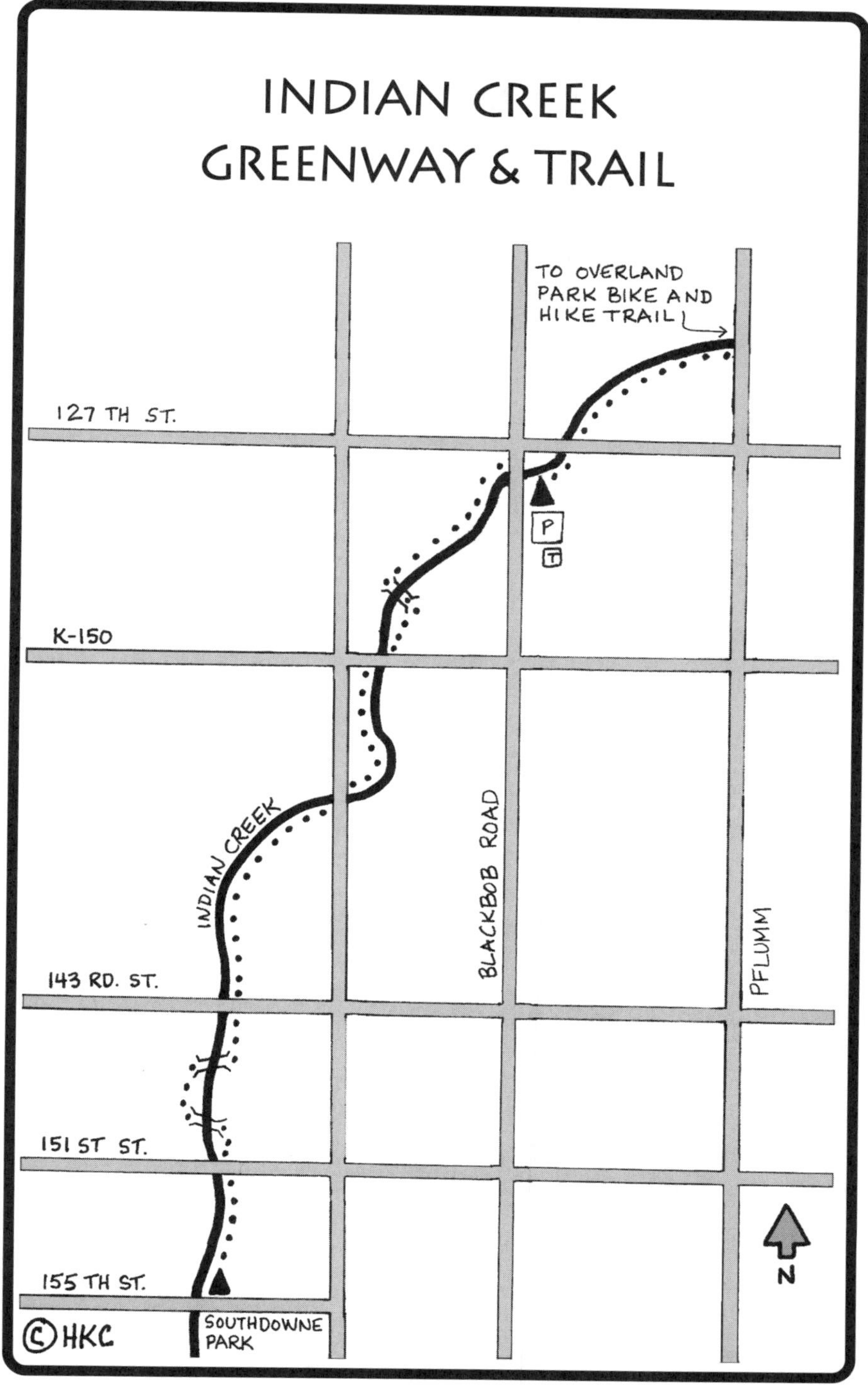
INDIAN CREEK
GREENWAY & TRAIL
TO OVERLAND PARK BIKE AND HIKE TRAIL
127 TH ST.
K-150
INDIAN CREEK
BLACKBOB ROAD
PFLUMM
143 RD. ST.
151 ST ST.
155 TH ST.
SOUTHDOWNE PARK
P
T
N
©HKC

34
OVERLAND PARK ARBORETUM

City of Overland Park, Kansas

Time: 1 to 3 Hours
Distance: 5 Miles
Rating: Easy to Moderate
Drinking Water: Yes
Accessible: Portions

The Arboretum is a very well planned and developed 300-acre preserve on the southwestern edge of the metropolitan area. It offers walking trails, woodland gardens, a water garden, a plant demonstration area, childrens' play areas, an environmental education and visitors center, and paved, connecting sidewalks.

Directions: Take Hwy 69 south to 179th Street. Turn right (west), go past the corner of Antioch Road and 179th Street and turn left into the Arboretum. Directions at the parking area show you where to begin the hikes.

Trail System: Five miles of interconnecting trails loop through the preserve, crossing bridges, circling ponds and ascending bluffs. Most paths are wood-chipped. There is also a 0.5-mile asphalt walkway. The trails cross Wolf Creek, a tributary of the Blue River. Flowers bloom throughout the season. One can wander the trails without fear of being lost. Sooner or later, they all return you to the beginning point. Maps and brochures, available at the visitors center, provide more complete information about the arboretum and walking paths.

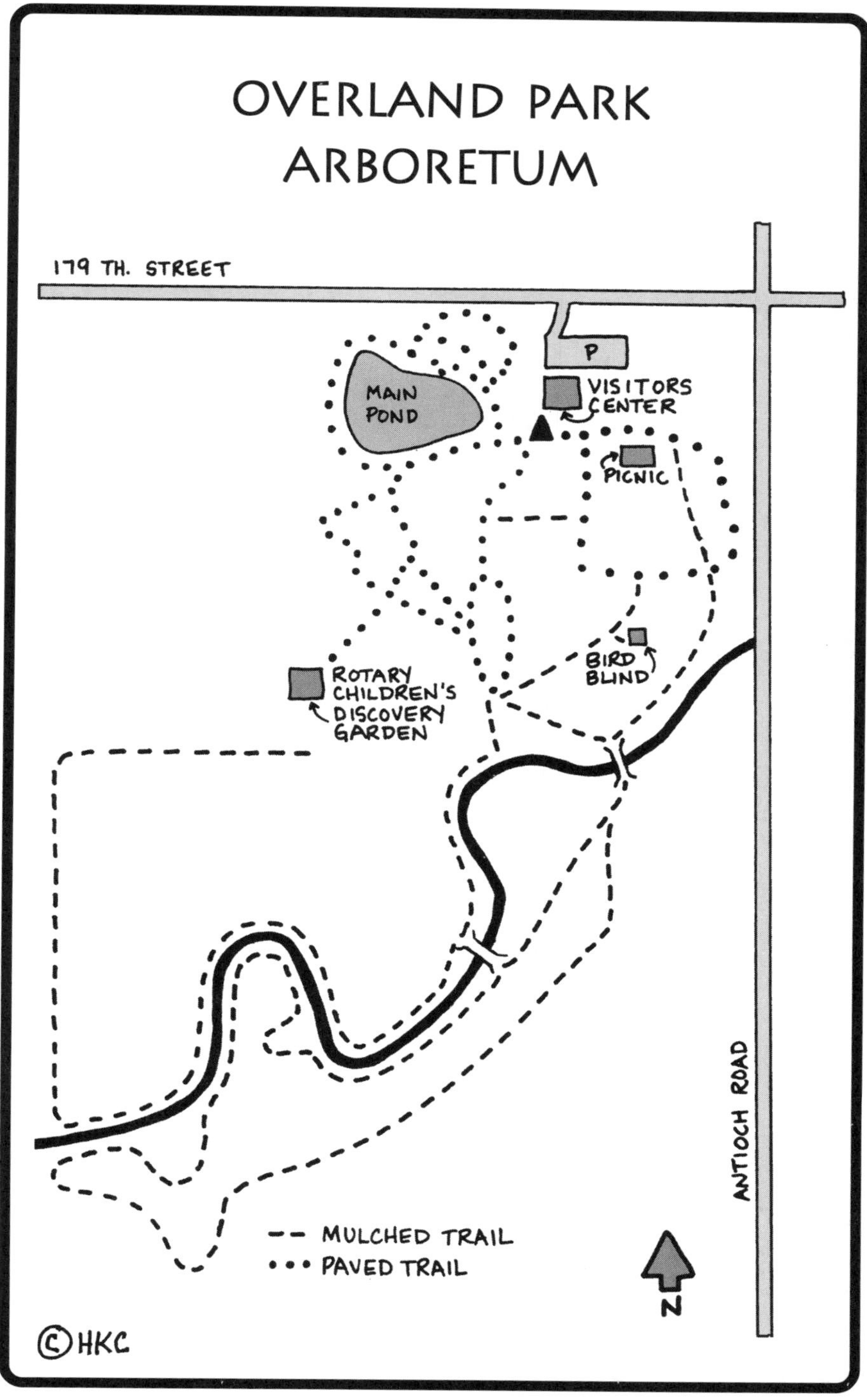
OVERLAND PARK
ARBORETUM
179 TH. STREET
P
MAIN
POND
VISITORS
CENTER
PICNIC
BIRD
BLIND
ROTARY
CHILDREN'S
DISCOVERY
GARDEN
ANTIOCH ROAD
MULCHED TRAIL
PAVED TRAIL
N
©HKC

Shawnee Mission Park offers every kind of trail, from the steep and rocky North Shore Trail to flat, paved trails.

35
SHAWNEE MISSION PARK
Johnson County Park & Recreation District

Lake Trail:
Time: 2.5 Hours
Distance: 6 Miles
Rating: Moderate
Drinking Water: Yes
Accessible: No

North Shore Trail:
Time: 1 Hour
Distance: 3 Miles
Rating: Moderate
Drinking Water: Yes
Accessible: No

Shawnee Mission Park Trail:
Time: 0.5 hour
Distance: 1 Mile
Rating: Easy

One of the Kansas City area's first dedicated walking trails was built in Shawnee Mission Park, along the south side of the lake. Once posted for foot travel only, it is now designated a horseback trail. In addition to the trails described here, there are other horseback trails suitable for hiking shown on park guides at information shelters.

Directions: Drive west from Overland Park on 87th Street to Renner Road. Turn north on Renner and go to the main park entrance at 79th Street. Enter the park and follow the park road that goes south from the visitors center. In a hundred yards or so, the road divides. Take the right branch. In 0.25 mile, you will come to Walnut Grove picnic grounds and parking area. Park at the west end of this area. The trail may also be accessed from the parking lot at Shelter 8.

The Lake Trail: Walk southwest past some softball fields to the edge of the woods, where a footbridge across a stream leads to the trail. Turn west (right) and follow the trail, which is not blazed or marked, but is heavily traveled. It wanders south and west along the lake for about 3 miles, ending at the dam. This trail passes through heavy woods, along rocky hillsides and up some fairly steep hills. It is a pleasant walk, but muddy in wet weather and rough in places in dry weather because of equestrian use. A party with two cars can reduce the walk to 3 miles by leaving one car in the parking area south of the dam.

North Shore Hiking Trail: A maze of trails may be found north of the lake. This area is designated a mountain biking area but hikers can enjoy it as well. Follow the park road past Walnut Grove and past Ogg Road to the northwest corner of the lake. Do not cross the dam. Park beside the road. There is a sign marking the trailhead. The trail takes you northeast up the hill through thick woods, where we saw deer and many birds. The route of this trail is difficult to describe. Our recommendation is to follow the map. This is a nice walk through interesting uplands.

Shawnee Mission Park Trail: A nice, 1-mile paved path leads from just south of the visitors center to the intersection of Barkley Circle and Fitch Memorial Drive near the lake. It traverses prairie and woodlands. Plans are for it to be extended along the north side of the roadway to the dam.

Gary Haller Trail in the Mill Creek Streamway Park: This 16-mile asphalt trail extends from near Olathe to the Kaw River and may be accessed south of the dam near Shelter 8 (see Trail Sites 38 to 42).

Phil Ratterman checks his time as he crosses the finish line of the Shawnee Mission Park Triathlon.

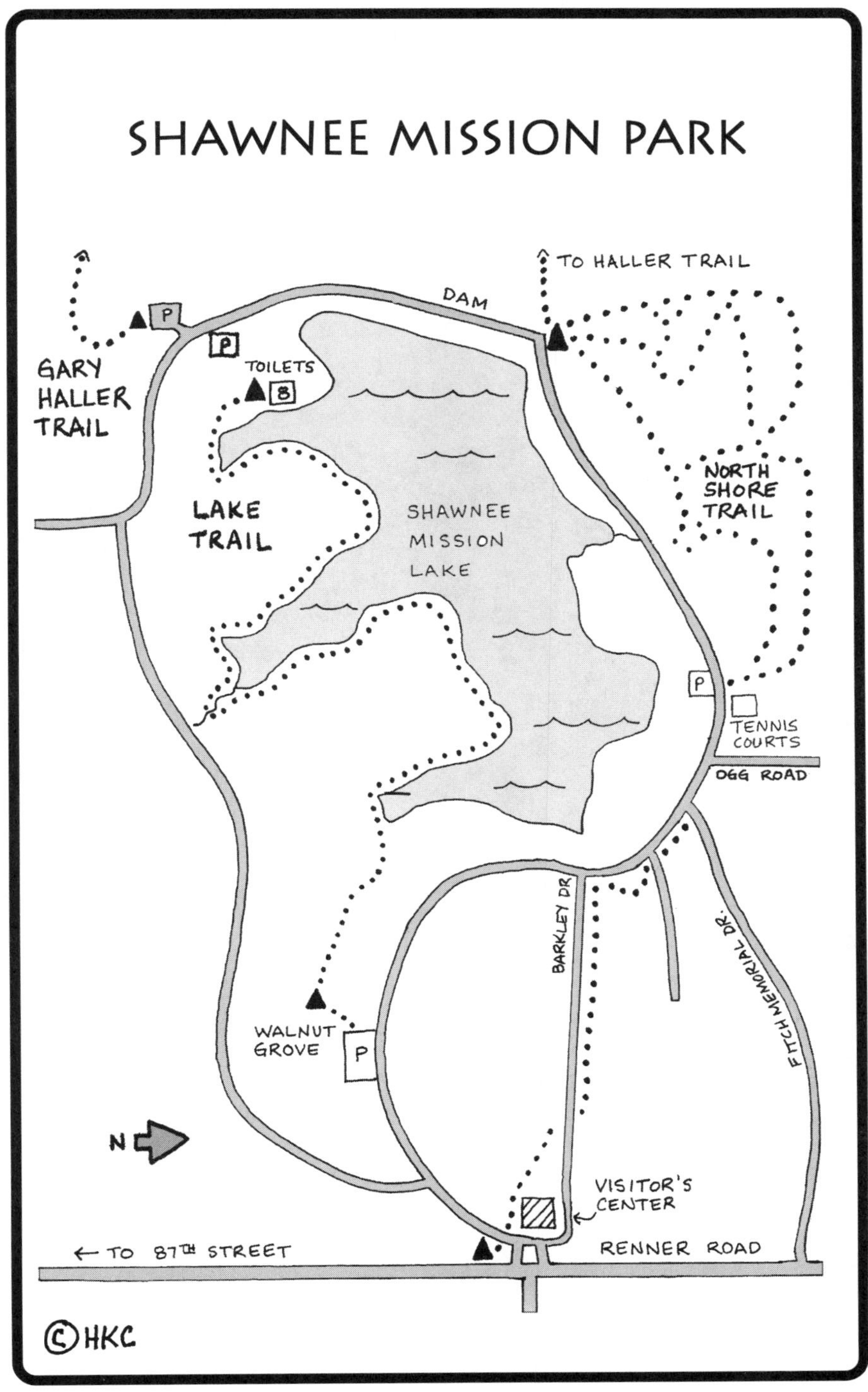
SHAWNEE MISSION PARK
TO HALLER TRAIL
DAM
P
TOILETS
8
GARY HALLER TRAIL
LAKE TRAIL
SHAWNEE MISSION LAKE
NORTH SHORE TRAIL
TENNIS COURTS
OGG ROAD
BARKLEY DR
FITCH MEMORIAL DR.
WALNUT GROVE
N
VISITOR'S CENTER
← TO 87TH STREET
RENNER ROAD
©HKC

Rent a sailboat at the marina and enjoy a day of hiking and sailing. Don't forget to pack a picnic.

TRAIL NOTES:

36
ERNIE MILLER PARK
Johnson County Park & Recreation District

Time: 1 to 2 Hours
Distance: 2 Miles
Rating: Moderate

Drinking Water: Yes
Accessible: Portion

We were pleased to find 2 miles of pleasant hiking trails in a small county park in western Johnson County. The area is an oasis among housing developments and other suburban establishments and is large enough to provide several hours of fairly isolated hiking. There are woods, meadows, hillsides, a stream and a nature center.

Directions: Drive south on Kansas Hwy 7 from Shawnee Mission Parkway, or north on Hwy 7 from Kansas Hwy 150 (Santa Fe Road) for 2 miles, to the north edge of Olathe. The park, on the west side of the road, is clearly marked. Park in the parking area near the entrance, adjacent to a shelter house. The trail begins on the south edge of the parking area.

Ernie Miller Park Trail: This trail is blacktop for a few feet, then wood chips and later a dirt path. It winds along the eastern edge of the park through woods and meadows and turns west into a valley. Follow the trail north along the route of a dirt road to the right at the edge of the hill and up the valley. The trail connects with another at a large footbridge. After you cross the bridge, you can take the trail straight ahead up a steep hill. Or, you can go immediately to the right after crossing the bridge. The trail up the hill divides at the crest. The left branch leads to old cement picnic benches and the western boundary of the park. Return to the branch where you turned left and take the other fork toward the north. The trail follows the stream and crosses at a rocky ford. Immediately after crossing the creek, take a sharp right. The trail leads across a small valley and joins the marked, asphalt nature trail. Take this trail to the left to the nature center. There you can see exhibits and maps of the area. It is a short walk to the parking lot. Prairie Center (Trail Site 37) is an easy drive from here.

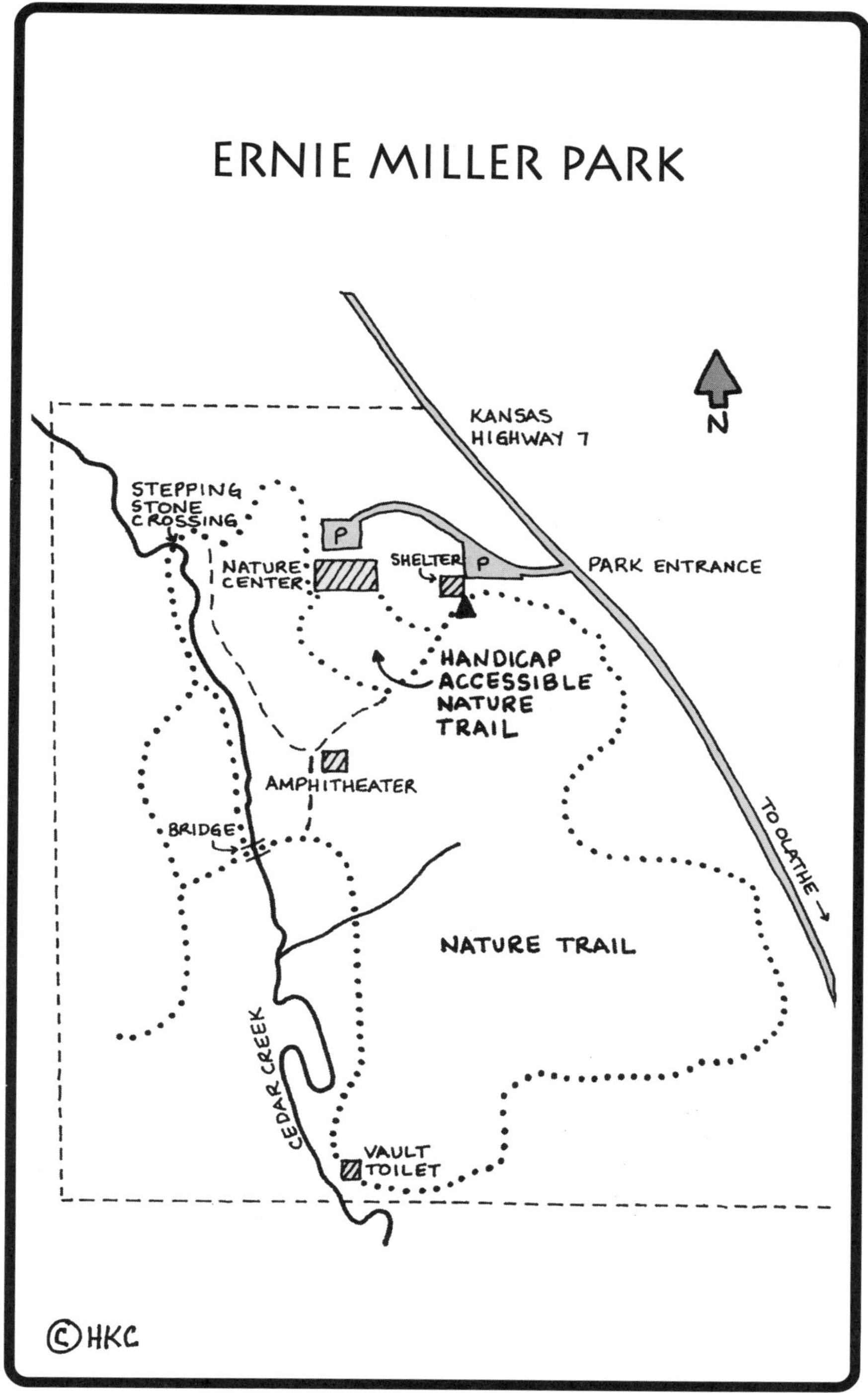
ERNIE MILLER PARK
KANSAS
HIGHWAY 7
N
STEPPING
STONE
CROSSING
P
NATURE
CENTER
SHELTER
P
PARK ENTRANCE
HANDICAP
ACCESSIBLE
NATURE
TRAIL
AMPHITHEATER
BRIDGE
TO OLATHE
NATURE TRAIL
CEDAR CREEK
VAULT
TOILET
©HKC

37
PRAIRIE CENTER
Kansas Wildlife & Parks

Time: 1.5 to 2 Hours
Distance: 3.1 Miles
Rating: Moderate

Drinking Water: No
Accessible: No

This 300-acre native prairie in Johnson County is owned by the state of Kansas and is supported by the Grassland Heritage Foundation, which originally purchased it for preservation. In addition to festivals and exhibits, walkers will find a well-marked nature trail and a system of pleasant paths across streams and through woods and prairies in the western undeveloped part of the preserve.

Directions: Kansas Hwy 7 runs north and south on the western edge of the metropolitan area. It can be reached by following Shawnee Mission Parkway or Kansas Hwy 10 to the west. Proceed south on Hwy 7 to its intersection with Santa Fe Road (135th Street) at the edge of Olathe. Take Santa Fe west for 3 miles to Prairie Center, marked by a stone house at the intersection. Go a few feet south to the parking area.

Nature Trail: The guided nature trail begins just west of the parking area. There should be booklets with a map of this trail and descriptions of the sights along it. Follow the nature trail southwesterly. You will pass a small pond and proceed up a hill to a larger pond with a cedar grove on the far side of the dam, about 0.5 mile from the starting point. In the grove, there is the foundation of an old settler's cabin. At this point, we depart from the guided nature trail (which proceeds up the hill to the southwest) and walk the back trails of Prairie Center. Later, we will rejoin the nature trail south of this grove.

Back Trails: At the cedar grove, take the gravel road to the right (north) down the hill to Sycamore Crossing over Cedar Creek. Unless the creek is high from recent rains, you can walk across without getting your feet wet. If the water at the crossing is deep, fast moving or you can't see the bottom, don't attempt to cross. Go back and continue the nature trail.

After the creek crossing, the unmarked trail proceeds uphill for a couple of hundred yards, where it divides. Take the fork to the left and walk for 0.25 mile. At this point a path joins from the right, just before you reach a stream bed. There is a bench located here. If you wish to take a side loop walk, take this path to the right. This leads you into a loop past a pond and through some deep woods—thick with ticks and poison ivy in summer—and to the west trailhead. When the loop rejoins the original trail, turn right.

If you do not wish to take the loop trail, proceed straight ahead, across a small stream, and bear left. The trail progresses to the south edge of the preserve and then back northeast, uphill through woods and across streams. When you reach the top of the hill, you will see a stone structure that houses restrooms, and beyond, the cedar grove where we departed from the guided nature trail. At the structure, rejoin the nature trail (gravel road) and follow it south through the open prairie, where the grasslands are evolving back to their native state. Just before the gate to Cedar Niles Road, the trail turns left. It ends at the parking area where you began.

There is a trailhead on the western boundary of the preserve that provides access to the back trails when streams are too high to cross. To reach it, proceed west on 135th Street to Moonlight Road. Turn south for 0.3 mile. The trailhead sign is on the left near a pond.

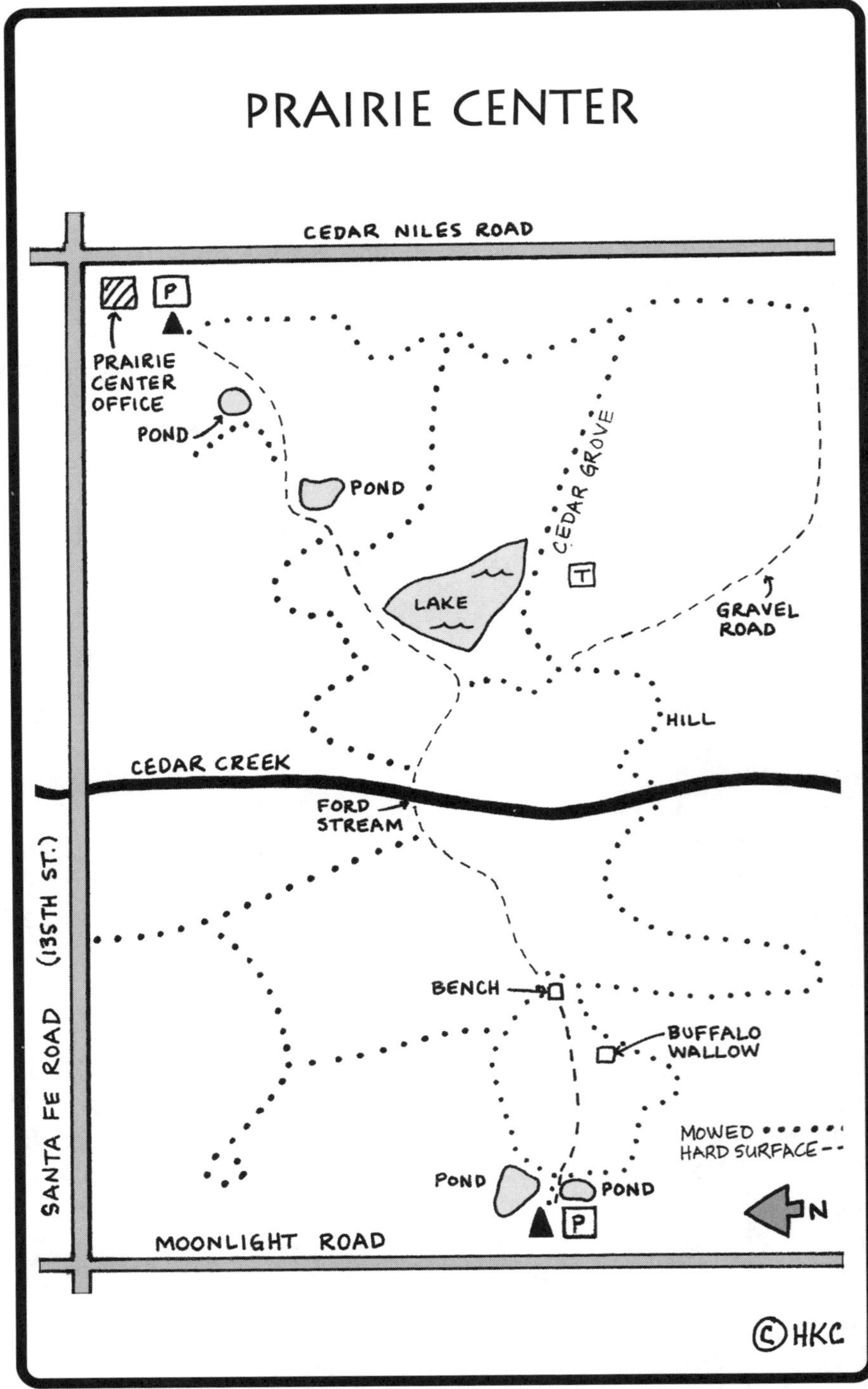
PRAIRIE CENTER
CEDAR NILES ROAD
P
PRAIRIE CENTER OFFICE
POND
POND
CEDAR GROVE
T
LAKE
GRAVEL ROAD
HILL
CEDAR CREEK
FORD STREAM
SANTA FE ROAD (135TH ST.)
BENCH
BUFFALO WALLOW
MOWED
HARD SURFACE
POND
POND
P
N
MOONLIGHT ROAD
©HKC

Walkers will enjoy a system of pleasant paths through woods and prairies at Prairie Center.

38
MILL CREEK STREAMWAY PARK GARY L. HALLER TRAIL (NORTHGATE ACCESS TO 95TH STREET SEGMENT)

Johnson County Park & Recreation District

Time: 2 Hours
Distance: 8 Miles (Round-trip)
Rating: Easy to Moderate
Drinking Water: No
Handicap Accessible: Portions

The Gary L. Haller Trail through Mill Creek Streamway Park provides 16 miles (one-way) of asphalt trails through attractive eastern Kansas woods and park land. We have divided the trail into five segments (Trail Sites 38 to 42). This is the south segment. It is 4 miles long (8 miles round-trip). The trail takes you along Mill Creek through very pleasant wooded hills and prairie to a rest area with a shelter and restroom at 95th Street. You will likely see Eastern Bluebirds as you walk. This trail connects with Olathe's Mahaffie Trail just west of the parking lot (see Trail Site 43). Gary L. Haller, for whom the trail is named, was Director of Parks and Recreation for Johnson County for twenty-seven years and was instrumental in growing park acreage, building trails and providing leadership for a dedicated funding source for streamway parks.

Directions: Take I-35 to 119th Street. Exit and head west on 119th. Pass Ridgeview Road where the street name changes to Northgate Road. In 1 mile, there is a parking lot on the south side of the road. The trailhead is here. Walk north to 95th Street. There are a couple of short but steep hills at about 1 mile and at about 2 miles. High water may make the path inaccessible after rain.

The Gary L. Haller Trail offers the opportunity to hike from Olathe, Kansas to the Kaw River, through a landscape that includes peaceful creeks, rolling prairies and impressive stands of large, old-growth trees.

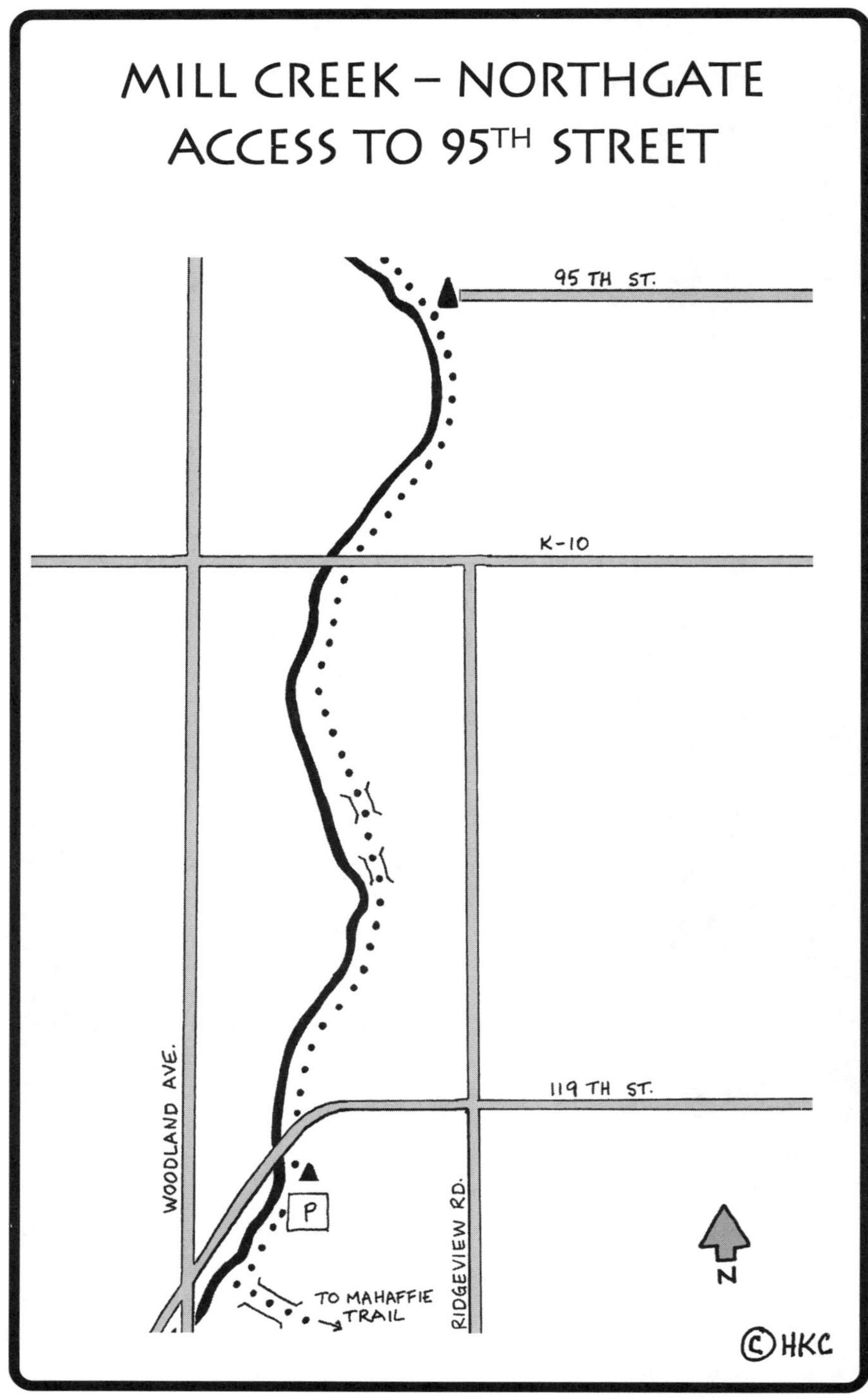
MILL CREEK – NORTHGATE
ACCESS TO 95TH STREET
95 TH ST.
K-10
119 TH ST.
WOODLAND AVE.
RIDGEVIEW RD.
P
TO MAHAFFIE
TRAIL
N
©HKC

TRAIL NOTES:

39
MILL CREEK STREAMWAY PARK GARY L. HALLER TRAIL (95TH STREET TO SHAWNEE MISSION PARK SEGMENT)

Johnson County Park & Recreation District

Time: 2 Hours
Drinking Water: Yes (Shelter 8 in Shawnee Mission Park)
Distance: 5 Miles (Round-trip)
Rating: Easy to Moderate
Accessible: Portions

The Gary L. Haller Trail through Mill Creek Streamway Park provides 16 miles (one-way) of asphalt pathways from Olathe, Kansas to the Kaw River, traversing attractive Eastern Kansas woods and park land. We have divided the trail into five segments (Trail Sites 38 to 42).

Directions: The north access to this segment is in Shawnee Mission Park. Drive west from Overland Park on 87th Street past Renner Road to the south entrance to Shawnee Mission Park on your right. Enter and pass the ball fields. At the first main intersection, turn left and follow the road to the parking area for the trails on the left (west) side of the road. If you come to the lake, you've gone too far. There are three other access points, one at a parking area south of 87th Lane, which can be reached by driving west on 87th Street past the park entrance and turning left on 87th Lane. The access is at the parking area on the south side of 87th Lane after crossing Mill Creek. Another is on Woodland Road south of 91st Street. The south access point is at a parking area at the end of 95th Street west of I-435.

Shawnee Mission to 95th Street: The well-marked asphalt trail enters the wooded area on the west side of the parking area and proceeds downhill for about 0.25 mile. At the first intersection, turn left. In another 0.25 mile, another trail intersects from the left. Turn left. This is the segment to 95th Street. The trail passes through deep woods and crosses a bridge over Mill Creek. It then proceeds through meadows along Mill Creek, across 87th Lane, through two tunnels, past a park with restrooms and a shelter and eventually across another bridge before emerging south of 95th Street. Just past the park, a path enters from the right. This takes walkers through a marshland and across a wooden platform before returning to the main trail. Hikers are likely to see bluebirds, meadowlarks and finches and may see deer, fox and even beaver. The hike is 2.5 miles one-way, and 5 miles round-trip back to Shawnee Mission Park.

Hikers may also continue south for 4 miles (one-way) to the Northgate Access (see Trail Site 38) or north 8 miles (one-way) to the end of the Gary L. Haller Trail at the Kaw River (see Trail Site 42).

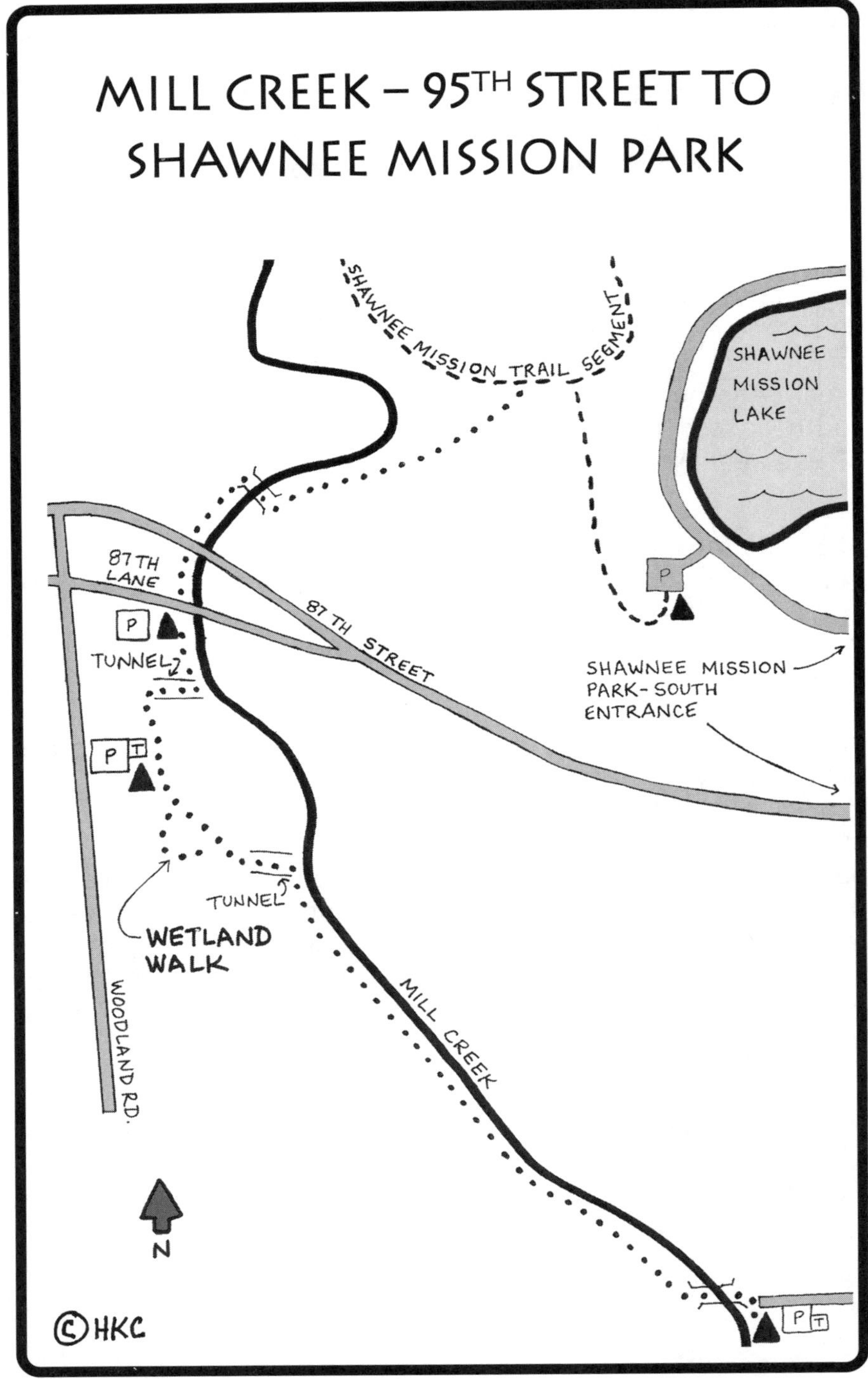
MILL CREEK – 95TH STREET TO SHAWNEE MISSION PARK
SHAWNEE MISSION TRAIL SEGMENT
SHAWNEE MISSION LAKE
87TH LANE
87 TH STREET
TUNNEL
SHAWNEE MISSION PARK-SOUTH ENTRANCE
TUNNEL
WETLAND WALK
WOODLAND RD.
MILL CREEK
N
©HKC

The trail from 87th Lane to 95th Street is one of the prettiest and most heavily-traveled in the area. Mill Creek Streamway offers a variety of amenities, including fences to keep children away from the riverbanks.

40
MILL CREEK STREAMWAY PARK GARY L. HALLER TRAIL (SHAWNEE MISSION PARK TO MIDLAND ROAD SEGMENT)

Johnson County Park & Recreation District

Time: 1 to 4 Hours
Distance: 2 to 6 Miles (Round-trip)
Rating: Moderate to Difficult
Drinking Water: No
Accessible: South Portions

This park and trail system extends for 16 miles (one-way) from Olathe to the Kaw River. We have divided the trail into five segments (see Trail Sites 38 through 42).

Directions: The trail may be accessed at either end. The south access is south of the dam in Shawnee Mission Park across from Shelter 8 (see Trail Site 39 for directions to the park), where there are signs and a parking lot. The north access is reached from Shawnee Mission Parkway. Turn south on Midland Road, which is 1 mile west of I-435. Proceed south 0.1 mile to a marked, paved parking area. The 2.7-mile Midland Road to Johnson Drive segment (see Trail Site 41) starts here.

Shawnee Mission Park to Midland Road: This 3-mile (one-way) trail runs between Shawnee Mission Park on the south and Midland Road near Shawnee Mission Parkway on the north and may be accessed at either end. The trailhead at Shawnee Mission Park is at the southwest corner of the parking lot. The walk north takes you through meadows and along Mill Creek before climbing steeply up wooded, rocky hillsides to vistas overlooking the valley. It was dubbed Kansas' "prettiest trail."

A 2-mile loop trail is also available from the Shawnee Mission Park access point. It is easy and takes you through meadows and along the creek. You can also access the segment to 95th Street (see Trail Site 39). The north access is reached from the paved parking area off Midland Road. From the parking area, walk west to the bridge, turn left across it and follow the paved trail 3 miles (one-way) south to Shawnee Mission Park. There are two steep hills to traverse on this segment of the trail, so be prepared.

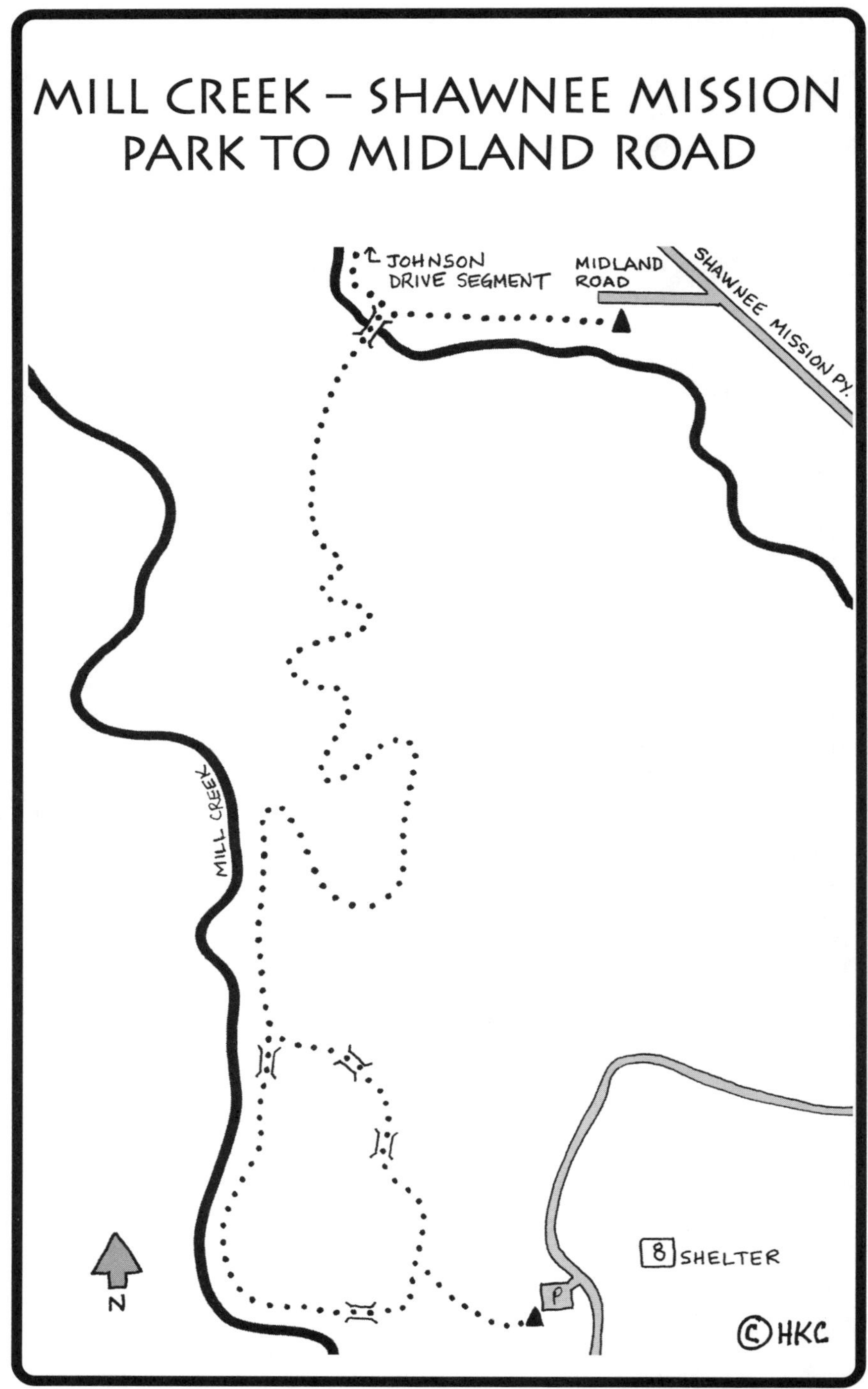
MILL CREEK – SHAWNEE MISSION
PARK TO MIDLAND ROAD
JOHNSON
DRIVE SEGMENT
MIDLAND
ROAD
SHAWNEE MISSION PY.
MILL CREEK
P
8 SHELTER
N
©HKC

Portions of the Gary L. Haller Trail have been designated "The Bluebird Capital of Kansas."

41
MILL CREEK STREAMWAY PARK GARY L. HALLER TRAIL (MIDLAND ROAD TO JOHNSON DRIVE SEGMENT)

Johnson County Park & Recreation District

Time: 2.5 Hours **Drinking Water:** At Barker Road Access
Distance: 5.5 Miles (Round-trip) **Accessible:** Portions
Rating: Easy

The Gary L. Haller Trail through Mill Creek Streamway Park extends for 16 miles from Olathe to the Kaw River. We have divided the trail into five segments (see Trail Sites 38 through 42).

Directions: Take Shawnee Mission Parkway west of I-435 1 mile to Midland Road. Proceed south on Midland Road 0.1 mile to a marked, paved parking area. Here you can access the segment described below or the Shawnee Mission segment to the south (see Trail Site 40). The trail described below can also be accessed from Barker Road 0.8 mile north of Shawnee Mission Parkway. The closest parking near the Johnson Drive access point is in the Mid-America West Sports Complex north of Johnson Drive.

Midland Road to Johnson Drive Segment: This 2.75-mile (5.5-mile round-trip) asphalt trail is suitable for walking, jogging or cycling. It parallels Mill Creek through woods and meadows. From the south access point, the trail proceeds north under Shawnee Mission Parkway and crosses Mill Creek two times before reaching the Barker Road parking area at about 1.5 miles, where restrooms and water are available. The trail proceeds north, eventually skirting a large sports complex and passing under Johnson Drive. The Johnson Drive to Nelson Island Segment (see Trail Site 42) may be accessed from Johnson Drive near the Mid-America West Sports Complex.

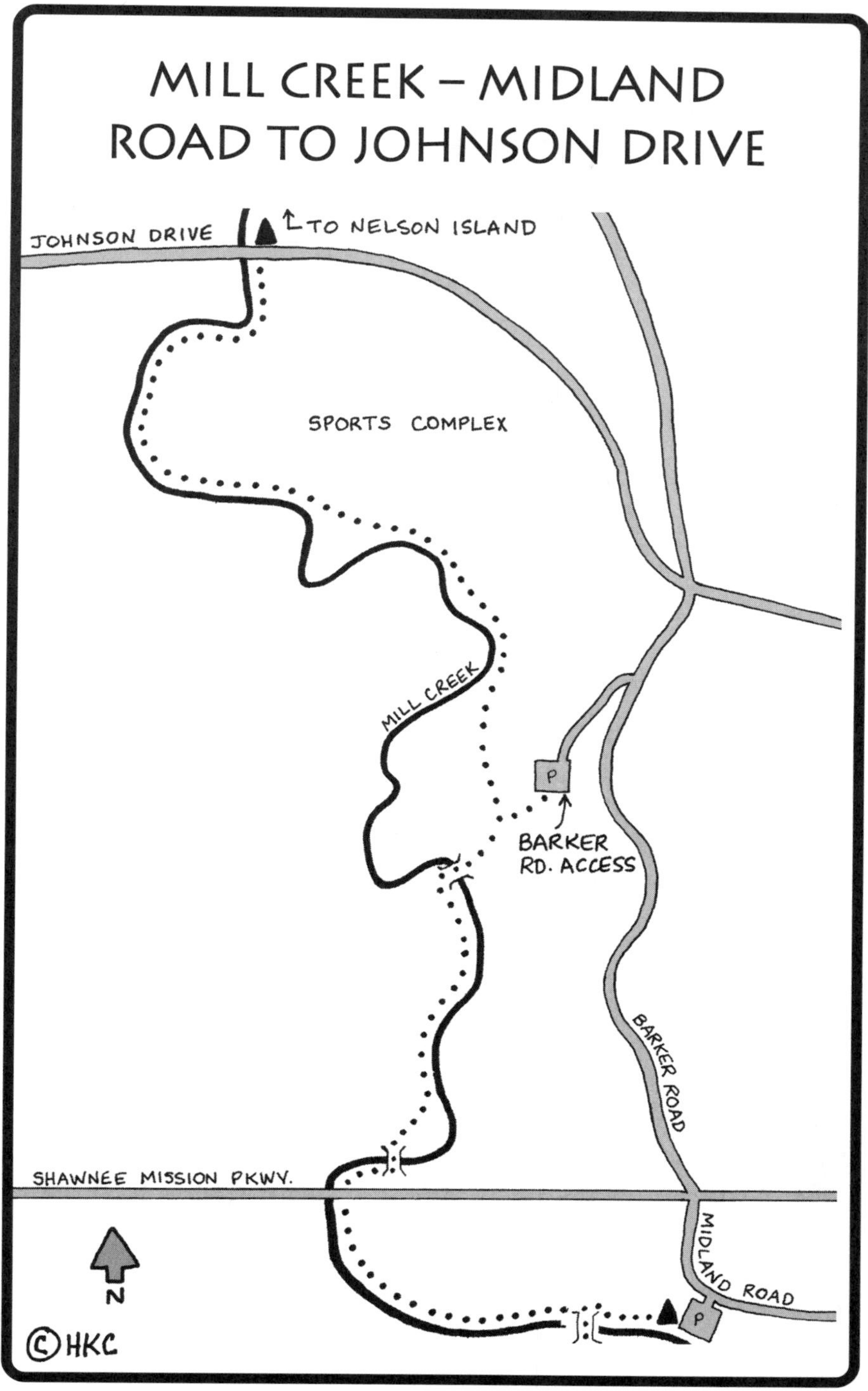
MILL CREEK – MIDLAND ROAD TO JOHNSON DRIVE
JOHNSON DRIVE
TO NELSON ISLAND
SPORTS COMPLEX
MILL CREEK
P
BARKER RD. ACCESS
BARKER ROAD
SHAWNEE MISSION PKWY.
MIDLAND ROAD
N
©HKC

Views of the Kaw River are similar to those enjoyed by early explorers and settlers.

42
MILL CREEK STREAMWAY PARK GARY L. HALLER TRAIL (JOHNSON DRIVE TO NELSON ISLAND SEGMENT)

Johnson County Parks & Recreation District

Time: 3 Hours
Drinking Water: At Wilder Road Access
Distance: 7 Miles (Round-trip)
Accessible: Yes
Rating: Easy

The Gary L. Haller Trail through the Mill Creek Streamway Park extends 16 miles (one-way) from Olathe to the Kaw River. We have divided the trail into five segments (see Trail Sites 38 through 42). This segment extends from Johnson Drive on the south to Nelson Island in the Kaw (Kansas) River on the north.

Directions: There is no parking area on Johnson Drive, so we suggest you go to the Wilder Road Access parking area. Go west on Shawnee Mission Parkway past I-435 approximately 1.5 miles to Woodland Road. Turn north on Woodland to 47th Street. Turn right (east) on 47th Street (which becomes Wilder Road and then Holliday Drive), and go approximately 0.5 mile to the Wilder Road Access parking area on the right (south). If you cross Mill Creek, you've gone too far. A reproduction of the original mill and an interpretive center adjacent to the parking area are planned for this site.

Nelson Island to Johnson Drive Segment: To get to Nelson Island from the parking area, proceed north under the 47th Street bridge and through tallgrass prairie. Then cross the 130-foot bridge to heavily wooded Nelson Island in the Kaw River. The trail through this 15-acre island provides panoramic views of the river. From Nelson Island to Johnson Drive, walk south about 3 miles. At about 1 mile, just beyond the second bridge across Mill Creek, the trail splits. The right (north) fork goes 0.65 mile (one-way) to Shawnee's Charles Stump Memorial Park. The left (south) fork goes to Johnson Drive. This segment of the trail connects with the Midland Road to Johnson Drive segment at Johnson Drive (see Trail Site 41).

Bridges across creeks and streams make the Mill Creek system accessible to cyclists, strollers and those with disabilities.

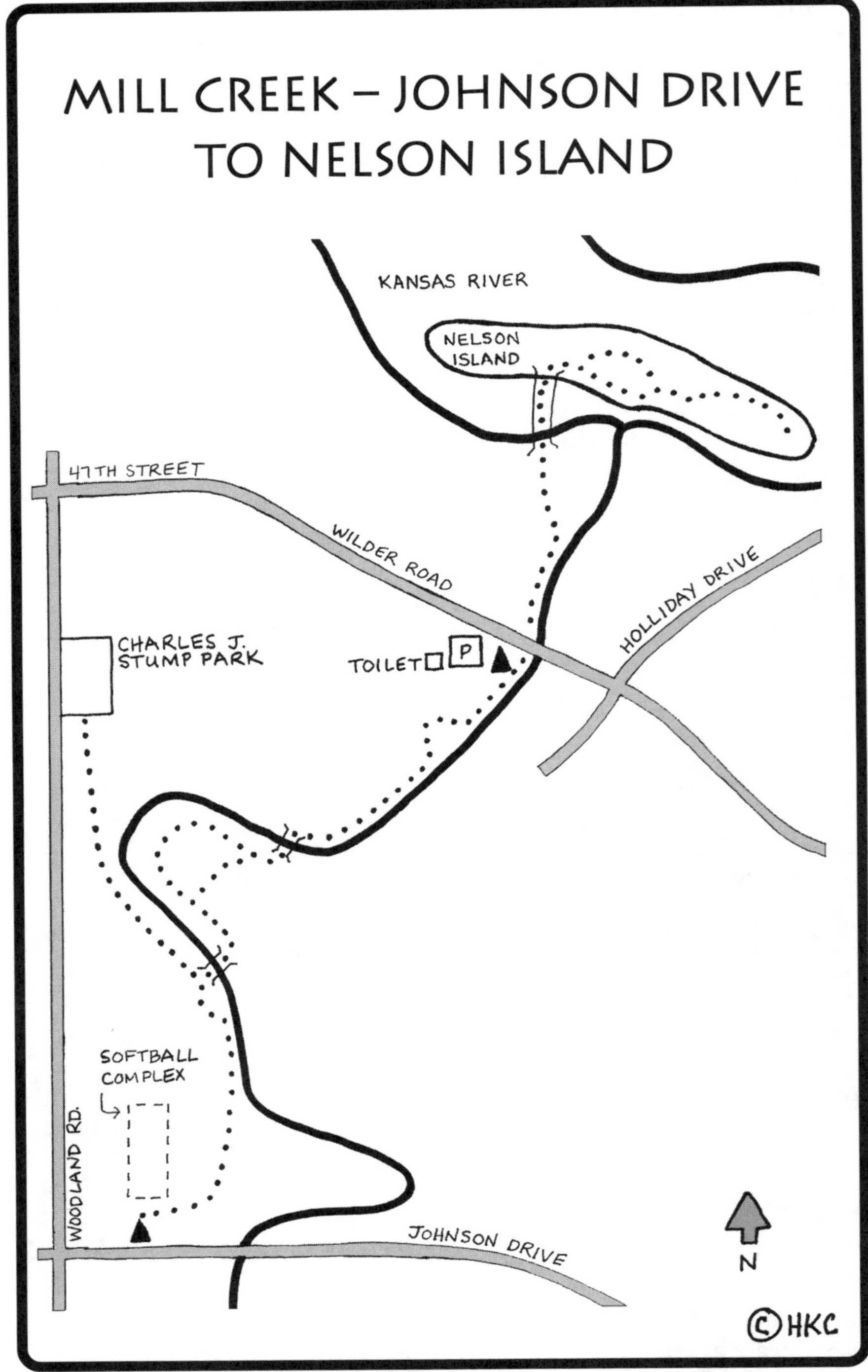
MILL CREEK – JOHNSON DRIVE TO NELSON ISLAND
KANSAS RIVER
NELSON ISLAND
47TH STREET
WILDER ROAD
HOLLIDAY DRIVE
CHARLES J. STUMP PARK
TOILET
P
SOFTBALL COMPLEX
WOODLAND RD.
JOHNSON DRIVE
N
©HKC

Hikers will enjoy crossing several bridges over Mill Creek.

43 SIX WALKS IN JOHNSON COUNTY

Johnson County Parks & Recreation District

These walks, laid out along streamways, paths and sidewalks, provide pleasant, hard-surfaced routes for a moderate walk.

Turkey Creek Streamway Trail: Turkey Creek parallels this 3-mile path that extends between 75th Street and Werner Park, adjacent to the Farmer's Market in downtown Merriam. This trail is especially nice when there is foliage on trees. Easiest access is from 75th Street. Take 75th Street west and turn right (north) at the first intersection beyond I-35. Turn right again and you are at the trailhead. The path proceeds north through woods and along Turkey Creek and ends at Werner Park. Return on the same route for a 6-mile round-trip walk. Plans are to extend the trail north 1 mile to a waterfall park near 50th and Merriam Drive.

Sar-Ko Par Trail: Two walks of 3 to 5 miles (round-trip) can be enjoyed from Sar-Ko-Par Park on the south side of 87th Street Parkway, east of Lackman Road. Park in the lot and then cross 87th Street, locating the trailhead on the north side. Descend thirty-eight steps. The asphalt path follows a stream north for a mile where it crosses 79th Street, passes open fields and returns to the woods. At about mile 1.5, the path divides. Straight ahead leads to Blackfish Parkway, and left climbs to Lackman Road. Go left. At Lackman, follow the sidewalk left back to Sar-Ko Par Park, or proceed to the southwest corner of Lackman and 79th and follow the path southwest. At Ad Astra Park, turn left on the 83rd Street sidewalk back to Lackman Road, and then cross to the asphalt path on the southeast corner. Proceed east to the bridge across Little MIll Creek. Follow the path to the intersecting path and turn left (south) back to the 38-step beginning.

Sunflower Park Nature Trail: This 1.3-mile walk is located in 60-acre Sunflower Park near DeSoto, Kansas. It is a joint project of the Johnson County Parks and Recreation District. A portion of the trail is asphalt and is accessible. The rest of the trail is wood-chipped. Drive west on Kansas Hwy 10 from Kansas City to the Eudora exit, then south on Kansas Hwy 185 to the sign and parking area. Booklets for the nature trail may be available at the trailhead. The well-planned, three-loop trail passes through prairie, pond and marsh ecosystems. We hiked it on a snowy day and saw many birds and animal tracks.

Heritage Park Walk: This pleasant asphalt walking, jogging and biking path loops around the lake in Heritage Park. West of the dam, a branch leads south into woods and meadows and connects with several picnic areas. The path begins north of the parking lot at the marina. Distance around the lake plus a round-trip on the branch trail is about 4 miles. Heritage Park is on Pflumm Road, 1 block south of 159th Street.

Mahaffie Creek Trail: This Olathe trail provides a varied walk through woods and neighborhoods for about 2.5 miles (one-way). It runs from Northgate Park on the north (see Trail Site

38) to Stage Coach Park on the south and passes the Mahaffie farmstead and stagecoach stop where walkers can get a glimpse of what life was like for travelers on the old Santa Fe Trail. Parking is available in both parks. To access the trail on the north, walk west on the Gary L. Haller Trail to the bridge over Mill Creek. Cross the bridge. Follow the path uphill and at the split, take the right fork. The trail proceeds through evergreen woods and crosses Harold Street where it follows Mahaffie Creek. After crossing Nelson Road, it eventually emerges onto a wide sidewalk along Kansas City Road. Turn left and pass the Mahaffie farmstead. Turn right at the crosswalk to Stage Coach Park. Follow the path to the south end of the park.

Rolling Ridge Trail: This recent Olathe trail extends for 2.5 miles (one-way) from Oregon Trail Park on Dennis Avenue on the south to both Ernie Miller Park (see Trail Site 36) and Prairie Center Park on the north. The trail may be accessed on the north at Prairie Center Park or on the south at the Oregon Trail Park on Dennis Avenue (143rd Street) just west of Kansas Hwy 7. Parking is available in all the parks.

The Heritage Park Trail is popular with hikers, joggers and cyclists.

The Sar-Ko Par Trail's asphalt path follows a stream north for a mile where it crosses 79th Street, passes open fields and returns to the woods.

44
KILL CREEK PARK TRAIL
Johnson County, Kansas Parks & Recreation District

Time: 1.5 to 2 Hours
Distance: 3 to 4 Miles
Rating: Moderate
Drinking Water: Yes, Seasonally
Accessible: No

Kill Creek features tallgrass prairies, eastern Kansas woodlands, limestone outcroppings, wetlands, a nice creek and a large artificial lake. Dirt trails are available for hikers, horseback riders and mountainbikers, and asphalt paths are available for walkers and bicycle riders. A nice variety of native plants as well as deer, fox, raccoon and a large variety of birds may be experienced. The park has picnic shelters and public restrooms available. Plans call for the Kill Creek Streamway trail to connect DeSoto and Kill Creek Park. Walkers can access the completed portion of this trail on 95th Street west of Kill Creek Road.

Directions: Kill Creek is south of DeSoto, Kansas. Drive west on Kansas Hwy 10 and exit at Kill Creek Road (about 10 miles from I-35). Proceed south on Kill Creek Road about 3 miles to 115th Street. Turn right on 115th to Homestead Lane. Turn left to the park entrance on your right. Follow the park road to the first paved parking area on your right. Park here.

Kill Creek Park Trail: To reach the trailhead for the natural-surface hiking trail, walk first to the asphalt path on the west side of the parking area. Turn right (north) on the asphalt path for about 0.1 mile. The trailhead is on your right and there should be a sign marking it. Follow the trail, taking the right fork through the prairie grass. At 0.5 mile, a horse trail enters from the right. Proceed on the combined trails to the left for about 50 yards to the dirt path on your right. There should be a sign here indicating you are on the hiking path. Take it into the woods, crossing a creek at about 0.8 mile. Continue on, crossing the creek once again. Shortly, a trail will enter from your left. This is a part of the loop trail shown on the map. We recommend you pass it by and continue straight ahead. The next time you encounter the creek, you have a choice to turn right, cross the creek and take a longer hike that ends on the asphalt path. This route, which is a little more difficult to follow at the creek, results in a hike of about 4 miles.

Your other choice is to continue straight on the better marked path, then cross the creek and loop back to the trail you started on. At that point, turn right and then retrace your path to the parking lot for a hike of about 3 miles. If you choose the longer route, follow the trail to the asphalt path and then turn left on it. Stay left each time you have a choice and you will return to the parking area where you started.

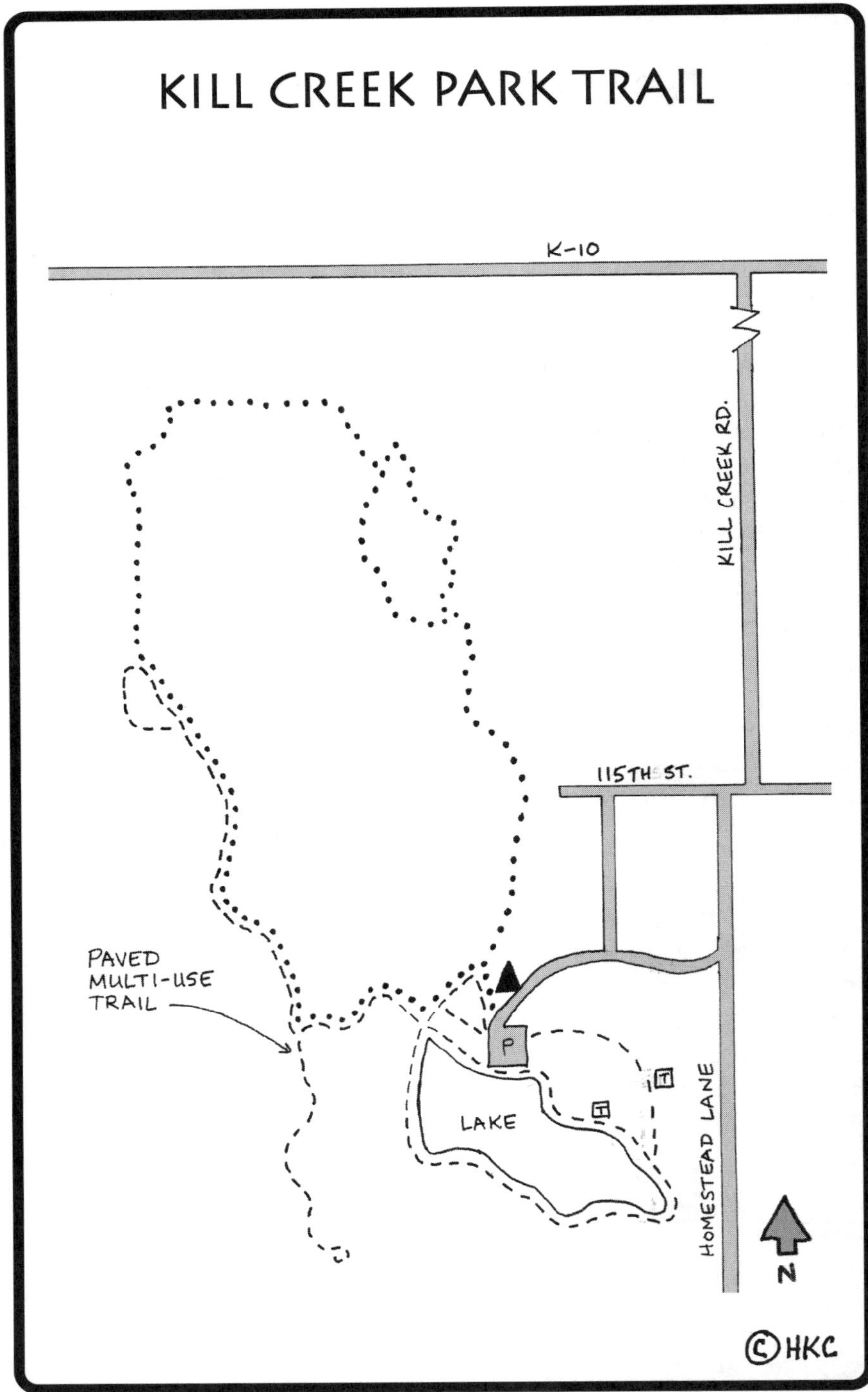
KILL CREEK PARK TRAIL
K-10
KILL CREEK RD.
115TH ST.
PAVED
MULTI-USE
TRAIL
P
LAKE
HOMESTEAD LANE
N
©HKC

(Above) Kill Creek Trail runs through old homestead sites. Park builders protected them from developers' bulldozers.

(Left) The park offers hikes through prairies and woods, skirting streams and lakes.

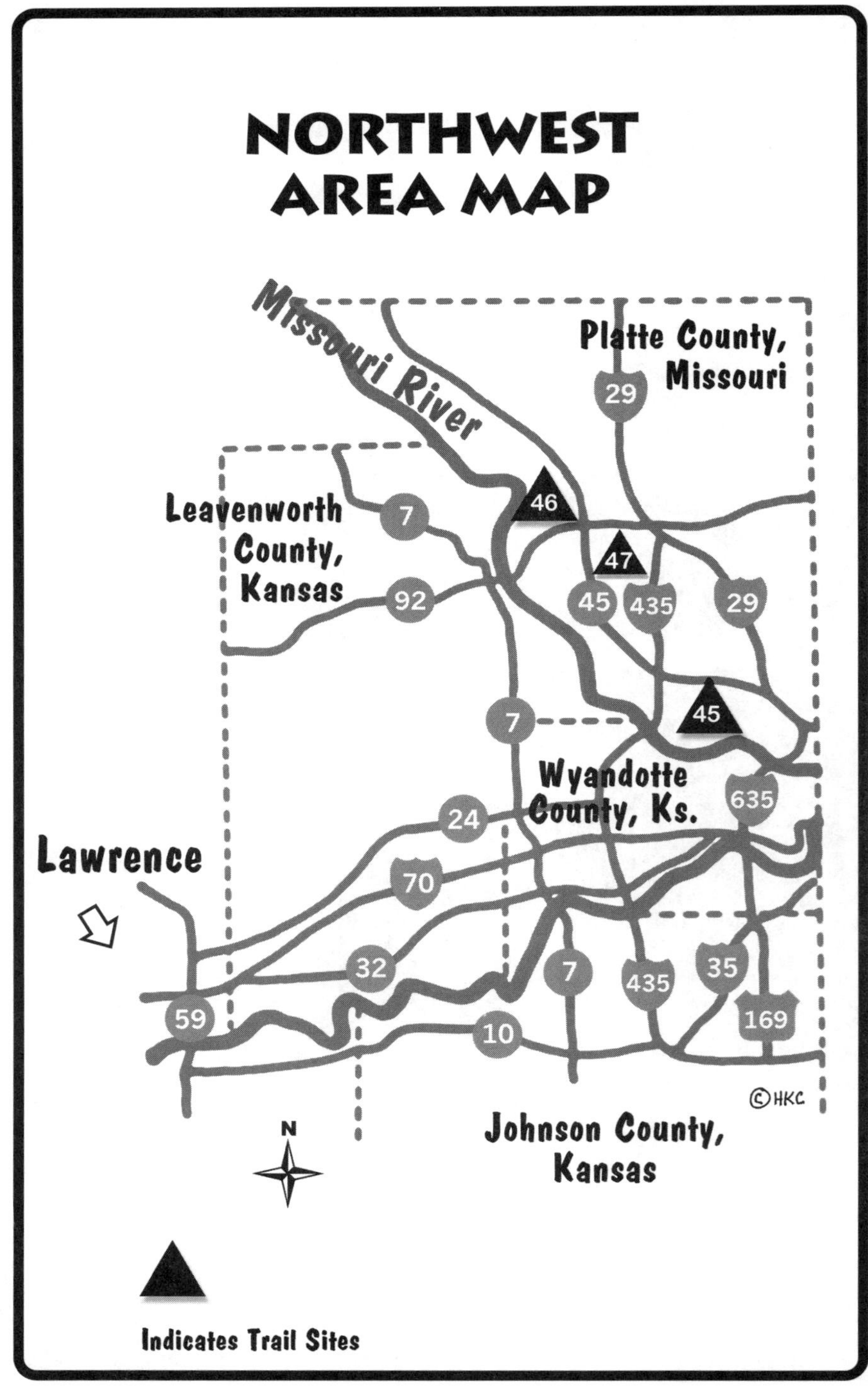
NORTHWEST
AREA MAP
Missouri River
Platte County,
Missouri
29
46
47
Leavenworth
County,
Kansas
7
92
45
435
29
45
7
Wyandotte
County, Ks.
635
24
Lawrence
70
32
7
435
35
59
10
169
©HKC
N
Johnson County,
Kansas
Indicates Trail Sites

TRAIL SITES IN THE NORTHWEST AREA

Note: ( ) denotes the number of trails at that location

Parkville, Missouri, located 9 miles from Kansas City, is one of the few places in the area where walkers can get close to the Missouri River.

45
PARKVILLE, MISSOURI TRAILS
City of Parkville, Missouri

Time: 1 to 1.5 Hours Each
Distance: 2.7 Miles and 3 Miles
Rating: Easy to Moderate
Drinking Water: Yes
Accessible: Some Sections

Parkville, Missouri is one of the few places in the Kansas City area where you can walk along the Missouri River. Two very worthwhile walks in the village, as well as interesting shops and restaurants to visit before or after a hike, are ample rewards for the 9-mile drive upriver.

Directions: Take Broadway north from downtown Kansas City, Missouri. Three miles north of the Broadway Bridge, turn onto Hwy 9 northwest to Parkville. Hwy 9 can also be accessed from I-635 a couple of miles north of the Missouri River.

A segment of the inviting trail system in Parkville's Nature Sanctuary.

English Landing Park and Trails: In downtown Parkville, turn south (left) on East Street where Hwy 9 turns right. Park near the City Market. The 2.7-mile route begins at the east side of the market area where there is a sign with map. The elongated loop path is crushed limestone with some asphalt sections. Follow the trail east between the Missouri River and high bluffs to the north. Enjoy the vistas of the river. After completing the east loop, cross an A-truss footbridge, follow the sidewalk around a ball field and return to the market.

Nature Sanctuary and Old Kate Trail: From the market, follow East Street (Hwy 9) to 12th Street. Turn right (east) at city hall and follow the street for a block to the parking area for the sanctuary. The lower loop, Old Kate Trail, in the 100-acre sanctuary is 1 mile long. It passes waterfalls, wetlands and old stone structures. The sanctuary and adjacent preserve are home to many birds and animals. Some portions of the path are wood-chipped, others are gravel. The upper loop, 3 miles long, is the White Tail Trail. It is a more challenging walk, with some switchbacks leading up steeper hillsides. The Bluebird Trail, 0.3 mile, is handicap accessible.

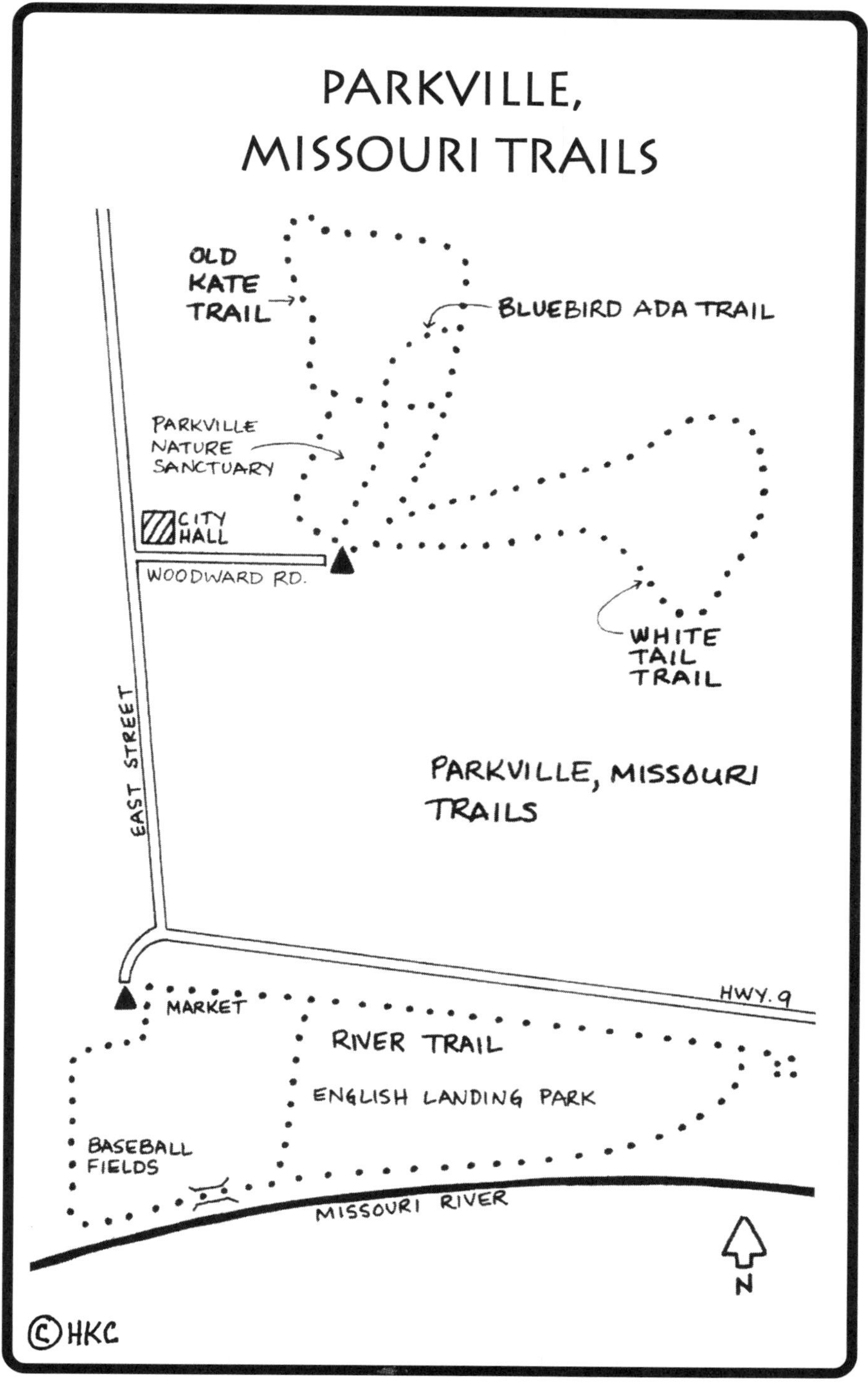
PARKVILLE, MISSOURI TRAILS
OLD KATE TRAIL
BLUEBIRD ADA TRAIL
PARKVILLE NATURE SANCTUARY
CITY HALL
WOODWARD RD.
WHITE TAIL TRAIL
EAST STREET
PARKVILLE, MISSOURI TRAILS
HWY. 9
MARKET
RIVER TRAIL
ENGLISH LANDING PARK
BASEBALL FIELDS
MISSOURI RIVER
N
©HKC

46
WESTON BEND STATE PARK
Missouri Department of Natural Resources

Time: 1.4 Hours (Each Trail)
Distance: 2 to 3 Miles (Each Trail)
Rating: Moderate to Difficult
Drinking Water: No
Accessible: Portions of Paved Trail

Four excellent trails, one asphalt, the others natural-surface, have been developed in this state park, which borders the Missouri River near Weston, Missouri. Much of the park is covered with trees interspersed with a few hilltop prairies along the bluffs. Lewis and Clark report that they stopped at a Kansas Indian Village in 1804 on the Kansas side of the river near the present-day park.

Directions: The park is 28 miles north of Kansas City on Hwy 45. One way to reach the park is to drive north on I-29 to Exit 20, and take Hwy 273 west until it intersects with Hwy 45. Turn left on 45 for 0.5 mile to the park entrance on your right.

Another way to reach the park from the Kansas side is to travel north on I-435 to the Hwy 45 Exit. From there, proceed north to the park entrance. The Bicycle Trailhead is 0.3 mile from the entrance. Turn into the parking lot on the left. If you reach the road to the campground on the right, you've gone too far. A useful trail guide booklet is available at the trailhead or at the superintendent's office on the main park road.

Bicycle Trail: The trailhead is on the west side of the parking lot, and is obvious. The asphalt trail follows a small creek through forests of cottonwood, sycamore and maple trees, and then returns along open prairie ridge tops. Most of the trail is easy, but there are two or three steep climbs that could be difficult for some. Benches are located along the way.

West Ridge and Harpst Valley Trails: These trails are well-marked and are at the end of the main park road near the overlook. The trailhead for the West Ridge Trail is at the end of the woods about 30 yards up the asphalt walk leading to the overlook. The trail proceeds south along a bluff and presents several views of the Missouri River and the Kansas plains. The trail proceeds through dense woods and down a hill where it connects with the Bicycle Trail. Turn left (north) on the Bicycle Trail at about 0.9 mile, where the trail again enters the woods on the left. This has been named Harpst Pass. If you take the left fork, Harpst Pass will proceed up a hill and connect with the West Ridge Trail. If you take the right branch of the trail after leaving the Bicycle Trail, you are on the Harpst Valley Trail. This trail proceeds uphill to the overlook parking lot. The West Ridge-Harpst Valley route is about 3 miles. The West Ridge-Harpst Pass route is about 2.5 miles.

North Ridge Trail: The trailhead for this 2-mile trail is at the end of the main road (past the turnoff to the overlook). Park in the designated parking area. The trail proceeds north up a hill and into the woods to the park border. Eventually, you will be able to walk into the picturesque village of Weston from this trail on a path that the city plans to build. The Bear Creek and Missouri River Trails, each 0.5 mile long, can also be reached from this parking area. The Missouri River Trail will take you to the bank of the river.

Weston Bluffs Trail: This trail skirts the western boundary of Weston Bend State Park. It runs 3.25 miles from Beverly on Missouri Hwy 45, north along the Missouri River to Weston on Old Bluff Road—an abandoned gravel and asphalt road suitable for hiking and biking. This trail is fairly level since it follows the river. There are views of the river, heavily forested bottomlands and marshes. Interpretive signs highlighting the journey of Lewis and Clark are located along the trail. To access the trail from Weston Bend State Park, park in the lot at the trailhead of the Northridge Trail. Follow the path west (toward the river) a short distance and intersect the Weston Bluffs Trail. If you walk north (right) for 1.3 miles, you arrive in Weston. Another 0.2 mile on village streets (Welt Street to Market Street) takes you to the train station—easily visible and the official trail terminus. Arrive in Weston early enough to enjoy lunch at one of many restaurants. If you walk south from the park access point for approximately 2 miles, you will arrive at a trailhead and a parking area just northwest of the Beverly crossroads. To drive to this trailhead, go south of the Weston Bend State Park entrance on Missouri Hwy 45 for 1.8 miles to Beverly. Just before the intersection with Missouri Hwy 92, turn right on a gravel road for 0.1 mile (at stone sign "Hill"), then right for 0.4 mile past farm buildings and turn off into the parking area. To walk the trail, follow the gravel road north for less than 0.1 mile to a gate.

One of the great views of the "Mighty Missouri" from Weston Bend State Park. The Lewis & Clark Corps of Discovery passed this area in 1804 and 1806.

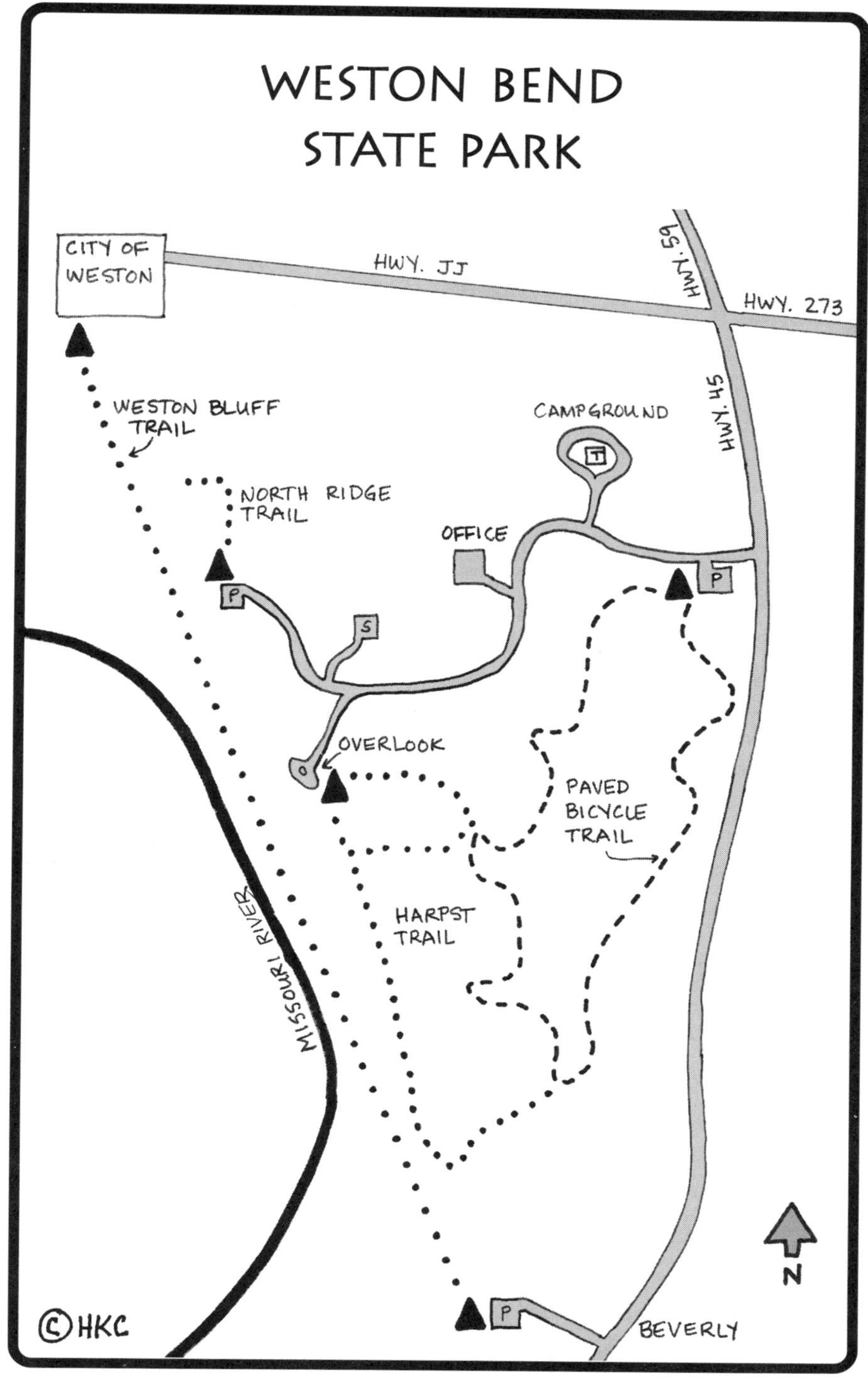
WESTON BEND
STATE PARK
CITY OF WESTON
HWY. JJ
HWY. 59
HWY. 273
HWY. 45
WESTON BLUFF TRAIL
CAMPGROUND
T
NORTH RIDGE TRAIL
OFFICE
P
S
OVERLOOK
PAVED BICYCLE TRAIL
HARPST TRAIL
MISSOURI RIVER
N
©HKC
BEVERLY

47
PRAIRIE CREEK GREENWAY
Platte County Parks Department

Time: 2 Hours
Distance: 4 Miles Round-trip (1st Stage)
Rating: Moderate
Drinking Water: No
Accessible: Yes

A project of Platte County, this asphalt trail follows 120-acre Prairie Creek Greenway south from Timber Park Subdivision. It is part of a growing system of trails in Platte County and other parts of the "Northland."

Directions: From I-29 south of Plattsburg, turn south on I-435 and immediately right (west) on Northwest 136th Street. Past Running Horse Road, turn south into the Timber Park Subdivision on Northwest 135th Street, then right on Timber Park Lane and right again on Northwest 134th Street. Follow Northwest 134th Street to Sycamore Drive, which leads to the north trailhead. To begin the trail at its south trailhead, turn south off 136th Street onto Hwy N. Follow Hwy N south for less than 2 miles and look for the trailhead parking area on the east side of the road. Immediately past the parking area, the highway curves to the southwest. If you continue on, you will reach Hwy D that leads back to I-435.

Trail: The Prairie Creek Greenway Trail offers opportunities to appreciate the unique beauty of Platte County, with views of the creek, a 20-acre prairie restoration area, native forest and a natural rock waterfall. A Native American stone axe head was found near the trail site. The first 2-mile segment ends at a parking area on Hwy N. The trail has been extended east to Running Horse Road. The county plans to develop the greenway along Prairie Creek and add 7.5 more miles of trail.

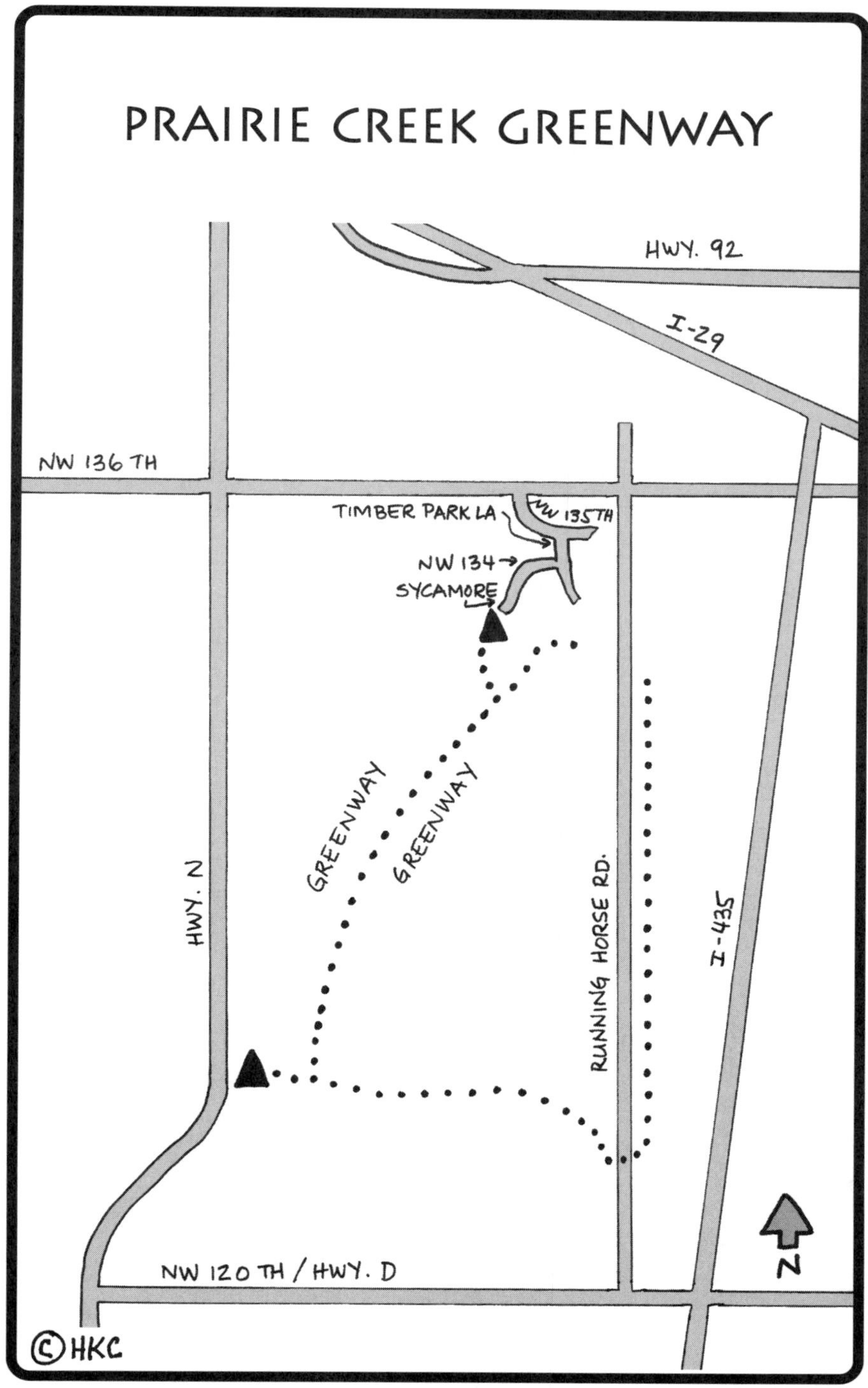
PRAIRIE CREEK GREENWAY
HWY. 92
I-29
NW 136 TH
TIMBER PARK LA
NW 135TH
NW 134
SYCAMORE
GREENWAY
GREENWAY
HWY. N
RUNNING HORSE RD.
I-435
N
NW 120 TH / HWY. D
©HKC

Brush Creek runs from State Line Road to the Little Blue River. It has been transformed from a drainage canal into an attractive waterway with paths.

URBAN WALKS

Urban Walks

Note: ( ) denotes the number of trails at that location

No matter the time of year: spring, summer, fall or winter, there's always a trail nearby that captures the mood of the season. Near the Plaza, great walking trails abound. They include the scenic Brush Creek Walk (opposite page), the Mill Creek Park Trail (above) and several others.

48
PLAZA AREA WALKS

Kansas City, Missouri Parks & Recreation Department

Time: 0.5 to 3 Hours
Distance: 0.5 to 6 Miles
Rating: Easy to Moderate
Drinking Water: Yes
Accessible: Some

Five short routes in parks in the Country Club Plaza area of Kansas City provide several pleasant hours of walking. A hike of more than 6 miles is possible if you choose to walk between the parks.

Gilham Park: This 1-mile loop extends from 42nd Street and Gilham Road on the north to Brush Creek Boulevard and Harrison Street on the south. You can park near either end. The trail surface is of shredded asphalt and proceeds through pleasant, wooded areas and mown grass beside limestone walls. There is a hill on the west side of the park. Walking time is about 0.5 hour. Reach Mill Creek Park (described on page 173) by going south on Harrison to 47th Street. Head west on 47th Street (which becomes Brush Creek Boulevard) about 0.8 mile to Main Street and an entrance to Mill Creek Park.

Kansas City Sculpture Park: Between Gilham Park and Mill Creek Park, stop to visit the Kansas City Sculpture Park at the Nelson-Atkins Museum of Art. A 0.5-mile walk takes you on a self-guided tour of a beautifully landscaped park built especially for the museum's sculptures.

Mill Creek Park: This asphalt loop runs parallel to J.C. Nichols Parkway from 46th Terrace to 43rd Street. Park along J.C. Nichols Parkway. The trail travels for 1 mile through trees and mown lawns and has several "fitness" stops along the way. There are nice views of the Plaza. While on the north portion of the trail, cross 43rd Street and visit the Vietnam War Memorial. (Further north about 5 blocks is Westport and the Santa Fe Trail Memorial erected in 1987 at Westport Road and Broadway.) Walking time is about half an hour.

Reach Loose Park (described below) by going west on 47th Street to Wornall Road. Walk south on Wornall, across Brush Creek, up the steep hill beside the hotel, to 51st Street, where the next walk begins. The walk between Mill Creek Park and Loose Park is about 0.9 miles.

Loose Park: This park extends from 51st Street to 55th Street along Wornall Road just south of the Plaza. The walking loop of more than 1 mile takes you through a variety of trees and rolling lawns. Many of the trees are identified. There is a nice evergreen grove in the southwest corner of the park. This park was the site of several military engagements during the Civil War Battle of Westport, and several plaques describe those events. Take time to visit the Rose Garden on the north side of the park. Walking time is about half an hour.

Brush Creek: (Shown opposite page) This is a pleasant 1.3-mile walk along Brush Creek from Roanoke Parkway on the west to Troost Avenue on the east. You can connect with the Harry Wiggins Trolley Track Trail (see Trail Site 49) at the intersection of Volker and Brookside Boulevards.

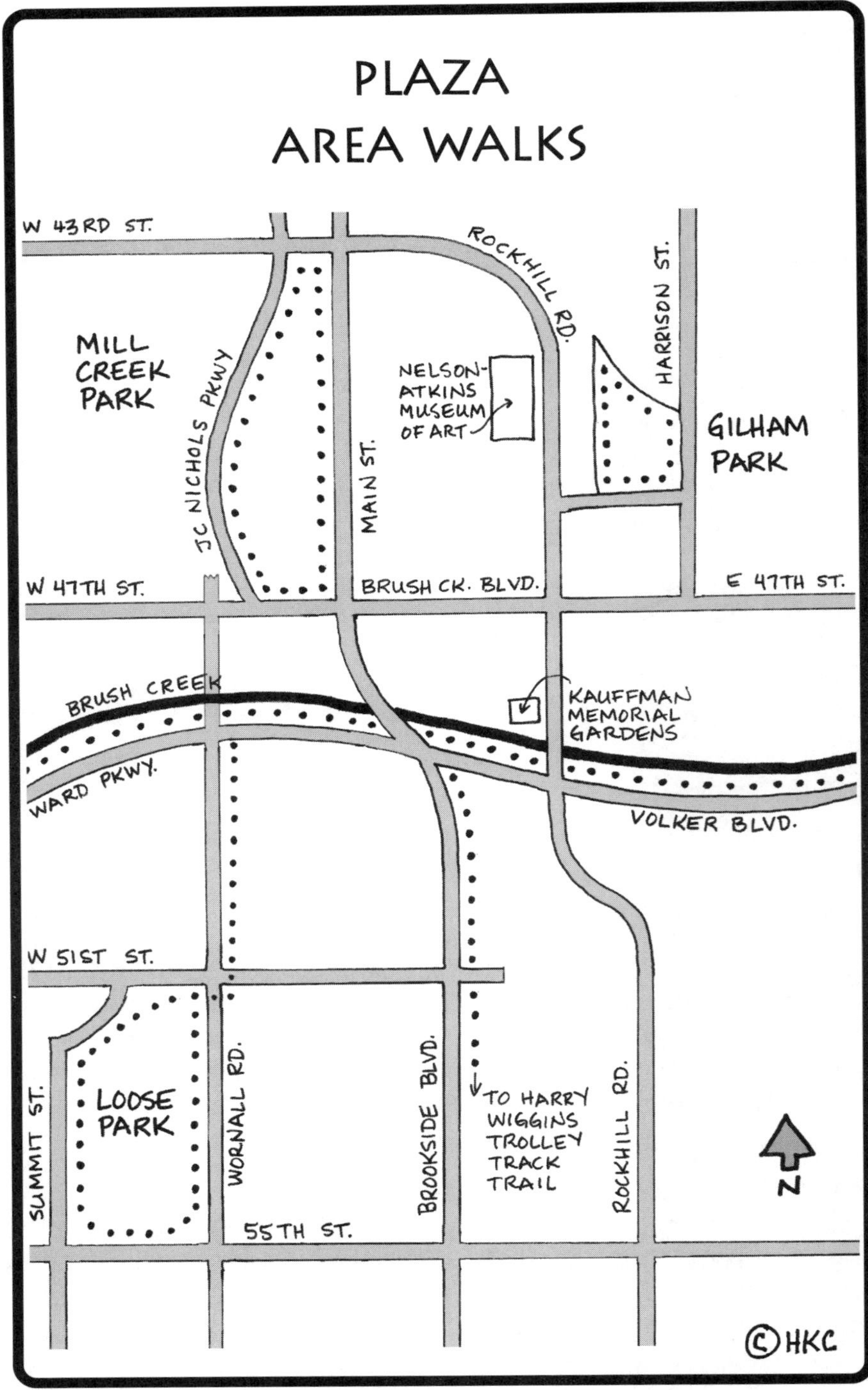
PLAZA
AREA WALKS
W 43RD ST.
ROCKHILL RD.
HARRISON ST.
MILL
CREEK
PARK
JC NICHOLS PKWY
NELSON-
ATKINS
MUSEUM
OF ART
GILHAM
PARK
MAIN ST.
W 47TH ST.
BRUSH CK. BLVD.
E 47TH ST.
BRUSH CREEK
KAUFFMAN
MEMORIAL
GARDENS
WARD PKWY.
VOLKER BLVD.
W 51ST ST.
LOOSE
PARK
SUMMIT ST.
WORNALL RD.
BROOKSIDE BLVD.
TO HARRY
WIGGINS
TROLLEY
TRACK
TRAIL
ROCKHILL RD.
N
55TH ST.
©HKC

The walking loop at Loose Park takes you past a variety of trees and rolling lawns. This park was the site of several Civil War engagements during the Battle of Westport. Plaques describe those events.

49
HARRY WIGGINS TROLLEY TRACK TRAIL
Kansas City Area Transportation Authority

Time: 3.5 Hours
Distance: 6.5 Miles (One-way)
Rating: Easy
Drinking Water: Yes
Accessible: Portions

This hike along the abandoned roadbed of the old Country Club and Westport Interurban Railway, which was established in 1890, is one of the best urban walks in Kansas City. It begins south of the Plaza and ends 6.5 miles later at Prospect Avenue, just south of 85th Street, where there is a small parking area. The entire trail does not have to be hiked at one time. You can walk segments such as the Plaza to Brookside or Brookside to the Waldo shopping area. Distances are shown on signs at main intersections. The trail surface is crushed rock from the Plaza to 85th Street, and from there to the end is asphalt. Harry Wiggins, for whom the trail is named, was a Missouri senator and a strong supporter of trails.

Directions: The trail begins at the intersection of Volker and Brookside Boulevards southeast of the Plaza. The right-of-way is easy to follow and is completely off-road (although it crosses several streets where you must exercise normal caution). The grade is slightly uphill to Waldo (75th Street) and downhill from there to the trail's end. The trail proceeds through parks, residential and commercial areas, and undeveloped property. Hikers will find benches and other amenities around the route. These distances may help walkers:

Volker to 55th Street: 0.75 mile
55th Street to Brookside: 1 mile
Brookside to Gregory Boulevard: 1 mile
Gregory to 85th Street: 1.75 mile
85th Street to Prospect: 1.75 mile

The popular Trolley Track Trail allows walkers to enjoy a number of neighborhoods and shopping districts.

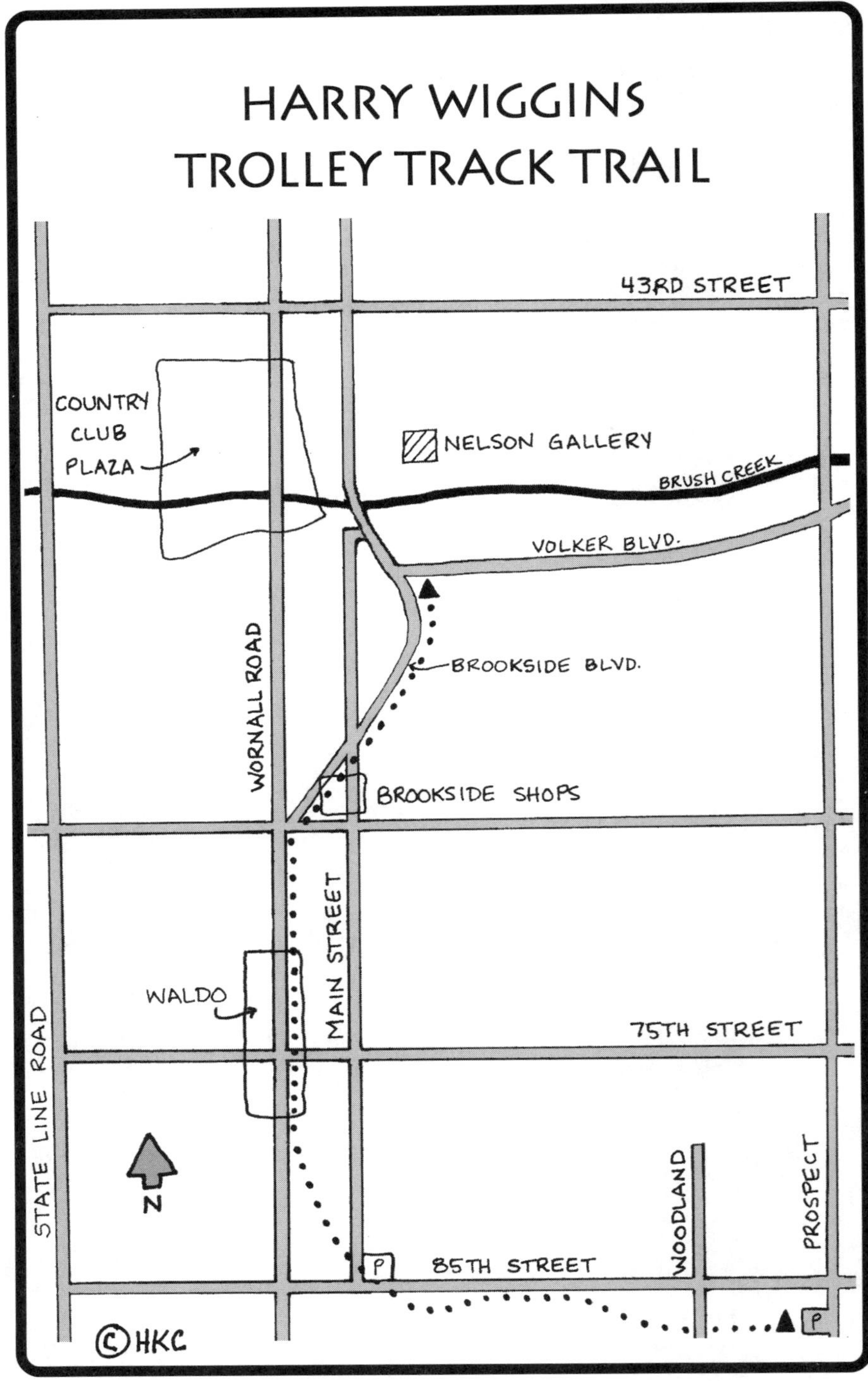
HARRY WIGGINS
TROLLEY TRACK TRAIL
43RD STREET
COUNTRY CLUB PLAZA
NELSON GALLERY
BRUSH CREEK
VOLKER BLVD.
BROOKSIDE BLVD.
WORNALL ROAD
BROOKSIDE SHOPS
MAIN STREET
WALDO
75TH STREET
STATE LINE ROAD
N
WOODLAND
PROSPECT
P
85TH STREET
P
©HKC

When the Riverfront Heritage Trail is complete, walkers will be able to hike between Berkley Park in Missouri and Huron Park in Kansas.

50
RIVERFRONT HERITAGE TRAIL

Kansas City, Missouri, Unified Government of Wyandotte County, Kansas City, Kansas, Kansas City River Trails, Inc., Faultless Starch

Time: From 1 to Several Hours
Distance: 9 Miles When Completed
Rating: Moderate
Drinking Water: Planned for Rest Stops
Accessible: Most

An ambitious system of pedestrian and bicycle paths is being developed along the Missouri and Kansas Rivers in downtown Kansas City, Missouri and Kansas City, Kansas. This bi-state project will connect riverfronts and business districts of both cities. A 9-mile long ribbon of green spaces, pedestrian and bicycle trails, historical markers and works of art will connect Richard L. Berkley Park on the east with Huron Park in downtown Kansas City, Kansas. Branches, some on-street, will extend south along the Kaw River in Kansas and also to Penn Valley Park on the Missouri side. The project will help achieve the long-term goal of reconnecting the community to our river heritage. It will be a major amenity for all in the metropolitan area and will complement the renaissance of downtown Kansas City.

At the time of publication of this book, the off-road segment of the trail was completed through Berkley Park and west along the Missouri River to Main Street. You can ascend a stairway at the foot of Main Street to an observation tower with great views of the river. Currently, a marked on-street biking route continues west via 3rd and 4th Streets to Wyandotte, south on Wyandotte, west on 9th Street to Case Park and the Lewis and Clark statue and lookout point. From there, the route meanders south, utilizing bike paths, bike lanes and greenways to 23rd Street. Another branch will lead south along the east side of the Kaw River.

As funding becomes available, the off-street trail will continue west through the bottoms and across the state line to Kansas City, Kansas. Future plans call for linkages to Kaw Point on the Kansas side and Cliff Drive on the eastern end.

Directions: To reach Berkley Park, take Grand Avenue north from downtown Kansas City, Missouri, past the River Market. The route curves to the east over a bridge and directly to Berkley Park. Park at the east end. From there, you can walk west as far as the trail is developed, or continue the alternative routes on streets. The Kansas City, Kansas segment can be accessed from Huron Park, 6th Street and Minnesota.

Trail: The Riverfront Heritage trail is developing as funding becomes available for the various segments. For the current state of the trail system, readers are advised to call the Mid-America Regional Council at (816) 474-4240.

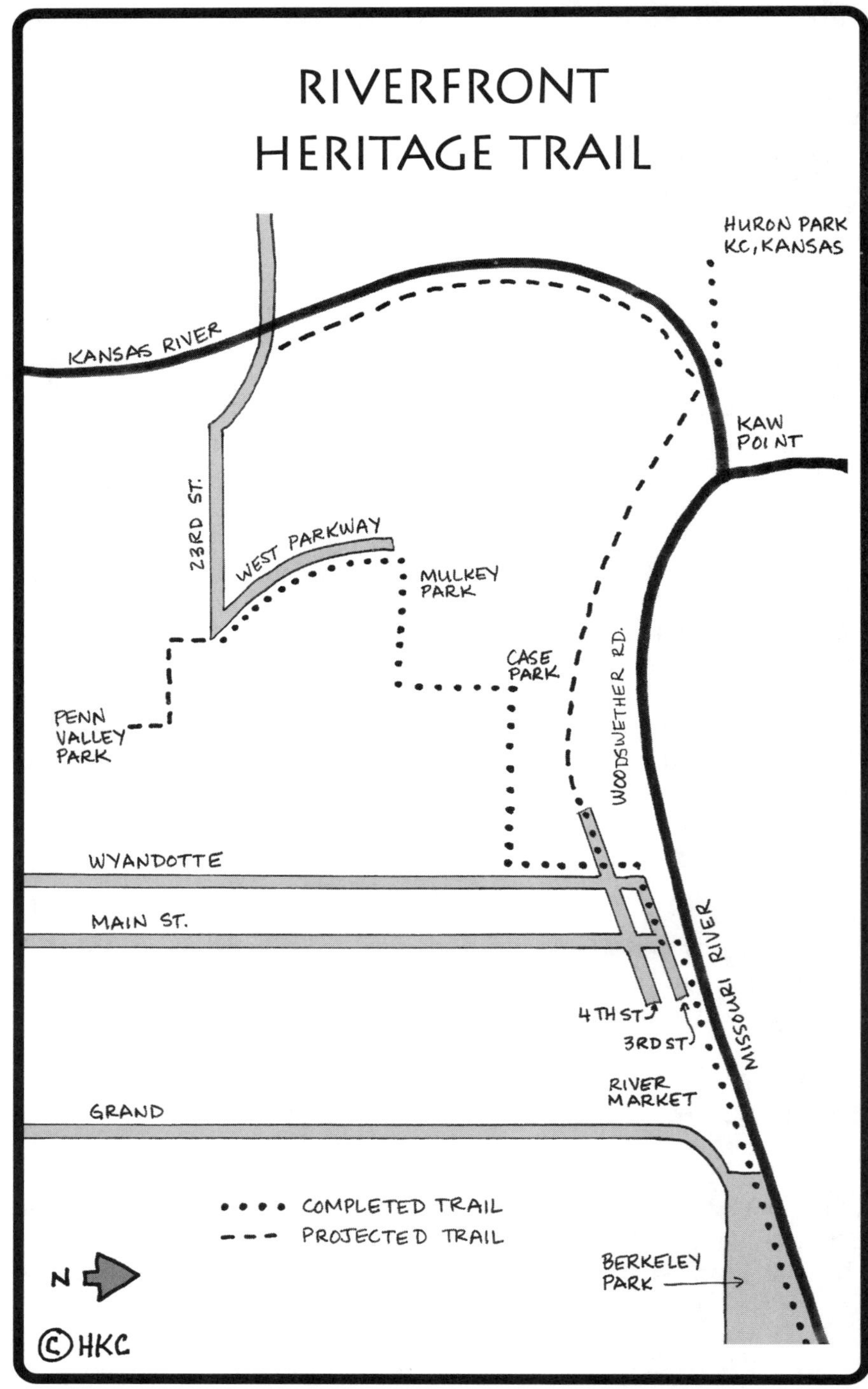
RIVERFRONT
HERITAGE TRAIL
HURON PARK
KC, KANSAS
KANSAS RIVER
KAW
POINT
23RD ST.
WEST PARKWAY
MULKEY
PARK
CASE
PARK
WOODSWETHER RD.
PENN
VALLEY
PARK
WYANDOTTE
MAIN ST.
4TH ST
3RD ST
MISSOURI RIVER
RIVER
MARKET
GRAND
COMPLETED TRAIL
PROJECTED TRAIL
N
BERKELEY
PARK
©HKC

An observation platform at the foot of Main Street provides a panoramic view of the Missouri River and its bridges.

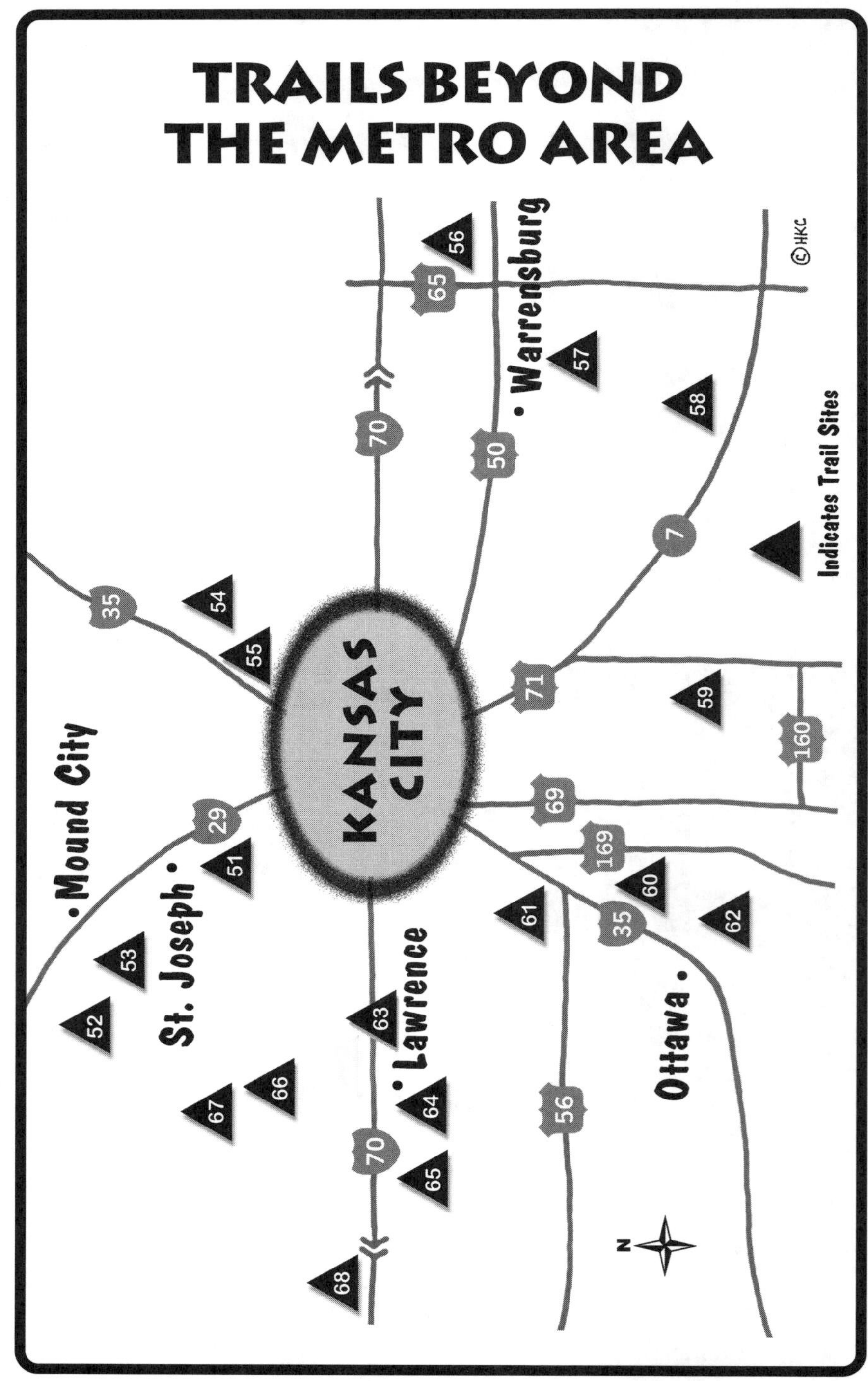
TRAILS BEYOND
THE METRO AREA
KANSAS CITY
Mound City
St. Joseph
Lawrence
Warrensburg
Ottawa
Indicates Trail Sites
51
52
53
54
55
56
57
58
59
60
61
62
63
64
65
66
67
68
35
29
70
50
7
71
69
169
160
56
65
N
©HKC

TRAILS BEYOND THE METRO AREA

Note: ( ) denotes the number of trails at that location

51
BLUFFWOODS CONSERVATION AREA
Missouri Department of Conservation

Time: Up to 5 Hours
Distance: 2 and 5 Miles
Rating: Moderate to Difficult
Drinking Water: No
Accessible: Some

This is a 2,300-acre forest reserve far enough from the city to provide isolation, along with rewarding trails and enjoyable vistas.

Directions: Drive north from Kansas City on I-29, past Kansas City International Airport to Exit 20, then take Hwy 273 north and west until it intersects with Hwy 45. Turn right and follow Hwy 45 until it joins Hwy 59. Proceed north on Hwy 59 to the community of Halls. Across from the intersection of Hwy KK, turn right (east) onto Bluff Road (County Road 233), which immediately crosses a railroad track. Follow this road for 0.6 mile until it intersects with Henman Road. Turn right (south) on this gravel road and follow it for 0.6 mile, across two small bridges. Just past the Kerlin Cemetery, turn left on 60th Road and proceed 0.1 mile across a bridge to a parking area on the left side of the road. A sign indicates "Kerlin Creek Picnic Area and Lone Pine Trail."

Maple Falls, Lone Pine & Turkey Ridge Trails: These three continuous trails total 5 miles. The hike described here involves walking the perimeters of the three trails for a total of 4.5 miles (see map). Proceed from the upper (east) end of the parking lot. At the far end of the picnic area is the trailhead. After a few yards there is a bridge with trail signs. Follow the Maple Falls Trail to the left. In less than 0.5 mile, it intersects the Lone Pine Trail. Take the Lone Pine Trail to the left. The route will take you up some steep hills past the "Lone Pine," a large, old, gnarled fir tree. Soon you will come to a bluff with a wide view of the Missouri River Valley. Continue on until the intersection with Turkey Ridge Trail. Follow Turkey Ridge Trail to the left where you will encounter another vista. Continue for about 1.5 miles, when you again intersect with Lone Pine Trail. Follow this trail to the left, where you will soon intersect with Maple Falls Trail. Follow Maple Falls Trail to the left and back to the trailhead at the picnic ground.

Forest Nature Trail System: In the northeast section of the park is a network of three short paved trails and two natural-surface nature trails. Drive northeast from Halls on Hwy 59. At Bethel Road, turn right (southeast) and follow the road to the trailhead, where interpretive booklets are available. Four loop trails and two connecting paths, which total 2 miles, provide pleasant walking through several ecosystems (see map for individual trail names).

Visitors to this region may enjoy the 1,100-acre Honey Creek Conservation Area. Turn off I-29 at Fillmore, Exit 29, and follow the blacktop road across I-29 and south. This site contains a number of trails, including 5.5 and 7.5-mile multi-use trails.

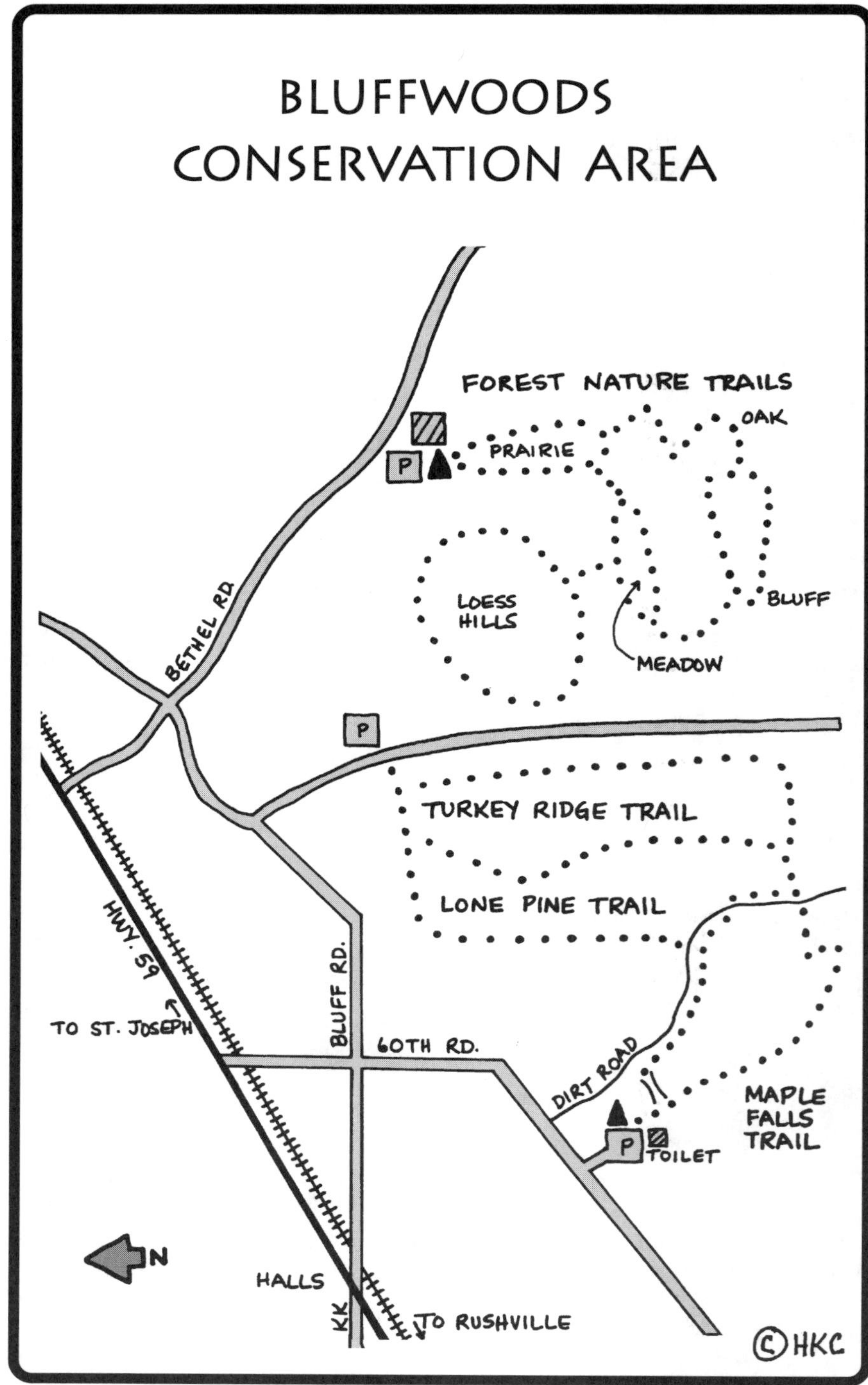
BLUFFWOODS
CONSERVATION AREA
FOREST NATURE TRAILS
OAK
PRAIRIE
P
LOESS HILLS
BLUFF
MEADOW
BETHEL RD.
P
TURKEY RIDGE TRAIL
LONE PINE TRAIL
HWY. 59
TO ST. JOSEPH
BLUFF RD.
60TH RD.
DIRT ROAD
MAPLE FALLS TRAIL
P
TOILET
N
HALLS
KK
TO RUSHVILLE
©HKC

Wildflowers.

Krista and Ellie Stigall enjoy the view at Eagle Days.

52
SQUAW CREEK NATIONAL WILDLIFE REFUGE
U.S. Fish & Wildlife Service

Time: 5 Hours
Distance: 10 Miles
Rating: Easy

Drinking Water: No
Accessible: No

Squaw Creek National Wildlife Refuge is a stopping point for thousands of migrating ducks and geese each spring and fall. The refuge roads and walking trails provide excellent opportunities to view and photograph an abundance of wildlife, including pelicans, blue heron, and in late fall and early winter, bald eagles. Nearby is the Jamerson C. McCormack Loess Mounds Preserve (see Trail Site 53), which overlooks the refuge on the east.

More than a hundred mature bald eagles can be seen at Squaw Creek in early December. The refuge is also a stopping point for thousands of migrating ducks and geese each spring and fall.

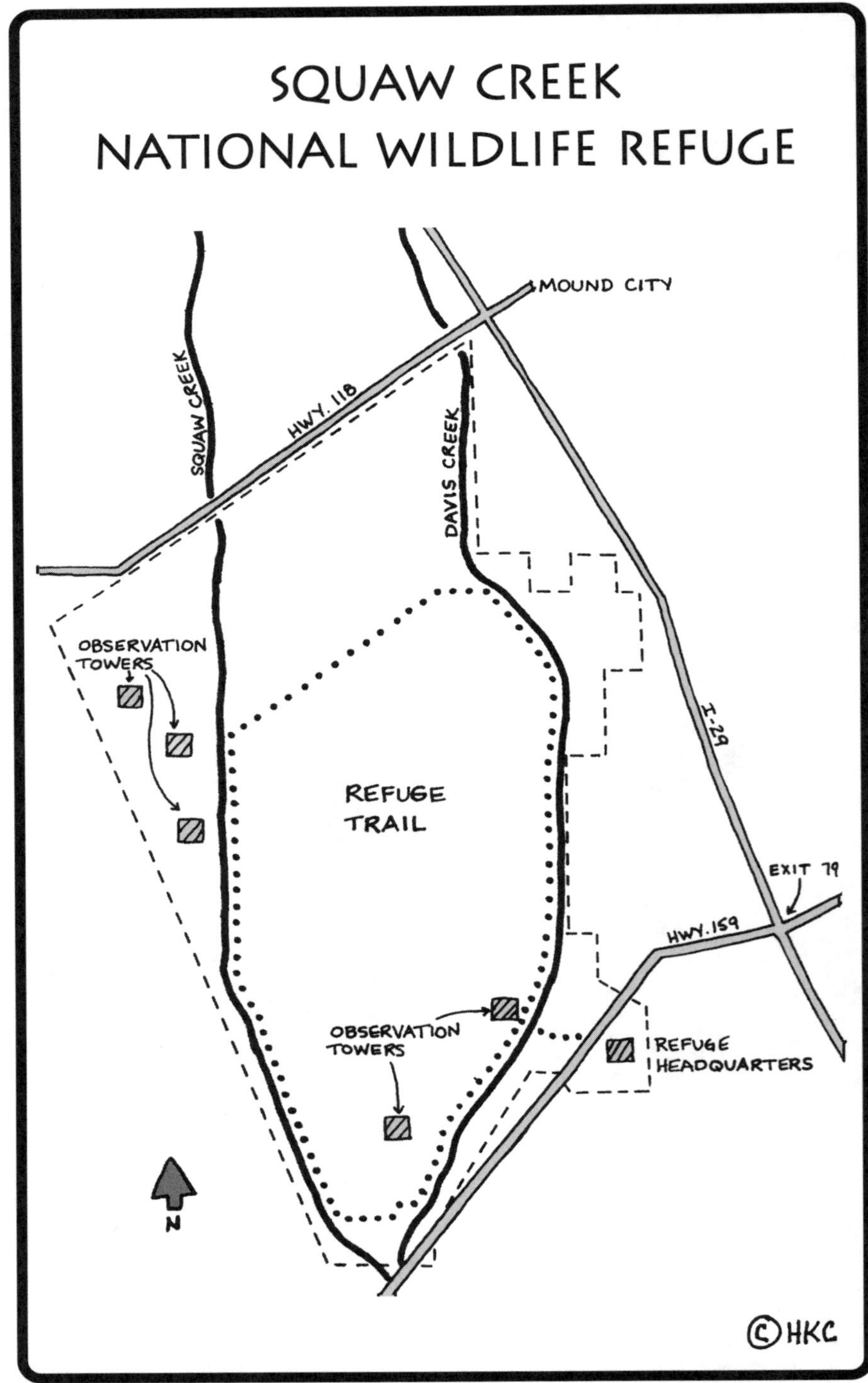
SQUAW CREEK
NATIONAL WILDLIFE REFUGE
MOUND CITY
SQUAW CREEK
HWY. 118
DAVIS CREEK
I-29
OBSERVATION
TOWERS
REFUGE
TRAIL
EXIT 79
HWY. 159
OBSERVATION
TOWERS
REFUGE
HEADQUARTERS
N
©HKC

Directions: The Squaw Creek National Wildlife Refuge is 95 miles north of Kansas City via I-29. Just south of Mound City, Missouri, take Exit 79. Go southwest on Hwy 159 to the refuge headquarters. The road into the refuge is on the right. A map and brochure are available at the headquarters on the left.

Refuge Trail: The trail, which circles the refuge, is a hard-pack surface road that must be shared with motor vehicles. There are several observation towers shown on the map, which may be reached only on foot. Also, different levees are open from time to time and available only to walkers. The walk around the refuge is 10 miles. However, if you walk to and from the observations towers, or to the ends of the levees, you can add several more miles to your walk.

53
McCORMACK LOESS MOUNDS PRESERVE

The Nature Conservancy
& Missouri Department of Conservation

Time: 1 Hour Minimum
Distance: 2 or More Miles
Rating: Difficult

Drinking Water: No
Accessible: No

Loess (pronounced *luss*) soil mounds are unusual, grass-dominated, steep vertical ridges, rarely seen except in northwestern Missouri, eastern Nebraska, western Iowa and southwestern South Dakota. They were formed 10,000 to 15,000 years ago by strong winds that deposited up to 150 feet of silt, clay and fine sand in valleys along the Missouri River. The loess hills overlook the Squaw Creek National Wildlife Refuge, where thousands of migratory pelicans, ducks, geese and bald eagles may be viewed in the spring and fall (see Trail Site 52). This 227-acre preserve also supports many species of endangered Missouri plants.

Directions: The preserve is 95 miles north of Kansas City, Missouri via I-29. Just south of Mound City, Missouri, take Exit 79 and head southwest 3.7 miles (1.6 miles south of Squaw Creek) on Hwy 159. A sign and parking lot marking the entrance are on the east (left) side of the highway. If you reach Hwy 111, you've gone too far.

Loess Mounds Trail: The trail proceeds east from the parking area, up a steep dirt road cut into the loess. At about 0.4 mile, there is a less defined trail to the left. This spur, about 0.1 mile long, leads to a scenic overlook with a spectacular view of the Missouri River Valley. A lookout at the end of the trail provides an excellent place to observe birds and other wildlife. The main trail ascends sharply and takes you to the hilltop and the eastern edge of the property, about a mile each way. You must return by the same route. There are several side trails that we did not explore, but looked interesting. Allow time to enjoy the birds, wildlife, geological features and plant life.

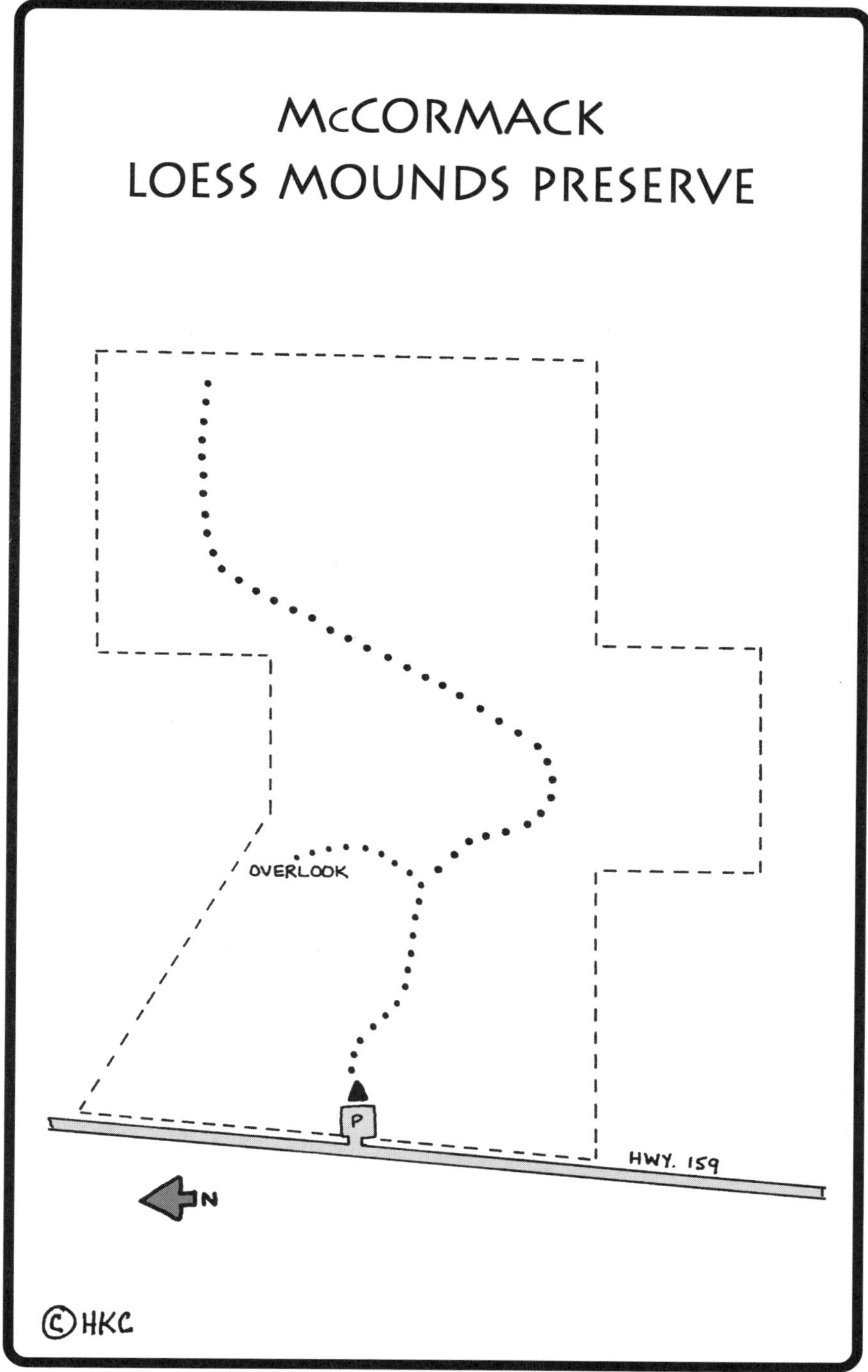
McCORMACK
LOESS MOUNDS PRESERVE
OVERLOOK
P
HWY. 159
N
©HKC

Author Bill Eddy takes a break on the Deer Creek Loop. This 1.5-mile loop is an interesting option for energetic hikers. It begins at the lower pond dam along Deer Run Trail and follows a ridge overlooking Deer Creek Valley.

54
WALLACE STATE PARK
Missouri Department of Natural Resources

Time: 2 to 3 Hours
Distance: 5 to 7 Miles
Rating: Moderate
Drinking Water: Yes
Accessible: No

One of the prettiest and most varied trail systems we walked was in Wallace State Park, north of the metro area. The trails are thoughtfully laid out through a variety of terrain in an area of dense woods, open meadows and streams. The trails are well maintained with directional signs at most intersections. With the aid of a map, one can connect loop trails and various campground trails to produce an interesting walk of up to 7 miles. There are benches on most trails. We saw many wildflowers, ferns and stately trees.

Directions: Drive north from Kansas City on I-35 to the Wallace State Park Exit, just south of Cameron. Pick up Hwy 121 at the exit and follow the directions 2 miles east to the park entrance. Just inside the entrance is a park office on the left, where further information may be obtained.

Rocky Ford Trail: The trailhead for this 0.75-mile trail lies on the right side of the road in a picnic area. This trail immediately takes you into the woods where you gently drop into the floodplain of Deer Creek. Following the creek upstream, water can be seen cascading over large limestone shelves. This may have been a Mormon Trail crossing. The trail ends in a picnic area south of the trailhead.

Deer Run Trail is 2 miles long, or 1 mile if you take the shortcut. The trailhead is at Lake Allaman spillway. This loop trail passes through a variety of habitats—mature oak forests, edges of recently abandoned fields, near ponds, across streams (crossings are generally dry except after heavy rains), along the north side of a hill rich in ferns and mosses and back through the Deer Creek floodplain, with many large trees. This trail ends in the picnic area below Lake Allaman dam.

Deer Creek Loop is 1.5 miles long. It is an interesting option for energetic hikers who would like to extend the length of Deer Run Trail. The trail begins at the lower pond dam along Deer Run Trail and follows a ridge overlooking Deer Creek Valley. It then enters the floodplain, where it follows the meandering stream for more than 0.5 mile before turning up a small valley and rejoining Deer Run Trail.

Skunk Hollow Trail is 0.75 mile long. The trailhead is in Campground 4. There is no parking at the trailhead, however, cars may be left at the entrance to the campground. This is a heavily wooded area with gentle hills. Intermittent streams offer little waterfalls as a highlight.

Old Quarry Trail is a 0.75-mile trail. The trailhead is in the scout camping area. You are welcome to walk this trail even if the scout area is occupied or the gate is closed. Park cars outside the gate and enter the area on foot. A sign along the road marks the trailhead. The trail passes a small limestone outcrop (where settlers may have quarried foundation stones), follows the edge of a hayfield, then returns through a small Scotch and Shortleaf Pine grove planted by school children in the 1950s.

Oak Leaf Trail: An intersecting, 1-mile loop trail that winds through Trice-Dedman Memorial Woods, located about 3.5 miles west of Lathrop on Hwy 116, 17 miles southwest of Wallace State Park. Perhaps the largest remaining old-growth oak woodland north of the Missouri River, this 50-acre tract was donated by the Dedman family to the Nature Conservancy and is maintained by the Department of Natural Resources. Parking is on the highway shoulder. The trailhead is on the north side of the road. Stop at the park office for more information.

The trails at Wallace State Park are thoughtfully laid out through a variety of terrain in dense woods, open meadows and streams. The trails are well maintained with directional signs at most intersections. With the aid of a map, one can connect loop trails and various campground trails to produce an interesting walk of up to 7 miles.

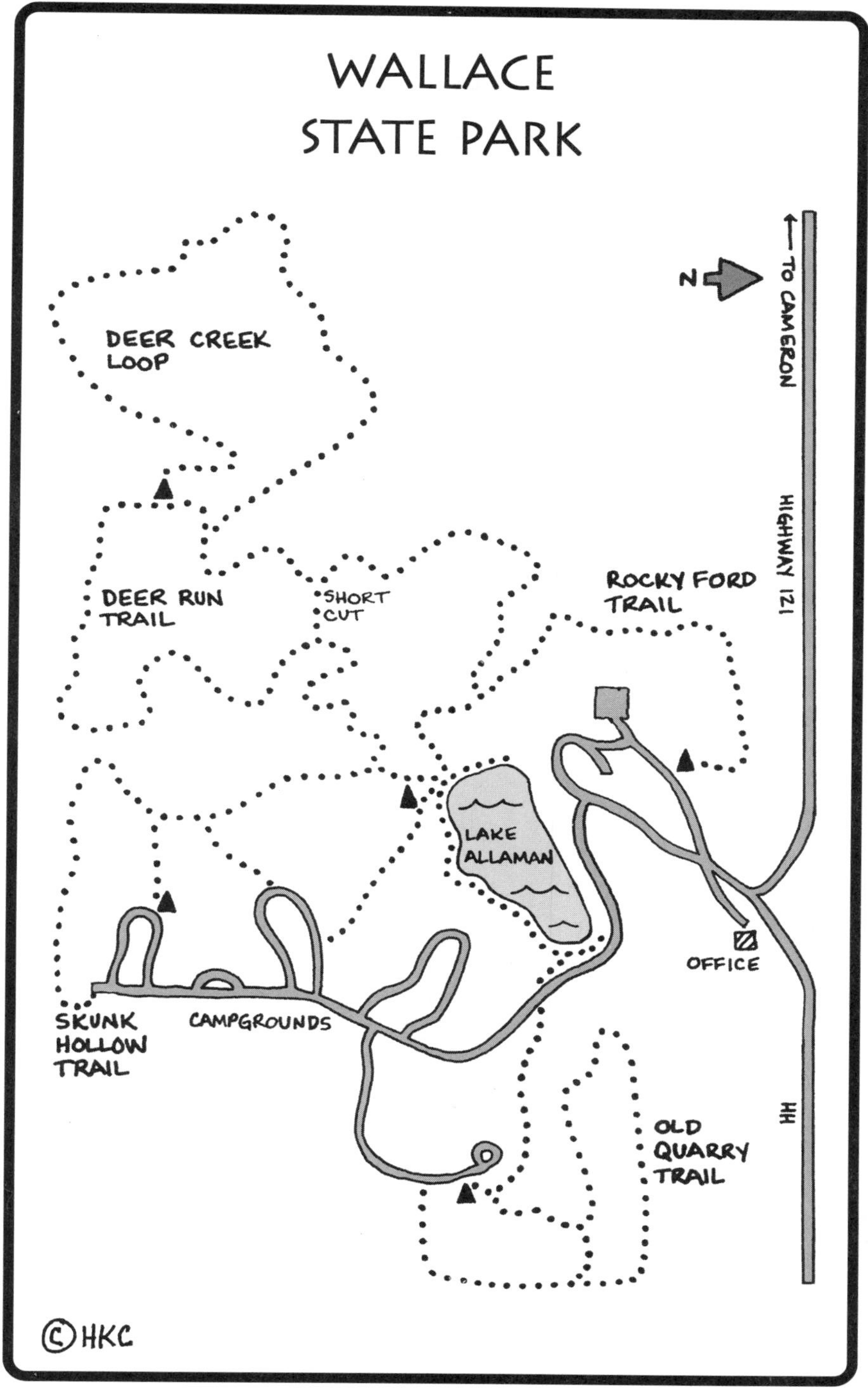
WALLACE
STATE PARK
N
TO CAMERON
HIGHWAY 121
DEER CREEK
LOOP
DEER RUN
TRAIL
SHORT
CUT
ROCKY FORD
TRAIL
LAKE
ALLAMAN
OFFICE
SKUNK
HOLLOW
TRAIL
CAMPGROUNDS
HH
OLD
QUARRY
TRAIL
©HKC

55
KEARNEY FISHING RIVER TRAIL
City of Kearney, Missouri

Time: 1.5 hours
Drinking Water: At Meadowbrook Drive
Distance: 4 miles
Accessible: Yes
Rating: Easy

This nice addition to walking paths in the northland forms a loop of over 4 miles on the south side of Kearney. The asphalt trail travels south from a trailhead on 19th Street east of Kearney High School, circles farms fields and follows the Fishing River as it makes its way westward. The trail runs under Missouri Hwy 33 and shortly turns northward as it parallels the Burlington Northern-Santa Fe tracks. At 19th Street) it travels eastward across Hwy 33 to the starting point. A spur leading north from near the starting point provides access to subdivisions. The hiker will see rich bottomland, large shade trees along the river and many kinds of birds.

Directions: To get to the trail, drive north from Kansas City on I-35 for about 25 miles (depending on where you begin) to the Kearney, Missouri State Hwy 92 exit. Follow Hwy 92 east for a few blocks to an intersection with Hwy 33. Turn right (south) on 33 and follow it for about a mile to 19th Street. Turn left (east) on 19th Street and follow it for 0.5 mile to the starting point, where the trail heads south through Whitegate subdivision. There is parking along the street and in a lot adjacent to the tennis courts.

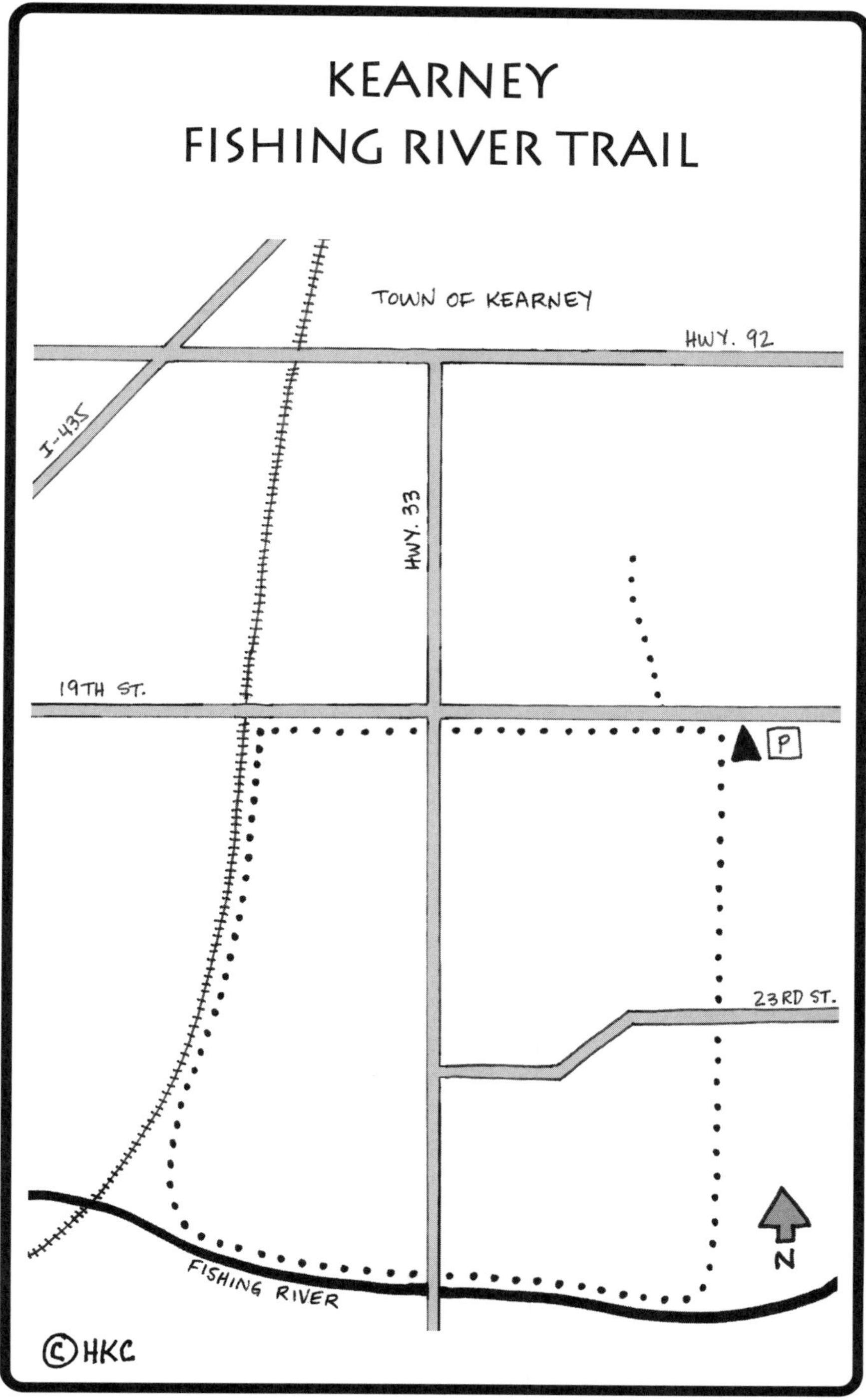
KEARNEY
FISHING RIVER TRAIL
TOWN OF KEARNEY
HWY. 92
I-435
HWY. 33
19TH ST.
P
23RD ST.
N
FISHING RIVER
©HKC

The trail from Rocheport towards Jefferson City passes high limestone bluffs, caves, springs, deep glens and river vistas.

56
KATY TRAIL STATE PARK
Missouri Department of Natural Resources

Time: Varies by Segments **Drinking Water:** At Trailhead
Distance: 225 Miles, With Trailheads Every 4 to 35 Miles
Rating: Easy, except for distance **Accessible:** Yes

The Katy Trail is the longest hiking and biking trail in Missouri, and is fast becoming one of the most popular. It is also America's longest rails-to-trails project. Stretching 225 miles from Clinton on the west to St. Charles on the east, the trail is built on the bed of the abandoned Missouri-Kansas-Texas (MKT or "Katy") rail line. Since it follows a railroad bed, the trail is level with only occasional gradual inclines. The surface is finely crushed rock called 'chat' that is well suited to walkers and cyclists. From Boonville east, the trail follows the Missouri River to the St. Charles area, progressing beneath high bluffs, through thick forests, past communities, and along other varied and scenic terrain, with frequent vistas of the Missouri River and its valley.

Most hikers will cover the Katy Trail in segments. Since it follows the railroad route, there are communities at intervals all along the way. Guidebooks and maps, outlined on the following pages, indicate the trailhead communities and distances between them. Parking is available at the trailheads and one can either walk from the parking area along the trail and back, or leave cars at two trailheads for a one-way trek. An effort to extend the trail to Kansas City is underway.

Clinton Trailhead: The Wagoner Sports Complex trailhead in Clinton is the westernmost Katy Trail trailhead. Clinton is located about 70 miles from Kansas City, at the junction of Hwys 7, 13 and 52. Here, the trail is more rolling than the flat river bottom portions from Boonville on eastward. This stretch is relatively secluded, passing primarily through prairie country, farms and cattle ranches. Clinton's restored town square is worth a visit (be sure and stop at the soda fountain).

Sedalia Trailhead: To get there from Kansas City, follow Hwy 50 southeast some 80 miles. There are two access points in Sedalia, one east and one west. Reach the west access point, closest to Kansas City, by turning south from Hwy 50 on Thompson Boulevard, then east on Y and south on Clarendon Road to a marked parking area. To reach the east access point, follow the highway through town to the intersection with Engineer Avenue. Turn north on Engineer and follow it to Griessen Road. Go right (east) on Griessen until you reach the trail. The trail traverses prairie, farmland and woods.

Rocheport Trailhead: Rocheport, another popular access point, is a two hour drive east of Kansas City on I-70. Take Exit 115 just past the bridge over the Missouri River. It is well-marked. Signs direct you to the trailhead. The town offers bike rental, several bed & breakfasts and numerous shops. Several gourmet restaurants will be a highlight of the afternoon. The trail eastward passes tall limestone bluffs, caves, springs, deep glens and river views. On the western end of Rocheport is the Katy Trail's only train tunnel. A must see. McBaine, the next trailhead, is 8.9 miles to the east—an easy round-trip for bikers, but a long hike. Mighty Mo Canoe Rental offers guided floats for those wanting to experience the river: www.mighty-mo.com.

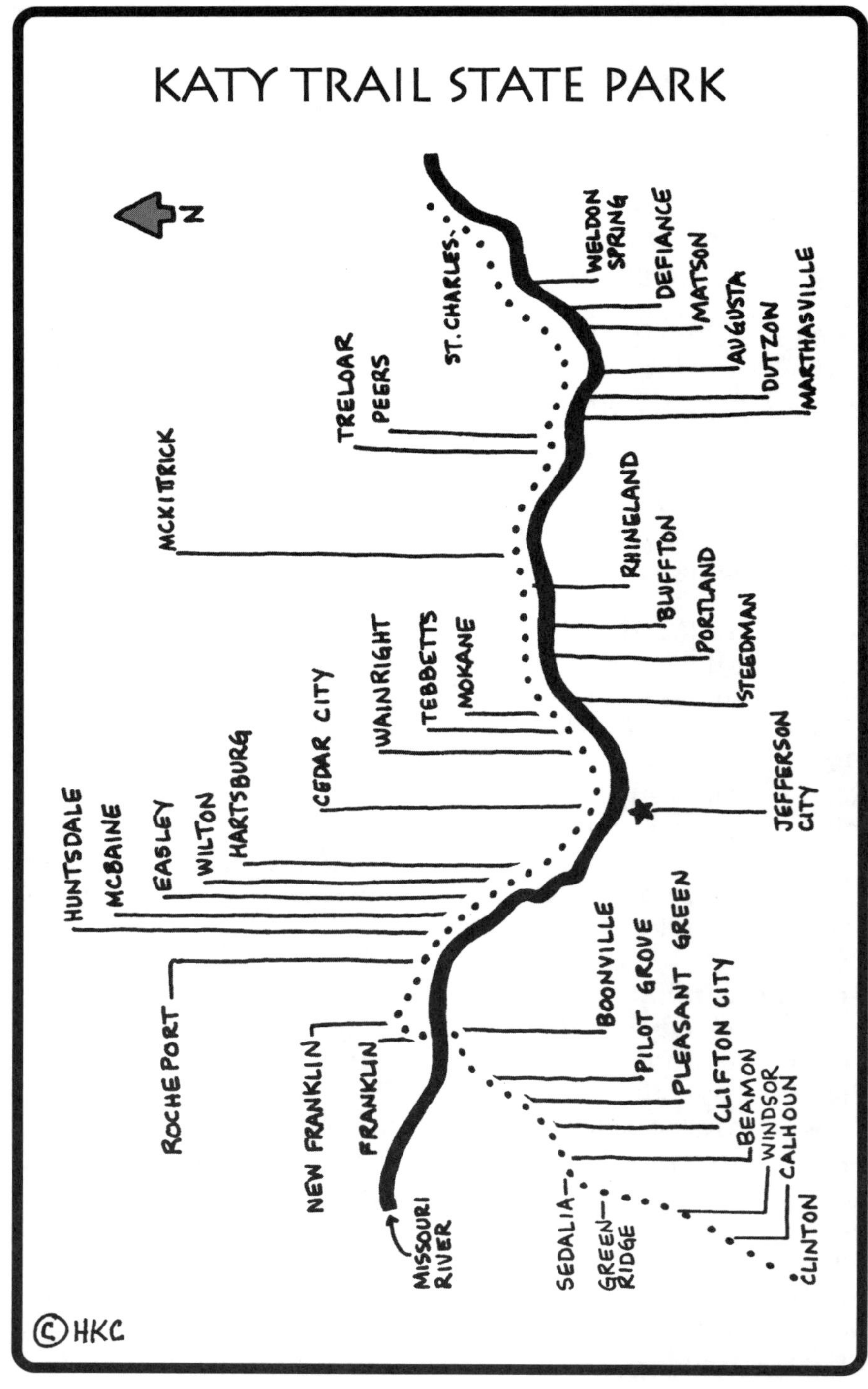
KATY TRAIL STATE PARK
N
ST. CHARLES
WELDON SPRING
DEFIANCE
MATSON
AUGUSTA
DUTZON
MARTHASVILLE
TRELOAR
PEERS
MCKITTRICK
RHINELAND
BLUFFTON
PORTLAND
STEEDMAN
CEDAR CITY
WAINRIGHT
TEBBETTS
MOKANE
JEFFERSON CITY
HUNTSDALE
MCBAINE
EASLEY
WILTON
HARTSBURG
ROCHEPORT
NEW FRANKLIN
FRANKLIN
BOONVILLE
PILOT GROVE
PLEASANT GREEN
CLIFTON CITY
BEAMON
WINDSOR
CALHOUN
CLINTON
SEDALIA
GREEN-RIDGE
MISSOURI RIVER
©HKC

Note: If you would like to plan a Katy Trail trip, go online to www.bikekatytrail.com. Or order Brett Dufur's *The Complete Katy Trail Guidebook* from Pebble Publishing. Pebble Publishing also offers a one-volume nature guide to commonly seen birds, trees, wildflowers, plants and more, called *The Katy Trail Nature Guide.* Call (573) 698-3903 or visit www.pebblepublishing.com. For a free Katy Trail brochure from the Missouri Department of Natural Resources call (800) 334-6946 or go online to www.katytrailstatepark.com.

The Katy Trail at the Rocheport trailhead.

57
KNOB NOSTER STATE PARK
Missouri Department of Natural Resources

Time: 1 to 5 Hours
Distance: 1.5 to 7.4 Miles
Rating: Moderate to Difficult
Drinking Water: Yes
Accessible: Portions

There are several developed trails in this attractive state park 60 miles southeast of Kansas City. Complete maps and directions are available in the park office.

Directions: Drive southeast on Hwy 50, past Warrensburg and to the western outskirts of Knob Noster. Turn south on Hwy 23 and follow the signs to the park entrance.

The Discovery & North Loop Trails start behind the office across the parking lot. Near the beginning, a path goes left. To complete the Discovery Trail, do not take this fork. Continue around the loop. At 0.5 mile you will return to the start. Now, start again but turn left at the fork. This leads to an amphitheater where the North Loop Trail begins in the northwest corner. This loop goes 2 miles through deep woods, along Clear Fork Creek and to a camping area with water and restrooms before crossing an access road and returning to the office.

Buteo Trail, Hawk Nest Trail & Clear Fork Savanna Trail: These trails begin on the south side of the campground access road. Buteo Trail begins at Lake Buteo near the picnic shelters. It circles the lake for a mile to connect with Hawk Nest Trail (2.3 miles including a 0.6-mile Clear Fork Savanna Trail loop).

The Opossum Hollow Trail begins at a park road west of the North Loop area. From the park office, take the road to the left past Lake Buteo south to Road DD. Go west to the first side road to the north. Follow this road for more than a mile. The trailhead is at the Morel Lake picnic area. This 1.5-mile trail loops past lakes and a savanna area, returning to Road DD.

There is a 7-mile **McAdoo Equestrian Trail** south of Road DD, and additional mountain bike trails opened recently. Ask for information at the park office.

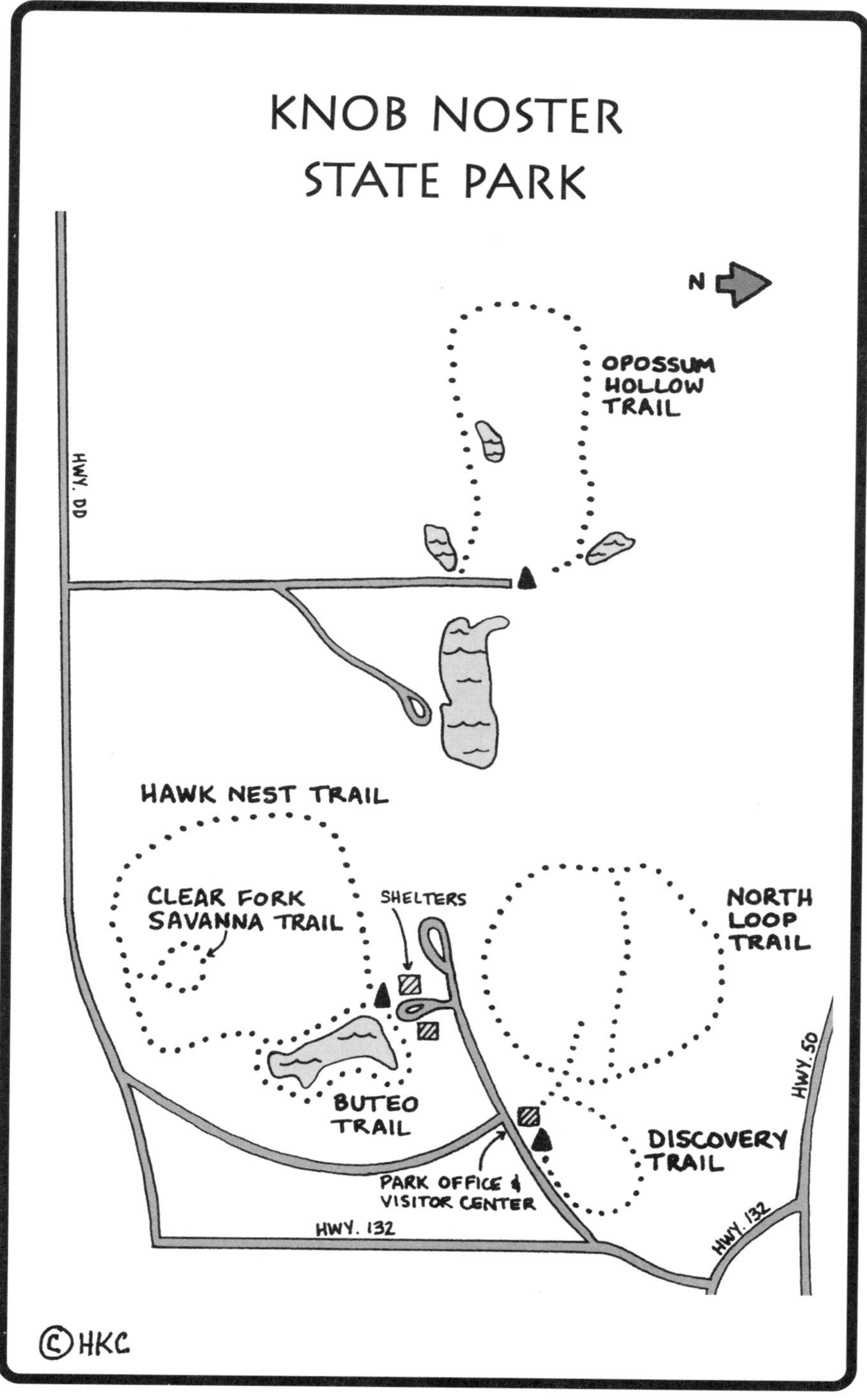
KNOB NOSTER
STATE PARK
N
OPOSSUM HOLLOW TRAIL
HWY. DD
HAWK NEST TRAIL
CLEAR FORK SAVANNA TRAIL
SHELTERS
NORTH LOOP TRAIL
HWY. 50
BUTEO TRAIL
DISCOVERY TRAIL
PARK OFFICE & VISITOR CENTER
HWY. 132
HWY. 132
©HKC

58
TRUMAN LAKE STATE PARK
Missouri Department of Natural Resources

Time: 1 hour
Distance: 2 Miles
Rating: Easy
Drinking Water: In Campgrounds
Accessible: No

Harry S Truman State Park is located southeast of Kansas City at Truman Lake, a large Army Corps of Engineers multi-use project. Facilities include camping and picnicking areas, a marina with ramps and boat rental and a sand beach.

Directions: Travel south from Kansas City on Hwy 71 to Harrisonville, where you pick up Hwy 7 heading southeast. Follow Hwy 7 to Route UU, and then north to the park entrance. The trip from Kansas City takes about two hours.

Bluff Ridge Trail: Inside the park, take the road to the left toward the park office where more complete information is available. If the office is closed, follow the road to the northwest, past the fee collection station for 0.7 mile, to a sign on the right indicating the Bluff Ridge Trail. If a gate to the side road accessing the trail is closed, park your car at the kiosk near the office and follow the campground road 0.2 mile to the trailhead. The trail is well-marked and maintained. It travels through oak and hickory forest, glades and savannas. After about 0.5 mile, a side trail to the right leads back to the campground. However, you should continue straight ahead to a bluff high above lake. This is a spectacular but dangerous spot. Keep children well away from the edge of the bluff. The trail continues to the right for 0.2 mile to the trailhead. There are interpretive signs along the trail.

Western Wild Flower Savanna Trail: This 0.75-mile nature trail begins at a kiosk north of the park office. The trail is well maintained and marked with wood chips in the path. There are also old roads running through the park that can extend one's walking adventure. Consult with the rangers at the office.

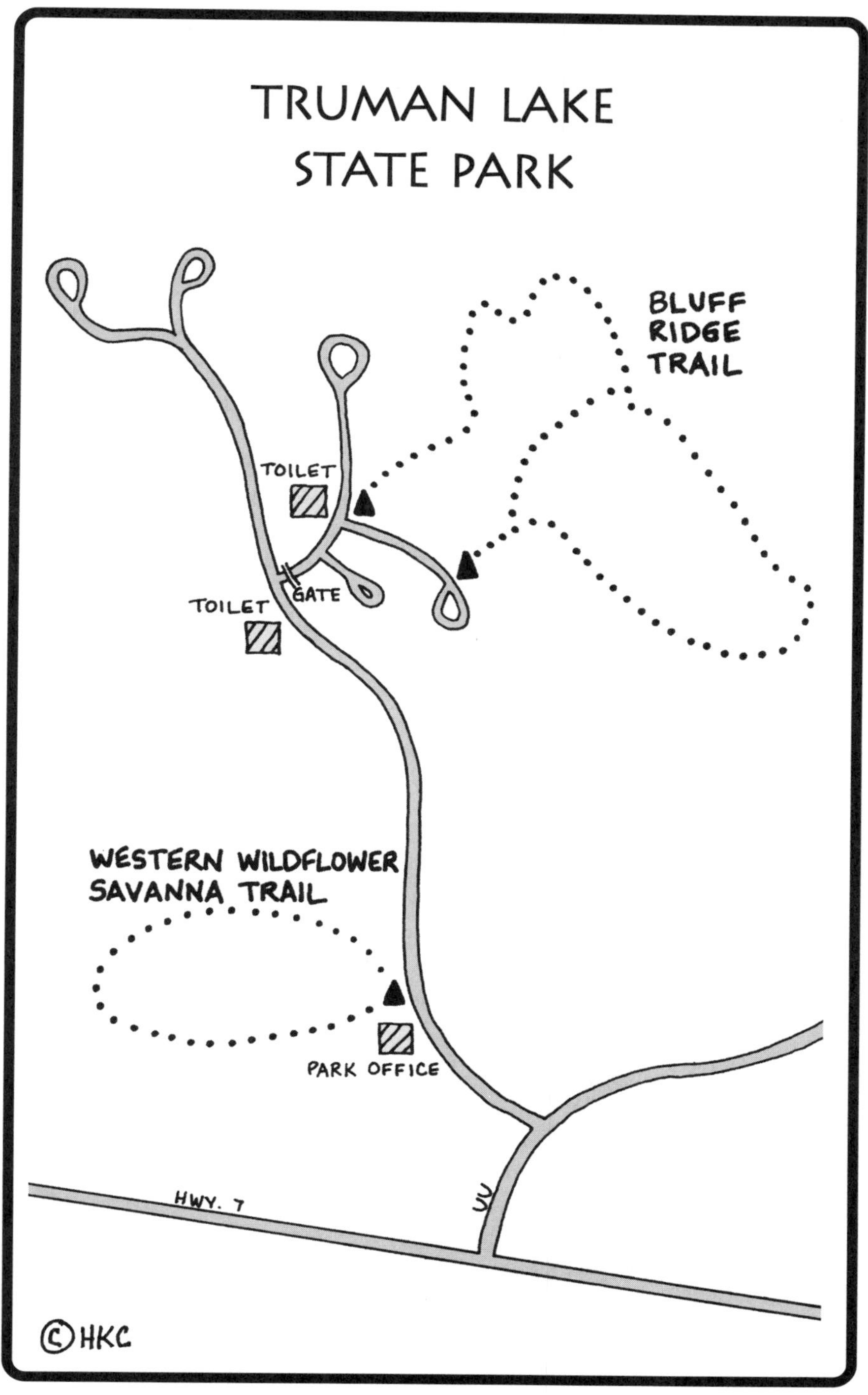
TRUMAN LAKE
STATE PARK
BLUFF
RIDGE
TRAIL
TOILET
GATE
TOILET
WESTERN WILDFLOWER
SAVANNA TRAIL
PARK OFFICE
HWY. 7
UU
©HKC

A herd of bison roam portions of Prairie State Park.

59
PRAIRIE STATE PARK
Missouri Department of Natural Resources

Time: 3 to 4 Hours
Distance: 7 Miles
Rating: Moderate
Drinking Water: At Visitors Center
Accessible: No

Prairie State Park is an impressive 2,558-acre preserve acquired with the aid of the Nature Conservancy to protect and interpret a sample of the rolling tallgrass prairies that once covered a third of the state. A visitors center provides exhibits, lectures and films that assist in understanding the natural features, plants and animals that inhabit this diverse environment. A herd of native bison (buffalo) roam segments of the park. Trails in the segment currently occupied by the bison are closed to hikers because it is unsafe to approach these large animals. Maps are available at the visitors center. The prairie is nearly treeless, with hot sun in the summer and chilling winds in the winter. Early morning and late evening are the best times to hike in the summer. A hat and water are strongly recommended. Smoking is prohibited due to the fire hazard in the grasslands.

Directions: Drive south of Kansas City on Hwy 71 for approximately 100 miles to Lamar, Missouri. At Lamar, turn west on Hwy 160. In 10 miles, turn north on Hwy 43. After 5 miles, turn west on County Road K. In about 3 miles, K turns right, but instead, turn left on (gravel) Road P and follow signs.

Trails: Three loop trails help the visitor gain an appreciation for the vastness, solitude and beauty of the prairie. The **Coyote Trail** (3 miles) begins at a picnic area just off the road leading into the park. It provides opportunities for wildlife observation, including prairie chicken, marsh hawk, coyote and scissor-tailed flycatcher. The **Gayfeather Trail** (1.5 miles) begins at a parking area at the south end of the park. It goes through a nearly undisturbed prairie community rich in wildflowers and other plant and animal life. A 0.2-mile spur trail provides access to the Coyote Trail. The 2.5-mile **Drovers Trail** begins at the visitors center. It provides good vistas of the rolling landscape.

Native prairie grasses provide food for the park's bison.

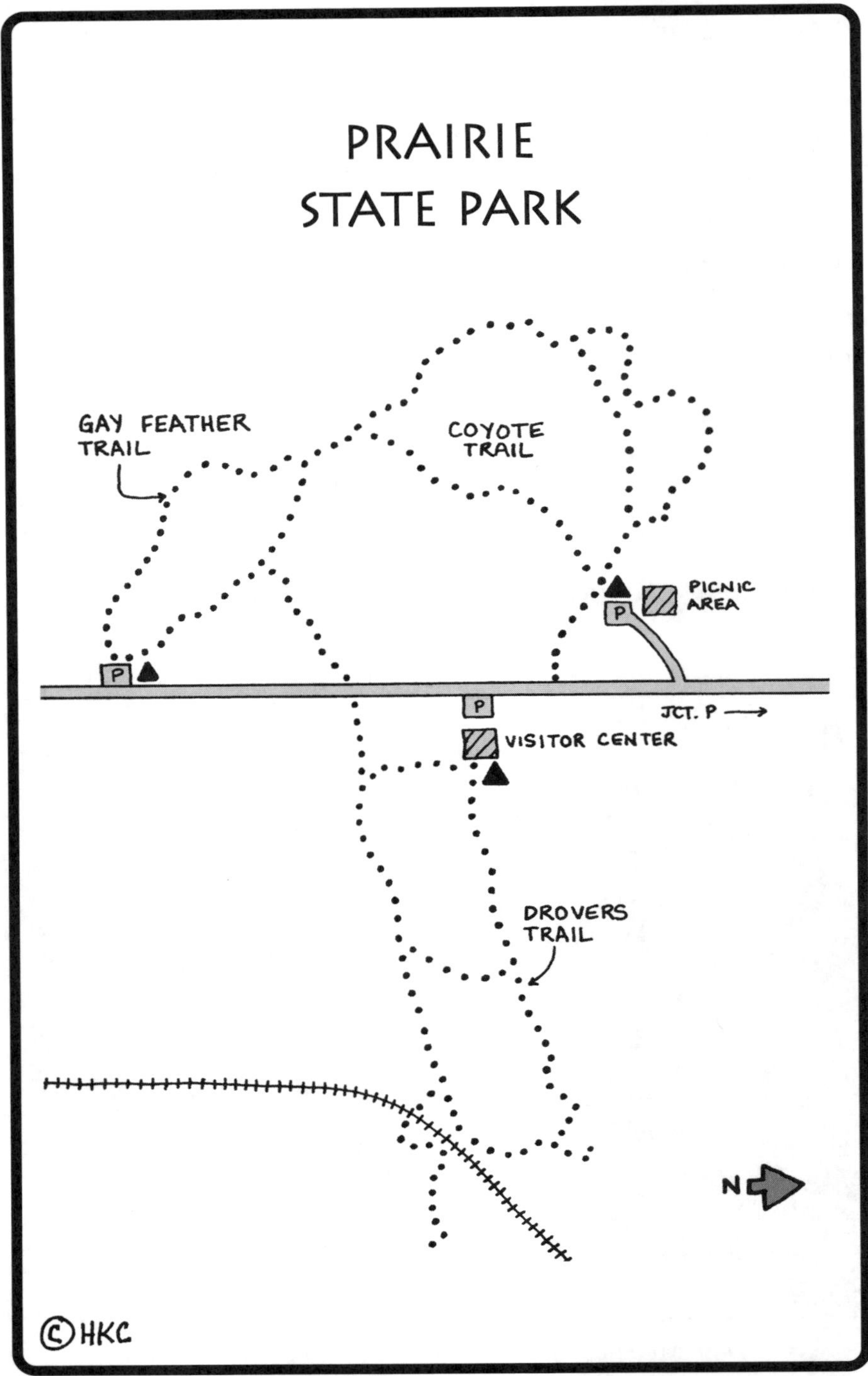
PRAIRIE
STATE PARK
GAY FEATHER
TRAIL
COYOTE
TRAIL
PICNIC
AREA
P
P
P
JCT. P
VISITOR CENTER
DROVERS
TRAIL
N
©HKC

60
HILLSDALE LAKE
U.S. Army Corps of Engineers

Time: 1 Hour
Distance: 1.5 Miles
Rating: Easy to Moderate

Drinking Water: Yes
Accessible: No

Hillsdale Lake is a 7,400-acre flood control area 40 miles south of Kansas City. It provides abundant recreation opportunities, including hiking, fishing, boating and bird watching. Hikers should stop at the visitors center for maps and literature and to view displays explaining the lake's resources. The area contains forests and meadows.

Directions: Drive south on I-35 to Hwy 169. Take Hwy 169 south. Turn right at Kansas Route 68 to the first intersection. Turn right (north) on Old Kansas City Road to 255th Street. Turn left towards the visitors center for parking, trail maps and restrooms.

Hidden Spring Nature Trail: The trail begins west of the visitors center beyond the water fountains. It is well-marked. For a longer walk, at 0.5 mile, take the spur loop trail to the left. At the next fork turn right, uphill to an observation deck. Continue on the trail for another 0.5 mile and return across a bridge to the beginning of the loop. Turn right about 25 yards to the main trail and turn left. Continue on the main trail that exits from the woods at about 1.5 miles.

The trail proceeds through woods and limestone outcroppings and skirts the lake. There are picnic tables at the trailhead and on the grounds of the visitors center.

Other Trails: There are other trails in the area, used principally by horseback riders. If you follow the blazes (blue or orange ribbons) you will find several miles of pleasant hiking. These trails are found north of the visitors center. Ask the Corps' rangers for directions.

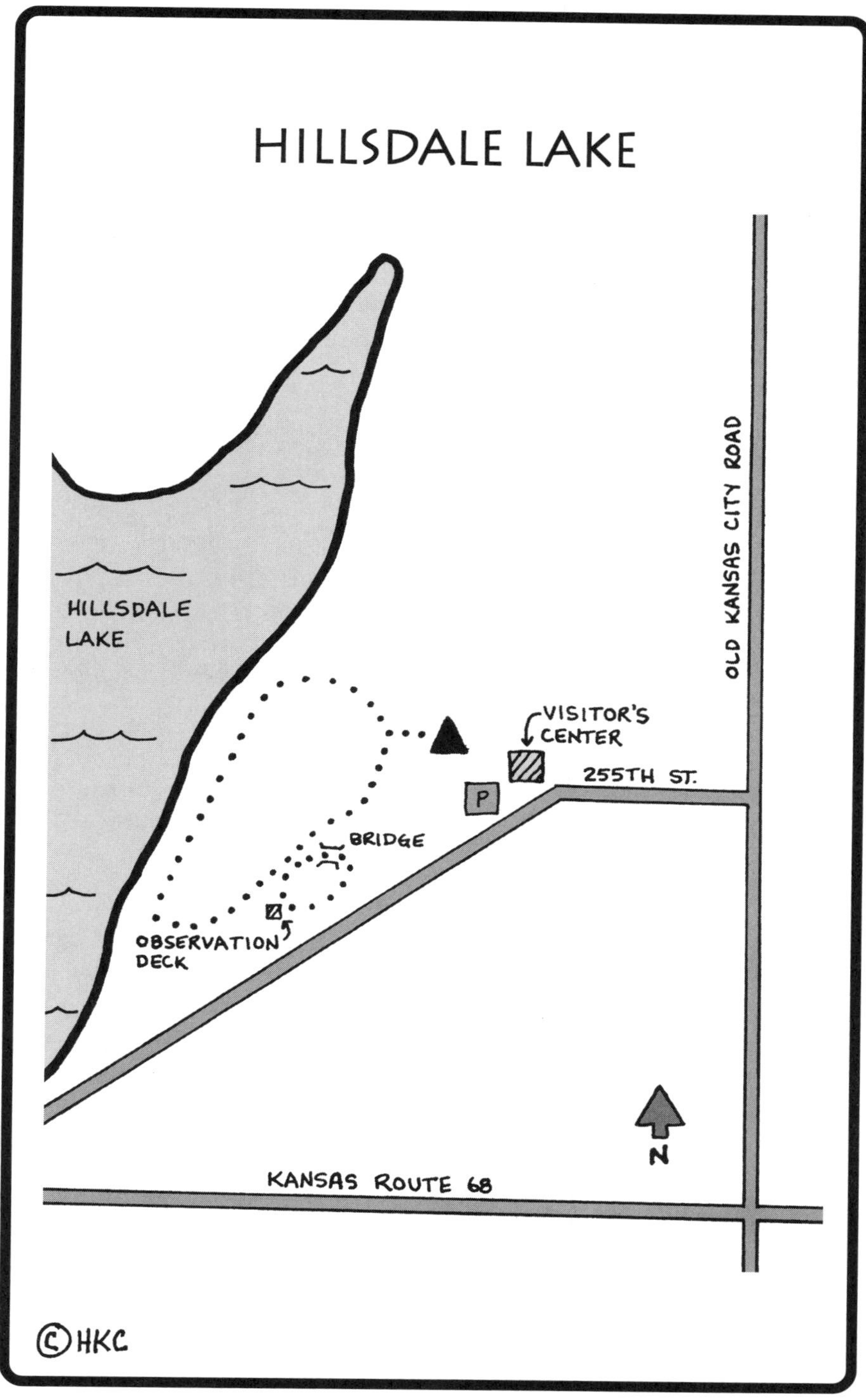
HILLSDALE LAKE
HILLSDALE LAKE
OLD KANSAS CITY ROAD
VISITOR'S CENTER
255TH ST.
P
BRIDGE
OBSERVATION DECK
N
KANSAS ROUTE 68
©HKC

61
LANESFIELD SCHOOL HISTORICAL PRAIRIE

Johnson County Museums, Kansas Department of Wildlife & Parks

Time: 1 Hour
Distance: 1.5 Miles
Rating: Easy to Moderate
Drinking Water: At Museum
Accessible: Short Circular Trail

This is an interesting historical site and prairie. Lanesfield is a ghost town whose only remnant is a restored stone school built in 1869. The town was founded in 1858 and at one time, in addition to the school, had a blacksmith shop, three stores, a hotel, three churches, seventeen homes and a population of about a hundred. It served as a mail stop on the Santa Fe Trail, which can be seen from the walking trail. Lanesfield was abandoned after the Santa Fe Railroad chose a depot in nearby Edgerton.

Directions: Drive south from Kansas City on I-35 to the Gardner 210 Exit, which is Hwy 56. Proceed on Hwy 56 through Gardner. At a split, stay right onto 175th Street to Dillie Road. Turn left on Dillie Road for 1.5 miles to the Lanesfield School Museum parking area.

Prairie Trail: The trailhead is at the shelter just east of the museum. The trail passes through the site of the pre-Civil War Battle of Bull Creek, where 1,600 pro-slavery Missourians clashed with 400 Free-State Militiamen after the Missourians burned the town of Osawatomie.

In addition to native prairie grasses, walkers will enjoy trees and shrubs, including one of the largest hackberry trees in the state of Kansas. There is an informative, well-written, self-guided tour pamphlet that walkers should pick up before beginning the walk at the small, but well-kept, museum.

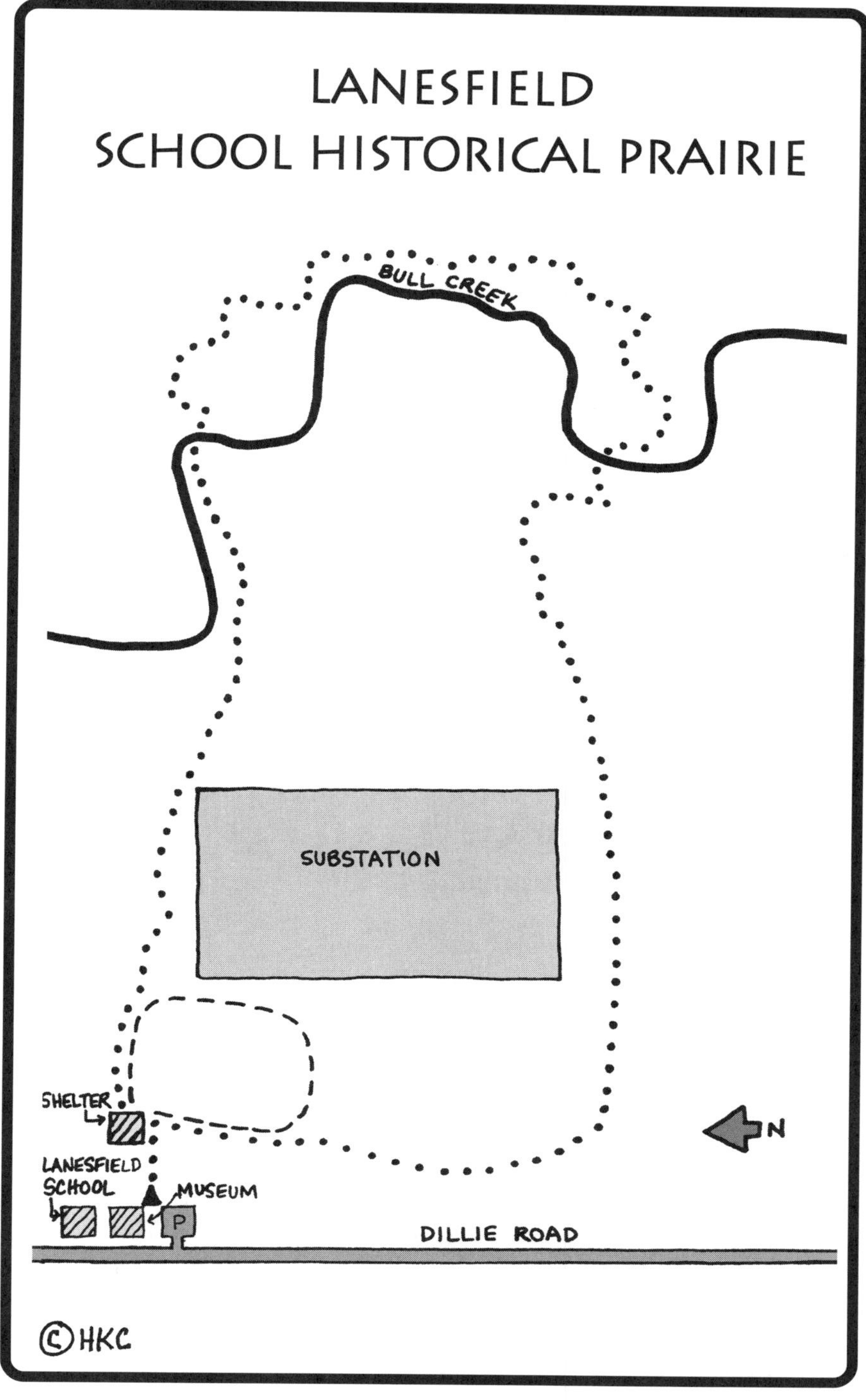
LANESFIELD
SCHOOL HISTORICAL PRAIRIE
BULL CREEK
SUBSTATION
SHELTER
LANESFIELD SCHOOL
MUSEUM
P
DILLIE ROAD
N
©HKC

Ottawa and Garnett, Kansas have made huge efforts to welcome users of the Prairie Spirit Trail. Take time to visit local businesses and museums.

62
PRAIRIE SPIRIT RAIL TRAIL
Kansas Department of Wildlife & Parks

Time: Varies by Segments
Distance: 33 Miles (One-way, Will Be 50 When Completed)
Rating: Easy
Drinking Water: At Communities Along Trail
Accessible: Portions

This trail follows the route of an abandoned Atchison, Topeka and Santa Fe Railroad line between Ottawa and Iola, Kansas. The Kansas Department of Wildlife and Parks has developed the trail between Ottawa and Richmond (15 miles) and between Richmond and Welda (18 miles). The final segment from Welda to Iola (17 miles) should be completed soon.

The 12-foot wide trail of crushed limestone provides a surface suitable for walking, wheelchairs and bicycles. There is a modest fee to use the trail. A wide variety of habitats can be encountered along the trail, from tallgrass prairie, deciduous forests and eastern floodplain forest to croplands. Wildlife includes deer, quail, hawks, owls, beaver and even bobcat.

Directions: Trailheads have been established in Ottawa, Princeton, Richmond, Garnett, Welda, Colony, Carlyle, Iola and other communities. Ottawa, the closest trailhead, is about 60 miles south of Kansas City. Take I-35 south to Kansas Hwy 68. Turn west on Hwy 68 to Ottawa. A trailhead has been established at the Old Depot Museum, an interesting place to visit. You can reach Richmond by taking Hwy 59 south from Ottawa. Turn west from the highway to the center of town where there is a parking area and access to the trail. Garnett, in the middle of the trail, has a very nice restored depot and a paved trail through town. From Hwy 59, turn east to the center of town where you can see the trail, and signs will direct you to the depot and trail access. Iola is at the intersection of Hwys 69 and 54.

The trail is supported by the Friends of Prairie Spirit Trail, P.O. Box 71, Garnett, KS 66032. Their website has information about the trail, events in communities along the trail, restaurants and other services: www.prairiespirittrail.org.

The Kanza Rail-Trail Conservancy is developing two other rail-trails in Kansas. They are the 117-mile Flint Hills Nature Trail that passes through Ottawa and the Landon Nature Trail that extends from Topeka to near Pomona Lake. Maps and other information can be found at www.kanzatrails.org.

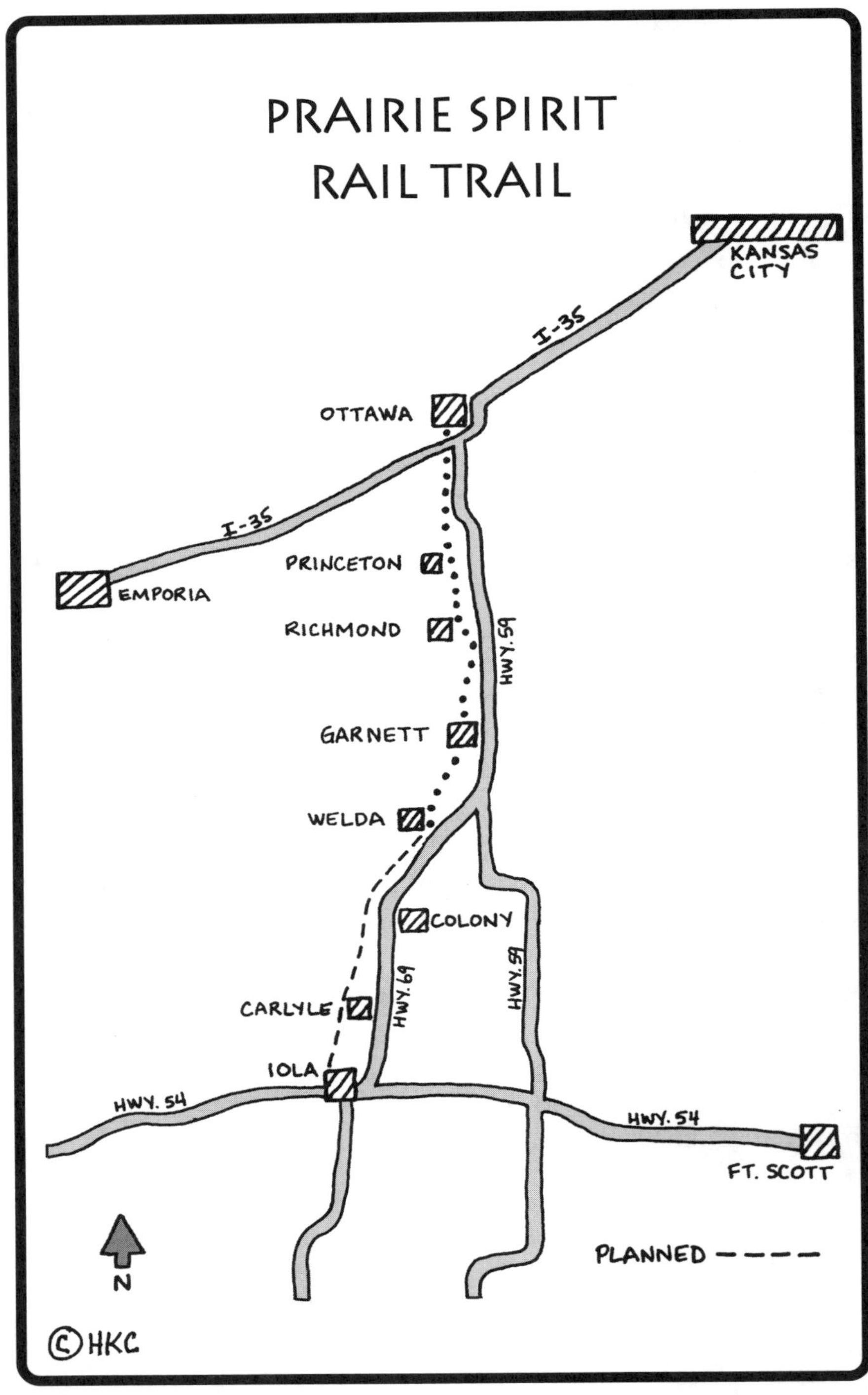
PRAIRIE SPIRIT
RAIL TRAIL
KANSAS CITY
I-35
OTTAWA
I-35
PRINCETON
EMPORIA
RICHMOND
HWY. 59
GARNETT
WELDA
COLONY
HWY. 69
HWY. 59
CARLYLE
IOLA
HWY. 54
HWY. 54
FT. SCOTT
N
PLANNED
©HKC

TRAIL NOTES:

63
LAWRENCE, KANSAS TRAILS
Lawrence, Kansas Parks & Recreation District

Time: 2 to 3.5 hours
Distance: 5 to 6.5 miles (One-way)
Rating: Easy
Drinking Water: No
Accessible: Portions

The Lawrence area has several trails for walkers to enjoy. Here are three of them. A good natural-surface nature trail can be enjoyed at Kansas University's Fitch Natural History Reserve north of I-70. Another trail, north of downtown, borders the Kansas (Kaw) River, where there are some very dramatic views of the river and where we have seen blue herons, egrets, ducks, geese and red tail hawks. Others have reported seeing bald eagle. A paved path generally parallels the South Lawrence Trafficway.

Fitch Natural History Reserve: Exit I-70 at the East Lawrence interchange and turn right on Kansas Hwy 59 for 0.5 mile. Turn right onto U.S. Route 40/Hwy 24 for 1.5 miles to just past the airport. Turn north on Douglas County 1600 E. Road. Continue on 1600, across the bridge over Mud Creek, for about 2 miles past Road 2000 N to the stone entrance to the reserve on your right. Proceed to the parking area. The nature trail consists of two loops, one of 1.3 miles and the other 0.8. There are thirteen "points of interest" along the way that feature ecology and history. There is elevation gain.

River Hike/Bike Trail: Exit I-70 at the East Lawrence interchange and turn left on Kansas Hwy 59 toward downtown. Proceed to Locust Street on the left before crossing the bridge to the visitor information center and parking area. The trail, which is atop the levee that borders the Kansas River, can be accessed from here. It may be followed east or northwest for about 5 miles in either direction. The path is also used by bikers, so hikers must use caution. The trail surface is finely crushed rock. Hikers going east will enjoy vistas of the river and stands of cottonwood, sycamore and other tree varieties. The path heading northwest is largely unshaded but provides many vistas.

Lawrence Trafficway Hiking and Biking Trail: This trail can also be reached from I-70 and Hwy 59. Follow Hwy 59 signs south (it is Iowa Street). Just south of 34th street is a shopping center on your right. At the south end, near the Holiday Inn Express, is an access point for the trail. If you reach the South Lawrence Trafficway (Route 10), you've gone too far. The trail heads west from the trailhead. It is a paved path that traverses wetlands, prairie grasslands and occasionally, residential areas. The west end, which climbs through a broad valley and limestone outcroppings, presents beautiful views. The path emerges near the road that crosses Clinton Dam just south of Clinton Parkway. From there, the path continues north to U.S. Route 40. We enjoyed crossing the dam road and going to the Corps of Engineers visitor center and walking to Clinton Lake, where there are viewpoints and shelters (see Clinton Lake at Trail Site 64). The path is 6.5 miles (one-way).

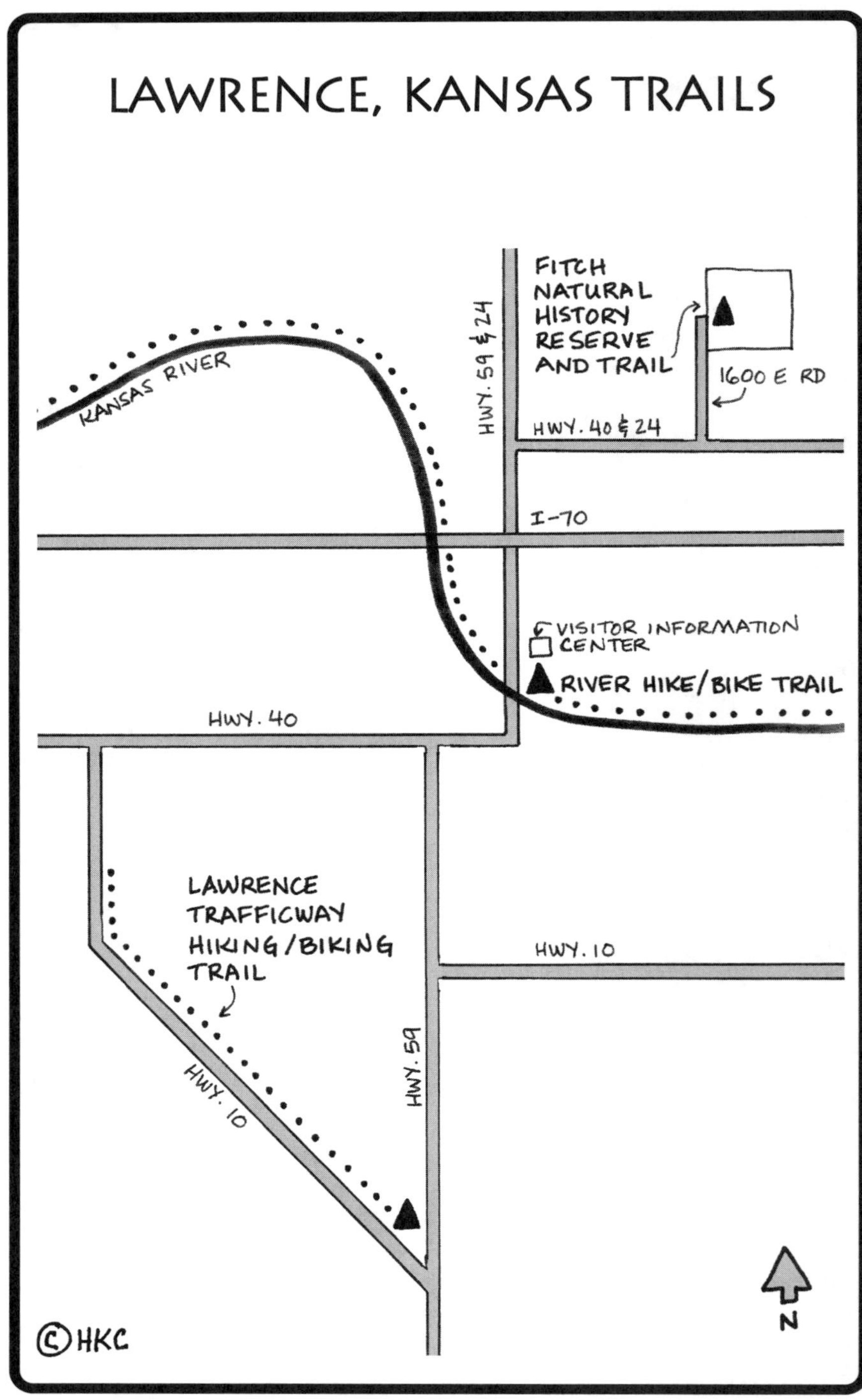
LAWRENCE, KANSAS TRAILS
FITCH NATURAL HISTORY RESERVE AND TRAIL
1600 E RD
HWY. 59 & 24
HWY. 40 & 24
KANSAS RIVER
I-70
VISITOR INFORMATION CENTER
RIVER HIKE/BIKE TRAIL
HWY. 40
LAWRENCE TRAFFICWAY HIKING/BIKING TRAIL
HWY. 10
HWY. 10
HWY. 59
N
©HKC

Sunshine filters through the canopy of trees that thrive along the Kaw River.

64
CLINTON LAKE
U.S. Army Corps of Engineers

Time: 4 to 7 Hours
Distance: 14 to 50 Miles
Rating: Moderate
Drinking Water: Some areas
Accessible: Being Planned

Clinton Lake is a 12,000-acre reservoir surrounded by forests and meadows. Bluebirds and beaver are abundant, and there have been sightings of eagle, gray fox, raccoon, deer and coyote.

Directions: Take Kansas Hwy 10 from Kansas City to Lawrence, Kansas. Stay on the road through south Lawrence. It will become Clinton Parkway. At the lake, continue right on Hwy 10, and in 0.1 mile, turn left at the entrance to the Corps of Engineers' visitors center. Stop by and pick up trail information.

North Shore Trail: The trailhead is located at Overlook Park, just past the visitors center at the north end of the dam. The surface is packed earth and rock with some steep slopes and obstacles. The Trunk Trail, blazed in blue, is about 7 miles (one-way) and takes about 4 hours to hike in each direction. The route is well used and generally easy to follow. The trail passes near park roads and picnic or camping areas, where water may be available, although carrying your own water is recommended. Some side loop trails, marked by white blazes, have been developed. They vary from 0.33 to 1.5 miles. A very worthwhile and pleasant walk on a well planned trail system.

Rockhaven Trail System: There are three trails called the Rockhaven Trails System, which we have not hiked. The system of roughly parallel trails runs west from the dam to 535th Road, following contours above the shoreline. The trails traverse scenic and rugged terrain on the south side of the lake.

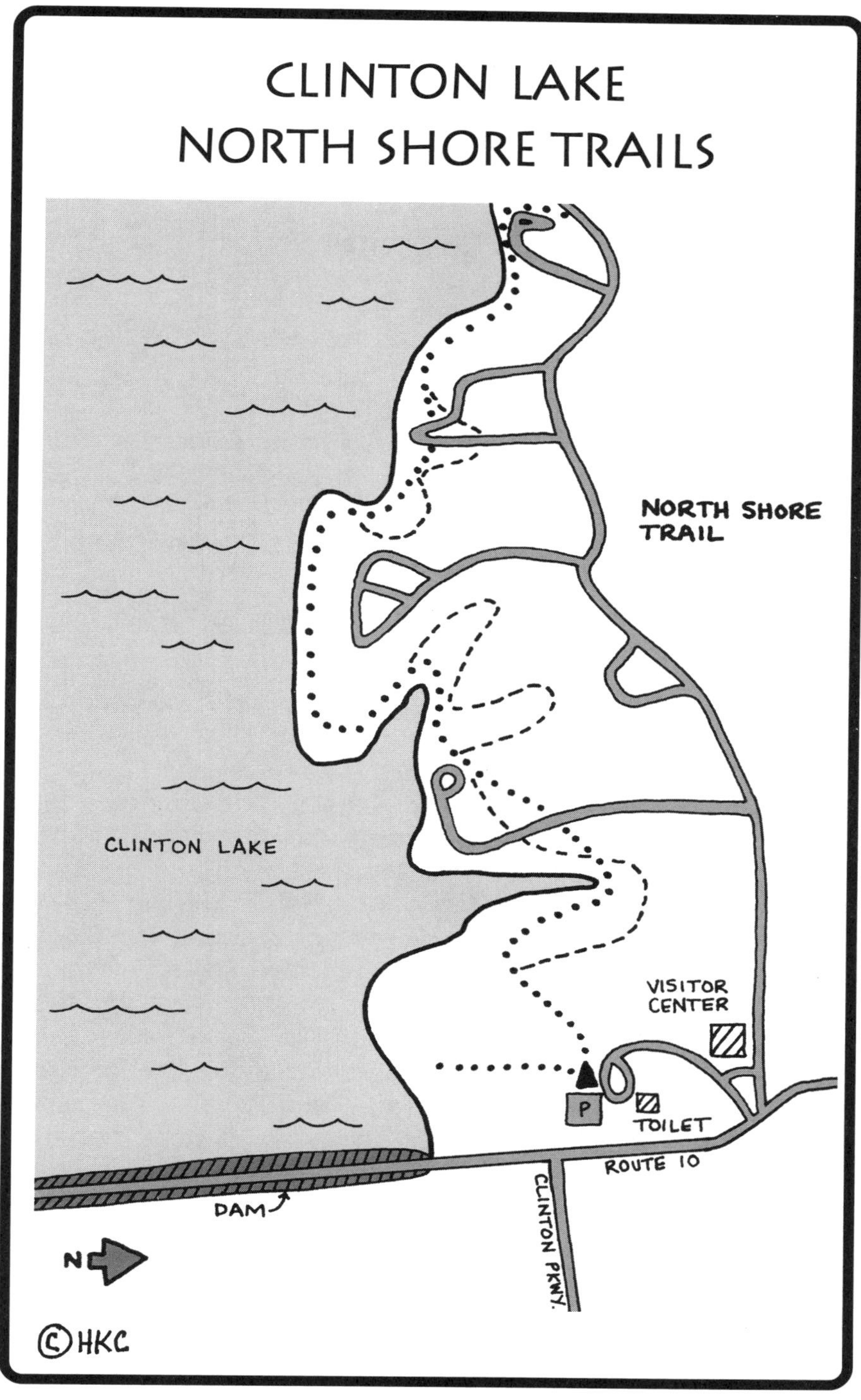
CLINTON LAKE
NORTH SHORE TRAILS
NORTH SHORE TRAIL
CLINTON LAKE
VISITOR CENTER
P
TOILET
ROUTE 10
CLINTON PKWY.
DAM
N
©HKC

Rimrock Trail (11 miles one-way) is most distant from the lake and is marked with blue blazes.

The **Benjamin Trail** is the middle route. It is 12.5 miles in length and blazed in yellow.

The trail nearest the lake is **Rockbottom Trail**, which is 8 miles long and blazed in orange.

Several side trails, which are often blazed in white, connect the main trails.

Clinton Pass Trailhead: The main trailhead is near the middle point of the trails at Clinton Pass in the Rockhaven Wildlife Area. This is accessible by taking County Road 458 east, which runs east-west a short distance south of the dam, and then turning north on County Road 700 east.

Interested hikers can obtain a current map and a report on trail conditions from the Corps of Engineers. Sections of these trails change, intersect and are sometimes flooded or obscured for other reasons.

Lynne Beatty, a member of the Kansas City Outdoors Club, suggests the following scenic route through some of the trails on the south side of Clinton Lake: "From the camping and day-use area, take the Rimrock (blue) trail to the left. Go past Burns Pass (white) and an unnamed crossover (white). After crossing a small creek several times, you'll see some houses up on the ridge. Drop down on the yellow trail into a sycamore-filled valley. A small cove of the lake will be in front of you. Look west for the eagle's nest. Continue along the lakeshore on the Rockbottom (orange) Trail. You'll pass a nice lunch spot with big logs and a rocky beach. Then head uphill on Clinton Pass (white) to your starting point. It is a leisurely 2.5 hour hike, about 4.5 miles depending on how far you walk on the beach before starting back up Clinton Pass."

The George Latham Trail (Trail Site 65) is on the west side of Clinton Lake.

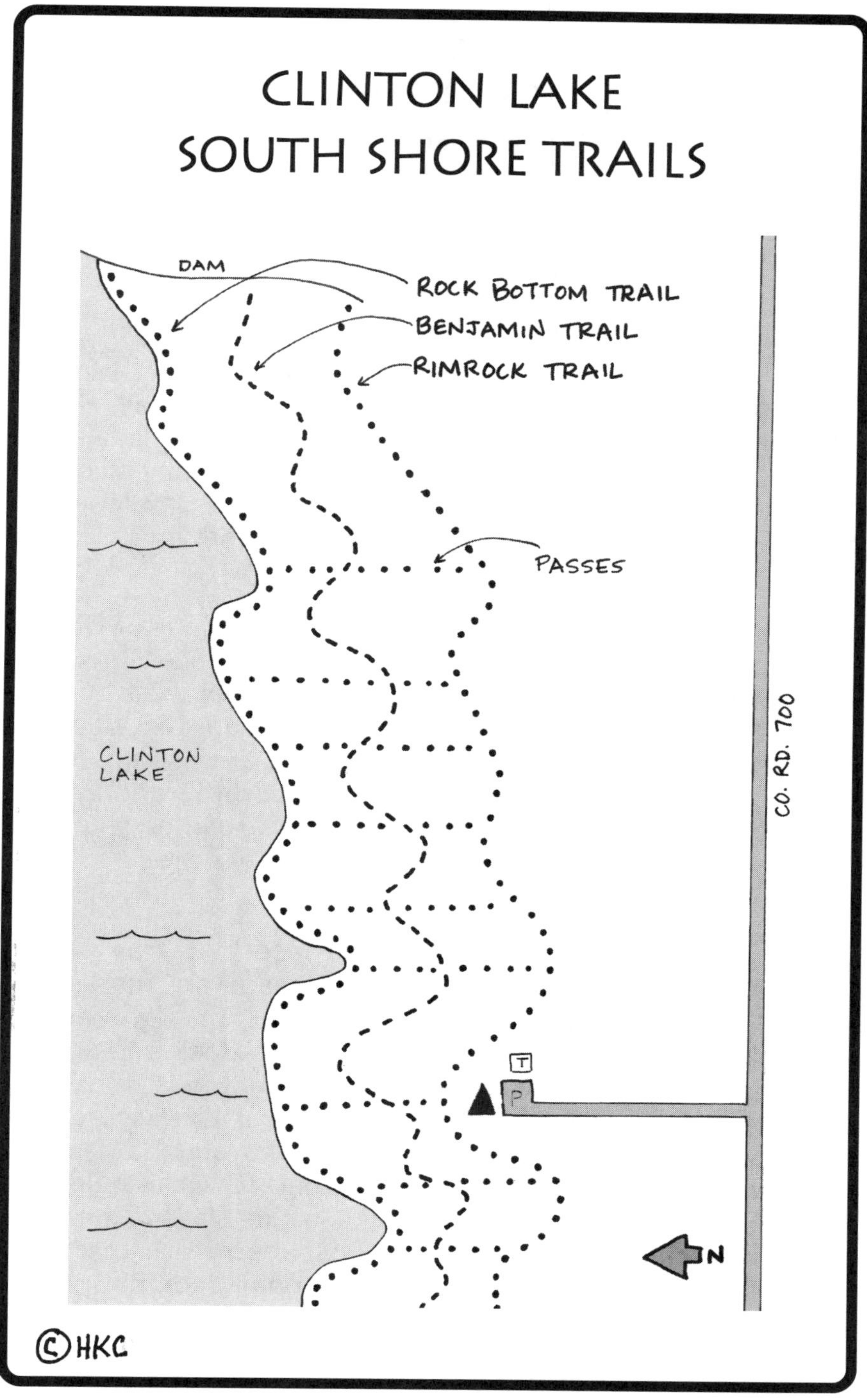
CLINTON LAKE
SOUTH SHORE TRAILS
DAM
ROCK BOTTOM TRAIL
BENJAMIN TRAIL
RIMROCK TRAIL
PASSES
CLINTON
LAKE
CO. RD. 700
T
P
N
©HKC

65
WOODRIDGE PRIMITIVE AREA
Clinton Lake, Kansas

Time: 2.25 Hours
Distance: 4.5 Miles
Rating: Moderate

Drinking Water: Yes
Accessible: No

Woodridge Primitive Area is a peninsula on the western edge of Clinton Lake near Lawrence, Kansas. Hikers are rewarded with beautiful views of the lake while walking through wooded hills. A fall hike is especially nice. The George Latham Trail described below has been developed by the Kansas Trails Council in memory of Mr. Latham.

Directions: Take Kansas Hwy 10 west from Kansas City to Lawrence. Stay on the road through south Lawrence. Turn right at Clinton Lake to Hwy 40. Turn left and travel west on Hwy 40 to Douglas County Road 442. Proceed on 442 to Stull. Turn left on Douglas County Road 1023 and drive south. At the intersection of Douglas County Roads 1023, 458 and 2, turn left (east) on Road 2. Go for 1 mile to a dirt road on your left. This road takes you to the Woodridge Primitive area.

George Latham Trail: This natural-surface loop trail begins and ends at the parking area. The trailheads are marked by signs. We began at the southeast trailhead on the right (as you face the woods). The trail proceeds counter-clockwise around the perimeter of a peninsula through heavy woods, meadows and rock outcroppings and presents several lake vistas. The area is home to a variety of birds. Beaver, coyote and deer are commonly seen. The main trail is well-marked with single blue blazes. Side trails are marked with double blue blazes. Chestnut, oak, black walnut, red cedar, and hackberry are the most common trees of the forest. During summer months, poison ivy and insects may be troublesome.

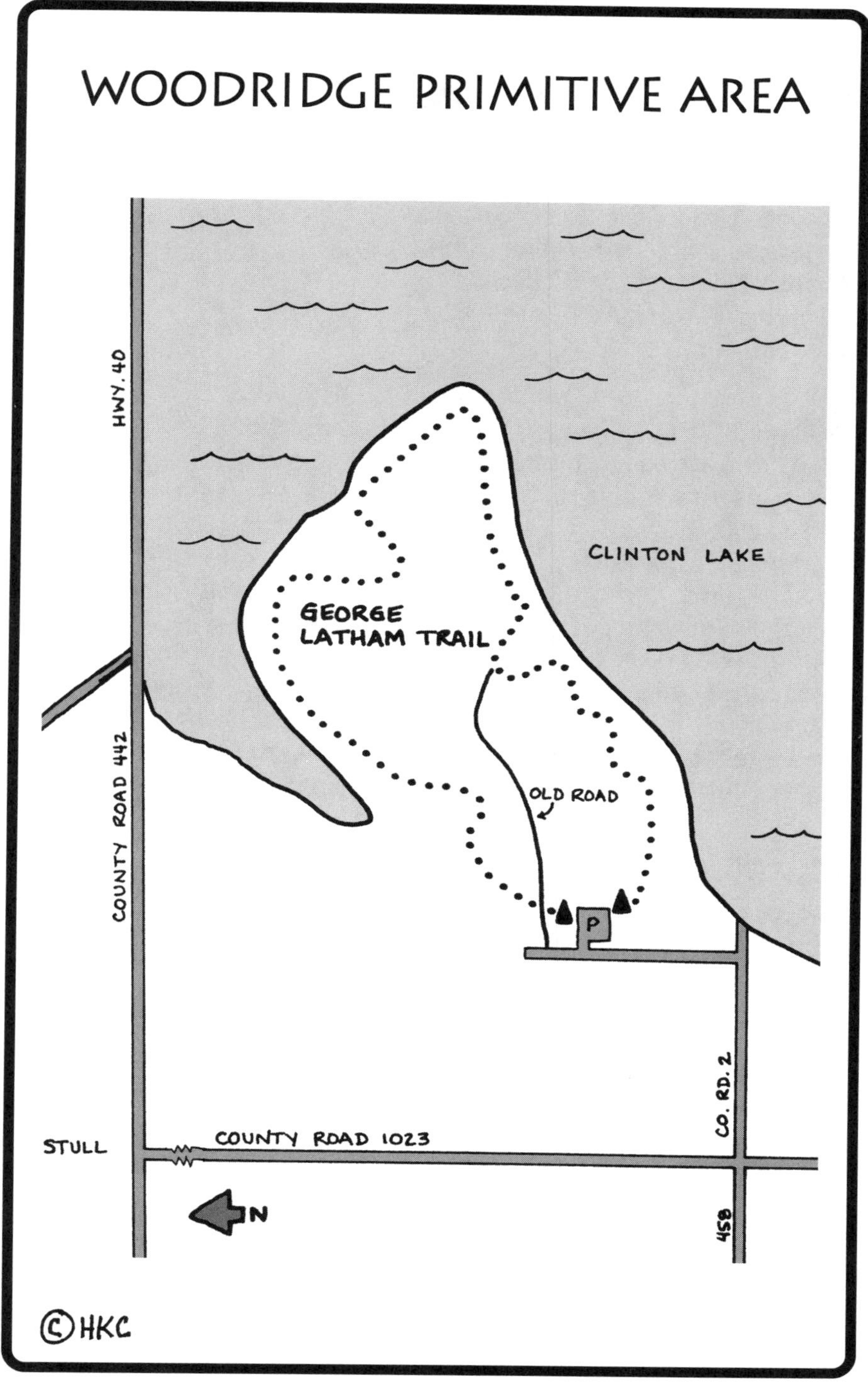
WOODRIDGE PRIMITIVE AREA
HWY. 40
CLINTON LAKE
GEORGE LATHAM TRAIL
OLD ROAD
P
COUNTY ROAD 442
CO. RD. 2
STULL
COUNTY ROAD 1023
N
458
©HKC

66
PERRY LAKE TRAIL
U.S. Army Corps of Engineers

Time: 1.5 to 8.5 Hours (One-way)
Distance: 2 to 14.5 Miles (One-way)
Rating: Moderate to Difficult
Drinking Water: At Access Points
Accessible: No

Perry Lake Trail, a National Recreational Trail, is one of the most challenging in the Kansas City area. It is a natural-surface trail that follows the eastern edge of Perry Lake through a variety of terrain. It is too long to hike round-trip in one day, so most hikers walk to one of the 8 access points along the trail and return to their start, or they arrange a shuttle with a friend to go just one-way. The trail is marked with blue blazes on trees and posts, and each mile is designated with a marker. Topographic maps and other trail information is available at www.perrylaketrail.net. The trail is supported by the Corps of Engineers, Kansas Trails Council, Sierra Club–Kansas Chapter and Kansas City Outdoor Club.

Directions: From Kansas City, go west on Hwy 24 to Perry, Kansas (Or take I-70 to the East Lawrence Exit, and take Hwy 24 to Perry.) At Perry, turn north at the lake signs, and go to the Perry Lake office. Pick up a Corps brochure with a map and a complete trail guide marked with drinking water sites.

Perry Lake Trail is divided into four main sections. This was originally done for administrative reasons when dividing volunteer labor resposibilities, but also serves to separate the trail along the main access points.

Section 1—Slough Creek Park to Longview Park: Section 1 is a 6-mile hike starting in Slough Creek Park near the southern end of the lake. An information kiosk with maps and contact information is located at the trailhead. To get there from the administration area, go back to the road that brought you from Perry and go north until you see the Slough Creek Park sign. Turn left into the park and follow this road past the gate station. There are three roads on the left. Between the second and third is a shower building marked by a drinking glass symbol. Across the road is a parking area. The trailhead is to the left, at the edge of the woods. From Slough Creek, the trail travels north along the lake. At 6 miles, the trail intersects with the East Half or Section 4 Trail (see Trail Site 67), which leaves Section 1 and heads east. Continuing north on Section 1, the trail follows the shoreline for much of the first 4 miles. The trail crosses Old Parker Place Road at 2.7 miles, followed by Lakeside Village Road at approximately 3.3 miles and then a boat launch area. The 4 mile marker is just north of the boat ramp area. Here you'll encounter 'table rocks' and the Mobe Rucker Memorial Park Bench for a quiet break near the lake and a scenic view. Longview Park boat ramp can be seen on the opposite side of the cove from this location. Near mile marker 5, the trail crosses Hoover Creek. Section 1 ends at Longview Park, just south of Apple Valley Farm (a great place for a break after a day on the trail). Section 1 is characterized by gentle slopes, woodlands, some open field crossings and many views of Perry Lake.

Longview Park: At 0.5 mile in length, this short trail portion between Sections 1 and 2 offers a glimpse of conditions found along the entire trail. The trail starts just south of Apple Valley Farm and heads west through a small, open field. Once entering the woods, a short, uphill climb takes you through the 'table rocks' found throughout the entire trail. At hilltop, a mix of open meadows and woods is encountered before crossing the road at the northern boundary of Longview Park. This short trail section is good for day hikes and is located close to tent and RV camping.

Section 2 (West)—Longview Park to Old Quarry Road: Section 2 is divided into two sections. The west half is 4.2 miles long and provides terrain/elevation gains. From Longview Park, the trail goes north through woodlands and near the lake. Just north of mile marker 7 is a small cove and the Richard Douthit Memorial Park Bench. Richard was an early trail builder and advocate. This location offers a peacefull setting and lake views. At mile marker 8, you are near the southern end of the Lakewood Hills subdivision. Section 2 (West) continues around the perimeter of this subdivision for about 4 miles. Enjoy a lunch break and lake views from one of the several high bluffs. As the trail follows the shore, it eventually turns to the east and then south into a small cove, where the trail passes a small pond and eventually crosses Old Quarry Road Bridge.

Section 2 (East)—Old Quarry Road to Old Military Park Road: The 3.5-mile eastern half of Section 2 provides the most rugged terrain of the trail, with steep hillsides and rocky paths. From Old Quarry Road, the trail follows the south side of Little Slough Creek and eventually enters Old Military Trail Park (closed). There are many high bluff views of the lake. A short distance east of mile marker 12 is the Dorothy Moore Memorial Park Bench at Solitude Point near a large rock outcropping overlooking the lake. Solitude Point is approximately 2.2 miles from the parking lot at Old Military Trail (OMT) Park, and is a frequent destination for day hikers starting at the northern trailhead. At 0.6 mile before the trailhead, you'll cross a bridge on the historic Ft. Leavenworth–Fort Riley Military Road.

All sections of the main trail are marked in blue paint blazes, which appear on trees, signs or fenceposts. Spur trails, which lead to the hikers' campground or to alternate access points, are marked in white.

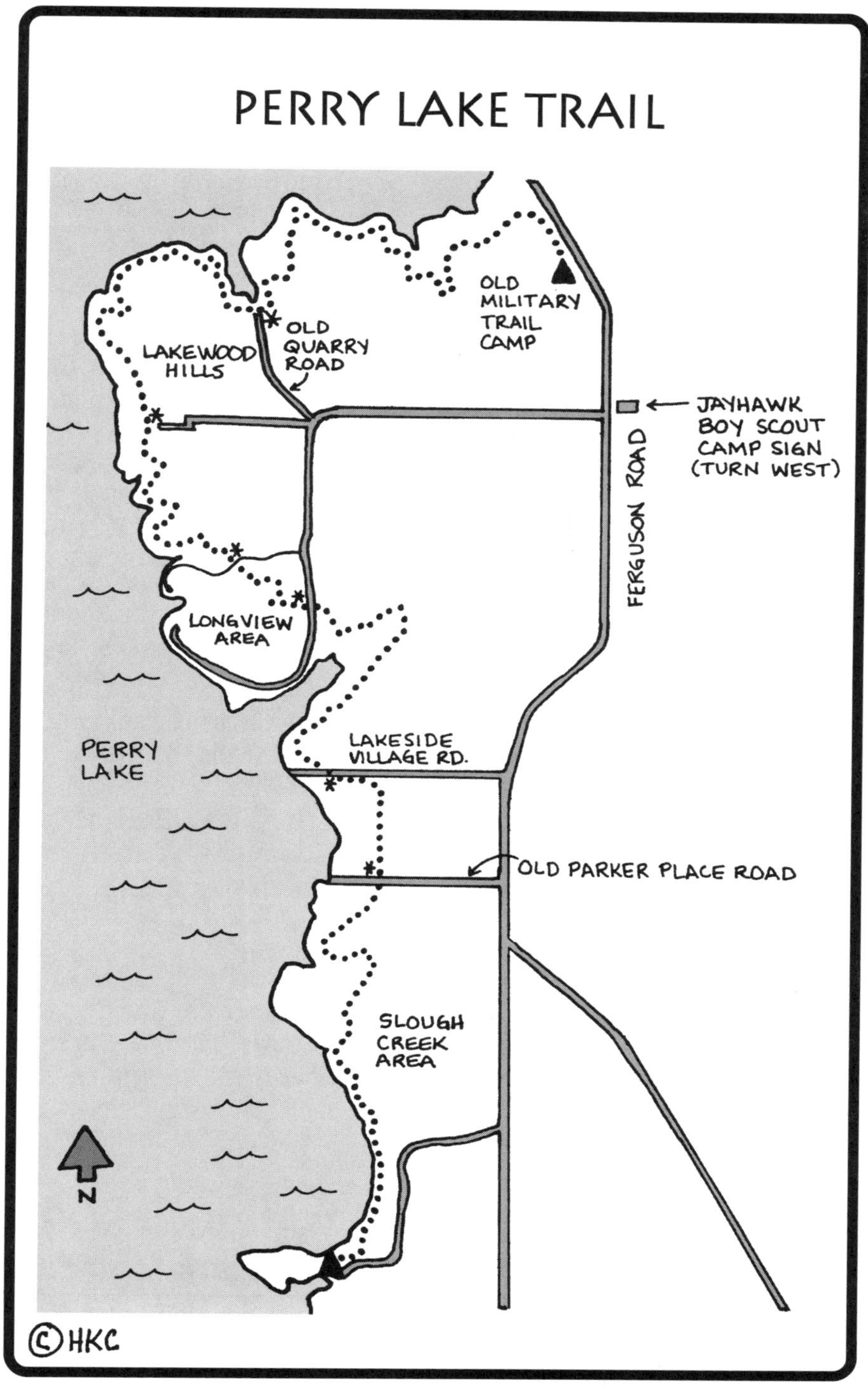
PERRY LAKE TRAIL
OLD MILITARY TRAIL CAMP
OLD QUARRY ROAD
LAKEWOOD HILLS
JAYHAWK BOY SCOUT CAMP SIGN (TURN WEST)
FERGUSON ROAD
LONGVIEW AREA
PERRY LAKE
LAKESIDE VILLAGE RD.
OLD PARKER PLACE ROAD
SLOUGH CREEK AREA
N
©HKC

67
PERRY LAKE TRAIL – EAST HALF

U.S. Army Corps of Engineers

Time: 2 to 8 Hours (One-way)
Distance: 3.5 to 14 Miles (One-way)
Rating: Moderate to Difficult
Drinking Water: At OMT Access Points
Accessible: No

Perry Lake Trail, a National Recreational Trail, is one of the most challenging in the Kansas City area. It is a natural-surface trail marked with blue blazes on trees and posts. The original trail (see Trail Site 66) follows the eastern edge of Perry Lake through a variety of terrain. The East Half, a more rugged and remote path, completes the 29-mile loop of the trail. We have not hiked the entire trail. Members of the Kansas City Outdoor Club have furnished much of the information in this description. The trail is too long to hike round-trip in one day, so most hikers walk to one of the access points along the trail and return to their start, or they arrange a shuttle with a friend to go just one way. Each mile is designated with a marker. Topographic maps and other trail information are available at www.perrylaketrail.net.

Directions: The East Half section of The Perry Lake Trail begins at the Old Military Trail (OMT) parking area on Ferguson Road. See directions at Trail Site 66. There are two other access points with parking. One is at the boat ramp parking area just north of the Ferguson Road bridge over Slough Creek; the other is at Slough Creek Park.

Perry Lake Trail is divided into four main sections. This was originally done for administrative reasons when dividing volunteer labor responsibilities, but also serves to separate the trail along the main access points. This description follows Sections 3 and 4 of the trail.

Section 3—Old Military Trail Park to Kiowa Road: Section 3 is 3.5 miles long and offers a more remote look at the Perry Lake area. The trailhead is on the southeast side of the Old Military Trail parking lot. The trail, marked by blue blazes, heads east into the backwaters of Little Slough Creek. At approximately 0.4 miles, you'll reach the site of the 94th Street Bridge. The bridge has been missing since October 2005, when flash flood waters carried it downstream several hundred feet. Another few hundred feet down the trail, you cross 94th Street (gravel), then climb to a hilltop view of Perry Lake to the west. The trail continues toward Little Slough Creek, generally following the south side of the creek, and ends at Kiowa Road (gravel, formerly Road 410A).

Section 4—Kiowa Road to Slough Creek Park: Section 4 is also very remote and begins on Kiowa Road (formerly Road 410A). This section follows the west/north side of Big Slough Creek, mostly along the road, for approximately 4 miles. There are many wooded areas and small field crossings. The trail passes Boy Scout Camp Jayhawk, follows the perimeter of the Audubon area, and eventually crosses Ferguson Road (at 4.5 miles) near a recent trail reroute. Heading west from Ferguson Road, the trail crosses near a boat ramp parking lot that has pit restrooms, a kiosk and a trailhead. After negotiating two substantial draws, the trail enters the Slough Creek Park north of the campground. It then crosses a road, connects with the original trail and returns to the Perry Lake Trail trailhead in the park (see Trail Site 66). From the Ferguson Road trailhead to the Slough Creek Park trailhead is 2.6 miles.

All sections of the main trail are marked in blue paint blazes, which appear on trees, signs or fenceposts. Spur trails, which lead to the hikers' campground or to alternate access points, are marked in white.

Other Trails: A trail system in the Delaware Area and two shorter nature trails are also available at Perry Lake.

The Thunder Ridge Trail is a 3-mile loop trail through the campground in the Slough Creek public use area at the south beginning of the Perry Lake Trail System. It passes through heavily wooded forests and connects with the campgrounds, making water and restrooms accessible to hikers.

The Prairie State Park Nature Trail is on the west side of the dam. It follows loops through woods, tall grass and vistas of the lake. It is accessible from a state park office parking area. A route for a 2.5-mile walk can be put together.

A series of loop trails in the Delaware Area's relatively undeveloped western side of the lake is maintained primarily for mountain bikers. There are 5 or more miles of trails that offer switchbacks, steep ascents and thick timberland.

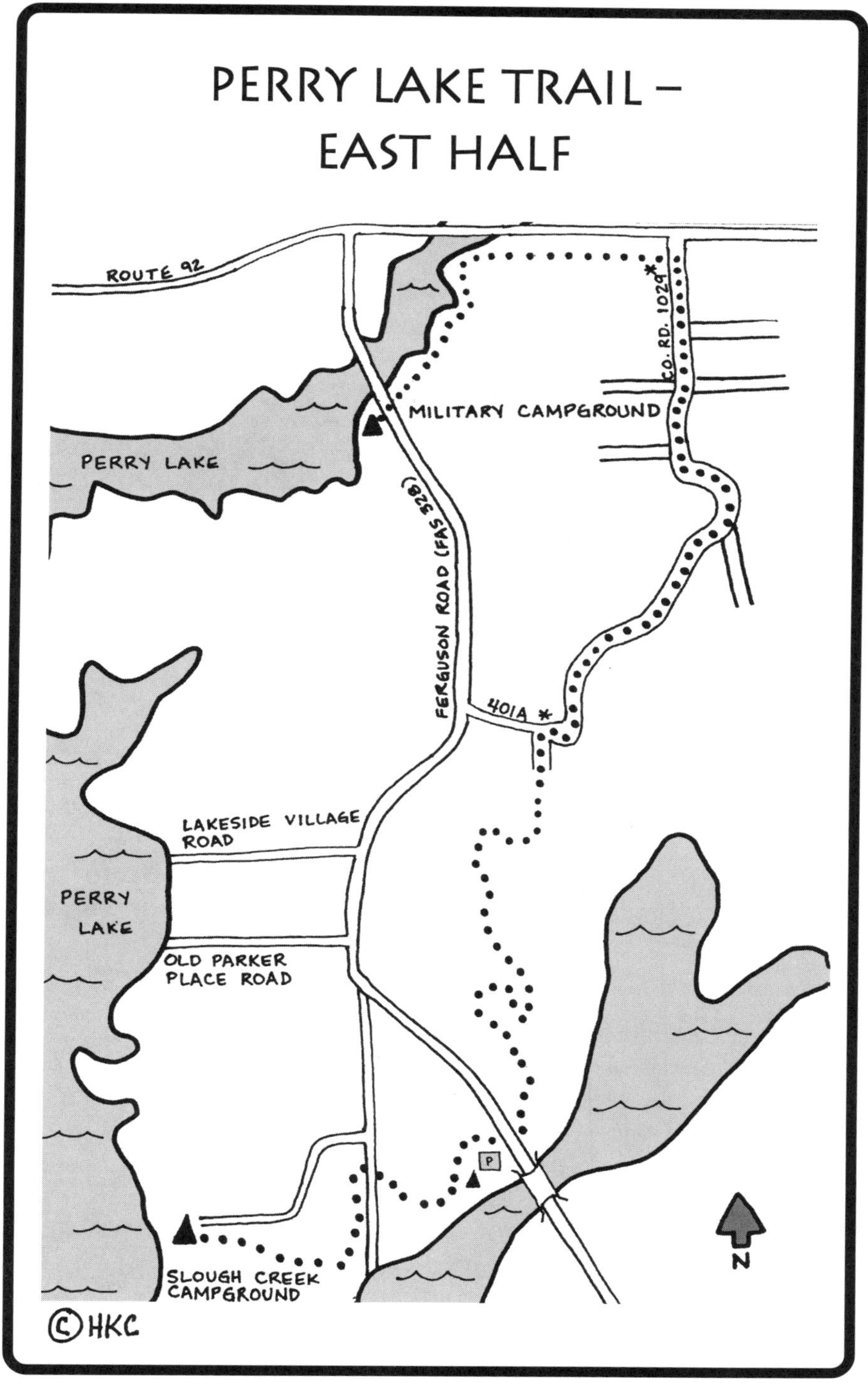
PERRY LAKE TRAIL –
EAST HALF
ROUTE 92
CO. RD. 1029
MILITARY CAMPGROUND
PERRY LAKE
FERGUSON ROAD (FAS 328)
401A
LAKESIDE VILLAGE ROAD
PERRY LAKE
OLD PARKER PLACE ROAD
P
SLOUGH CREEK CAMPGROUND
N
©HKC

The Flint Hills of Kansas are a national treasure. Take the opportunity to experience grasslands as far as you can see at the Konza Prairie.

68
KONZA PRAIRIE TRAILS
The Nature Conservancy & Kansas State University

Time: 2 to 3 Hours
Distance: 6.1 Miles
Rating: Moderate

Drinking Water: No
Accessible: No

Konza Prairie Research Natural Area provides a splendid opportunity to explore one of the unique geological features of the Midwest. The flint hills are a segment of the Great Plains. It was here, in a veritable sea of grass, "where the buffalo roamed." This 8,616-acre tallgrass preserve was part of the Dewey Ranch south of Manhattan, Kansas before it was purchased in 1977 by the Nature Conservancy.

It is now managed by Kansas State University as a research and education site for the study and preservation of the native tallgrass prairie. One hundred and fifty bison do, in fact, roam the preserve, although not in the area of the hiking trails. There are also deer, prairie chickens and hundreds of other animals, as well as more than five hundred species of wildflowers, shrubs and trees. The preserve is named after the Konza Indians Tribe, also the origin of the name of Kansas. It is said to mean, "People of the South Wind."

Directions: Drive west from Kansas City on I-70. In about two hours, you will pass the Kansas Hwy 177 turn-off to Manhattan. Continue west on I-70 for 6.5 miles to the McDowell Creek Road Exit (Exit 307). Drive north (right) on McDowell Creek Road for 5.1 miles, past the Ashland Cemetery, to Konza Prairie Lane, a gravel road. Turn right and continue for 0.5 mile to a parking area at the trailhead. A trail map and guide identify some of the major features of the trails.

Trails: The trail leads northeast along Kings Creek, crosses the creek on a footbridge and ascends to a high ridge. To the north, the Kansas River and Manhattan can be seen in the distance. To the south is the Kings Creek watershed. The trail follows fire breaks to the east. There are three concentric loops, with opportunities to loop back on the Nature Trail for a 2.8-mile walk, the Kings Creek loop for a 4.7-mile walk, or you can follow the Godwin Hill Loop for a trip of 6.1 miles. At the end of each loop, the trail drops down to the valley and follows Kings Creek back to the starting point, past the stone Dewey Ranch house.

The trail is open from dawn to dusk every day, except when the prairies are being burned (usually in April). Future plans include an accessible segment and an extension of the eastern end of the trail. For those who want to know more about the Konza Prairie we suggest *Konza Prairie: A Tallgrass Natural History* by O. J. Reichman, published by the University Press of Kansas.

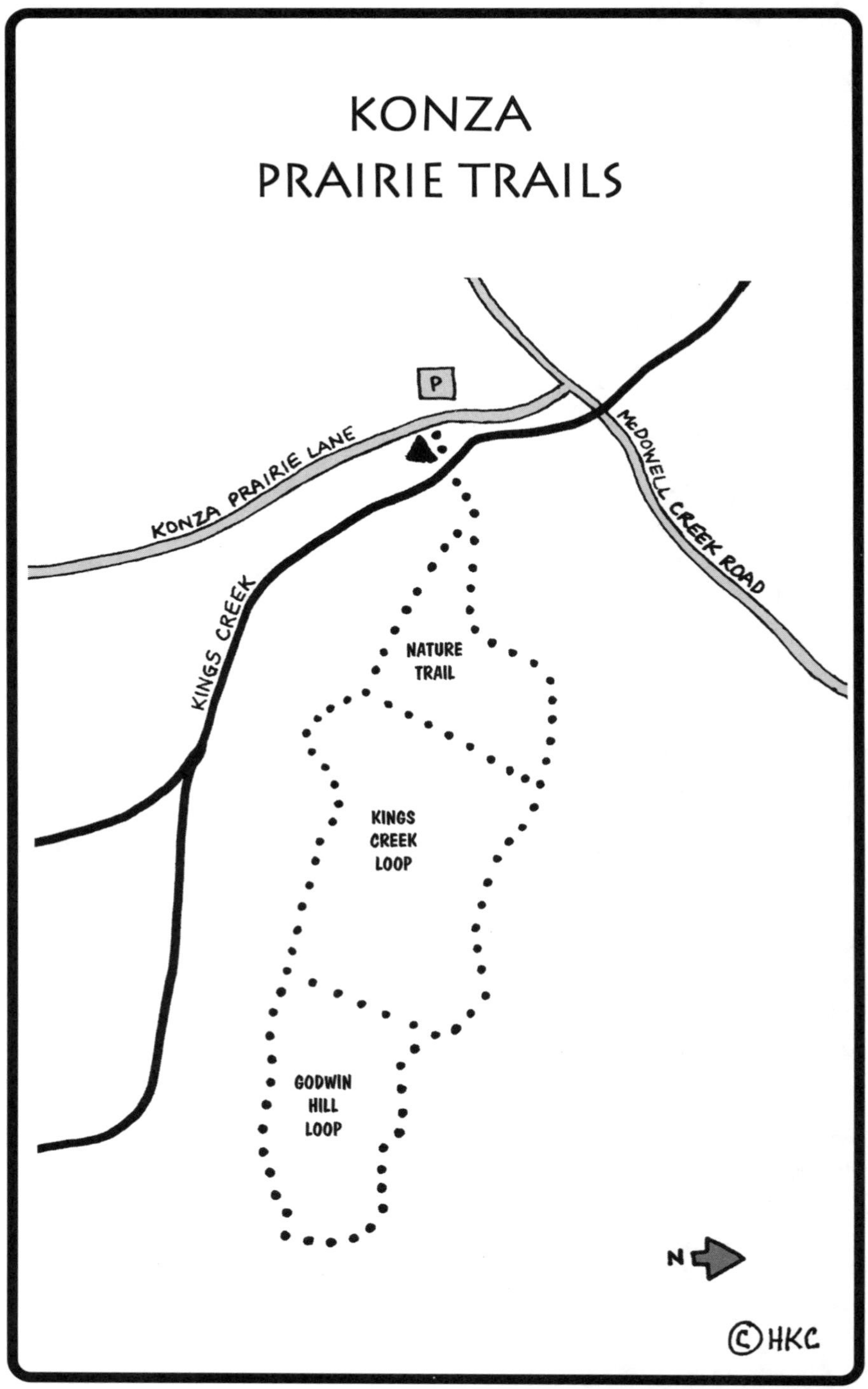
KONZA
PRAIRIE TRAILS
P
KONZA PRAIRIE LANE
McDOWELL CREEK ROAD
KINGS CREEK
NATURE
TRAIL
KINGS
CREEK
LOOP
GODWIN
HILL
LOOP
N
©HKC

TRAIL NOTES:

69
FAVORITE KANSAS HIKES

Since the original publication of this book in 1989, many new trails and trail directories have been developed in Kansas. We list the four trails below as some of our favorites, along with the other Kansas trails shown in this volume. The other hiking guides listed at the end of this book will provide more information about additional trails in Kansas.

Kanopolis State Park: On the north side of Kanopolis Reservoir, some 30 miles southwest of Salina, deep canyons have formed in the watershed of the Smoky Hill River. Horse Thief Canyon Trail (shown above) loops through five of these canyons, providing the hiker with impressive sights and unexpected vistas in the semi-arid hills of west-central Kansas, invisible to those driving the interstates. High walls of yellow and tan rock, flowing streams, rock formations sculpted by eons of wind and water, tall oak trees hidden deep in the canyons and sightings of many birds are some of the features of this 5.5-mile loop trail. Eight-mile Alum Creek Trail, which has some features similar to Horse Thief Canyon Trail, and the 6-mile Prairie Trail have been added to the system. Obtain a map and brochure from the park office at the lake.

Elk City Lake: One of the longest and best hiking trail systems in Kansas is at Elk City Lake, west of Independence in the southeastern part of the state. The 15-mile (one-way) Elk River Trail parallels the north shore of the lake and the Elk River. Beginning just west of the dam, it meanders south and west, much of the time on a shelf above the lake. The area is replete with rock formations and outcroppings, dense woods and vistas of the lake and surrounding hills. There are several other shorter trails that are well worth walking.

Tallgrass Prairie National Preserve: A national treasure in the Kansas Flint Hills is now open for hiking. Walkers can visit one of the few remaining areas of virgin prairie where a hundred and fifty years ago, the grass was as tall as a horse and supported countless bison. The preserve is located in Chase County, Kansas, the site of William Least Heat-Moon's book *PrairyErth*. The nearly 11,000-acre preserve is a partnership of the U.S. National Park Service, The Nature Conservancy and Kansas Park Trust. It is home to one hundred and fifty kinds of birds plus many reptiles and mammals. To reach the Preserve, drive 20 miles west of Emporia on U.S. Hwy 50 to Strong City and 2 miles north on Kansas Hwy 177.

The five trails begin at the historic Spring Hill Ranch House. The Southwind Nature Trail (1.75 miles) leads through tallgrass prairie, by the old, stone, one-room school, and past scenic overlooks. The Bottomland Trail (0.75-mile loop) has wayside exhibits and an information kiosk. It is wheelchair accessible.

There are three longer, backcountry trails: the Scenic Overlook Trail (6.4 miles round-trip); The 3 Pasture Loop Trail (3.8-mile loop); and the Red House Trail (6-mile hike), which takes you through wide open vistas of native rolling prairie and past limestone outcroppings, prairie flowers and old stone fences. Permits (free) are required for the backcountry hiking trails. Call (626) 273-8494. For much more information see www.nps.gov/tapr.

The Oregon Trail Education Center: For another taste of history, drive 4 miles west of St. Marys, Kansas on Hwy 24, then turn north at the Oregon Trail sign for 0.3 mile. The road that borders the center is on the track of the original trail, which carried 300,000 pioneers traveling west in the middle of the 19th Century. This site has been developed by the Jeffrey Energy Center at a point where the Oregon Trail veered north from the Kaw River and headed toward Nebraska. Located on a bluff overlooking the route of the trail, the center provides three pleasant and informative short trails through different ecosystems for about an hour of good walking. One of the trails is accessible. Signs provide directions to the walks and a history of this portion of the Oregon Trail.

TRAILS BY LENGTH

Distances are round-trip unless otherwise indicated

Trail	Miles
Katy Trail State Park (one-way)	225
Rockhaven Trail System, Clinton Lake (one-way)	50
Smithville Lake Trails (3) (one-way)	20
Tallgrass Prairie (5) (one-way)	18
Prairie Spirit Rail Trail (one-way)	33
Perry Lake Trails	30.5*
West Segment (one-way)	14.5
Northeast Extension (one-way)	16
Mill Creek Streamway Park Trails (one-way)	15.25
Northgate to 95th Street	4
95th Street to Shawnee Mission Park	2.5
Shawnee Mission Park to Midland Road	3
Midland Road to Johnson Drive	2.75
Nelson Island Segment	3
Elk City Lake (one-way)	15*
Clinton Lake–North Shore Trail	14
Clinton Lake–South Shore Trails (3) (one-way)	11*
Rimrock Trail	11
Fleming Park–Lake Jacomo (7)	10
Lawrence, Kansas River Trails	10*
Squaw Creek National Wildlife Refuge	10
Little Blue Trace (one-way)	10
Riverfront Heritage Trail (one-way) (developing)	9
Indian Creek Greenway & Trail	8.8
Longview Lake Bicycle & Hiking Trail (one-way)	8
Indian Creek Bike & Hike Trail (one-way)	7.75
Knob Noster State Park (6)	7.35
Burr Oak Woods (4)	7
Prairie State Park (3)	7
Wallace State Park (6)	7
Lawrence Trafficway Trail (one-way)	6.5
Harry Wiggins Trolley Track Trail (one-way)	6.5
Konza Prairie Trails (3)	6.1
Plaza Area Walks (5)	6
Shawnee Mission Park (2)	6
Monkey Mountain Nature Reserve (2)	6

Note: ( ) denotes the number of trails at that location

Parkville, Missouri Trails (3) 5.7
Horse Thief Canyon Trails 5.5*
Bluffwoods Conservation Area (3-trail loop) 5*
Overland Park Arboretum (system of loops) 5
Blue Springs Lake (2) (one-way) 4.7
Watkins Mill State Park 4.5
Woodbridge Primitive Area 4.5
Tomahawk Creek Greenway (one-way) 4.3
Blue & Gray Park (2) 4*
Blue River Parkway–South Trail 4
George Owens Nature Park (6) 4
Heritage Park Walk 4
Kearney Fishing River Trail (loop) 4
Kill Creek Trail (loop) 4
Prairie Creek Greenway (one-way) 4
Landahl Park–North Trail 3.6
Landahl Park–South Trail 3.5
Blue River Parkway–North Trail 3.5
Martha Lafite Thompson Nature Sanctuary (6) 3.5
Weston Bluffs Trail (one-way) 3.5
Byron Shutz Trail, Powell Gardens (loop) 3.25
Prairie Center (2) 3.1
James A. Reed Wildlife Area (3) 3
Shawnee Mission Park–North Shore Trail 3
Longview Lake 3*
Weston Bend State Park (4) 3*
Sar-Ko-Par Trails (one-way) .... 3 to 5
River Bluff Nature Reserve 2.6
Eddy-Ballentine/Blue River Glades Trails (2) 2.5
Jerry Smith Park (loop) 2.5
Mahaffie Creek Trail (one-way) 2.5
Rolling Ridge Trail (one-way) 2.5
Turkey Creek Streamway Trail 2.5
Fountain Bluffs Walks (circuit) 2.25
Little Cedar Creek, Unity Village (loop) 2.2

The following trails provide from 1 to 2 miles of walking: Ernie Miller Park, McCormack Loess Mounds Preserve, Truman Lake State Park, Klein Park–Cave Spring, Hillsdale Lake, Lanesfield School Historical Prairie, Hidden Valley Park Natural

* See descriptions for other trails in this area

Area, Sunflower Park Nature Trail, Maple Woods Nature Preserve, Powell Gardens Nature Trail, Hodge Park, Excelsior Springs Walks, Happy Rock Park, Gorman Park, Oak Grove Park, Stockdale Park, Westboro Park, Cates Creek Greenway, LaBenite Park, Fox Hollow Park and Marsh Trail.

TRAILS ACCESSIBLE TO PEOPLE WITH DISABILITIES

Trails listed below are considered accessible for people with disabilities. These trails are hard-surfaced pathways. When planning a trip to a trail not listed below, we suggest contacting sponsoring agencies (listed inside the back cover) for more information before heading out. Factors that may deem a trail non-accessible may include slope, surface, severe turns and a lack of resting places.

NATURAL SURFACE TRAILS

SELECT HIKING CLUBS & OUTDOOR ORGANIZATIONS

Burroughs Audubon Society, 21509 SW Woods Chapel Road, Lee's Summit, MO 64015. (816) 795-8177. Planned hikes, birdwatching and field trips. www.burroughs.org

Kansas City Outdoor Club, P.O. Box 95, Shawnee Mission, KS 66201. Planned hikes, camping and other outdoor activities.

Kansas Trails Council, Box 695, Topeka, KS 66601. Builds and maintains trails, holds camping and hiking activities. www.kansastrailscouncil.org

Possum Trot Orienteering Club of Kansas City, www.ptoc.org.

Sierra Club, Thomas Hart Benton Chapter, P.O. Box 32727, Kansas City, MO 64171. Hiking and camping as well as conservation projects. www.missourisierraclub.org

Sierra Club, Kanza Group, 9844 Georgia, Kansas City, KS 66109. Hiking, camping and field trips. www.kansas.sierraclub.org

Kansas City WildLands, 435 Westport Road, #23, Kansas City, MO 64111. (816) 561-1061 Extension 116. Volunteers restore, conserve and protect remnant natural areas. www.kcwildlands.org

OTHER
HEART OF AMERICA
HIKING GUIDEBOOKS

Discover Natural Missouri: A Guide to Exploring the Nature Conservancy Preserves. The Nature Conservancy, 1991.

Dufur, Brett, *The Complete Katy Trail Guidebook: America's Longest Rails-To-Trails Project.* Pebble Publishing, Inc., 2007.

Folzenlogen, Darcy and Robert. *Hiking Mid-Missouri: Scenic Trails of the Heartland.* Willow Press, 2000.

Lohraff, Keven. *Hiking Missouri.* Human Kinetics, 1999.

Hauber, Catherine, *Hiking Guide to Kansas*. University of Kansas Press, 1999.

Kight, Teresa, *Conservation Trails: A Guide to Missouri Department of Conservation Hiking Trails.* Missouri Department of Conservation, 1999.

Yanker, Gary and Carol Tarlow, *Mid-America Walking Atlas.* McGraw-Hill Publishing Company, 1990.

LIST OF TRAIL CONTACTS

Cave Spring Association, Inc., 8701 E. Gregory, Kansas City, Missouri 64133. (816) 358-2283. www.cavespring.org

Clay County Parks and Recreation, 17201 Paradesian Street, Smithville, Missouri 64089. (816) 407-3400. www.claycogov.com

Department of Parks and Recreation, 201 N. Dodgion, Independence, Missouri 64050. (816) 325-7360. www.ci.independence.mo.us/parksandrec

Excelsior Springs, Missouri Parks and Recreation, 112 S. Thompson Avenue, Excelsior Springs, Missouri 64024. (816) 630-1040. www.ci.excelsior-springs.mo.us

Jackson County Parks and Recreation, 22807 Woods Chapel Road, Blue Springs, Missouri 64015. (816) 503-4800. www.jacksongov.org

Johnson County Parks and Recreation District, 6501 Antioch, Merriam, Kansas, 66202. (913) 831-3355. www.jcprd.com

Kansas City Area Transportation Authority, Trolley Track Trail, 1200 E. 18th Street, Kansas City, Missouri 64108. (816) 346-0356. www.kcata.org

Kansas City Parks and Recreation Department, 4600 E. 63rd Street, Kansas City, Missouri 64130. (816) 513-7500. www.kcmo.org/parks

Kansas City Department of Wildlife and Parks, Kansas City District Office, 14369 95th Street, Lenexa, Kansas 66215. (620) 672-5911. www.kdwp.state.ks.us

Kansas State University, Konza Prairie Office, Manhattan, Kansas 66056. (785) 587-0441. www.ksu.edu/konza

Kansas Trails Council, P.O. Box 695, Topeka, Kansas 66601. www.kansastrailscouncil.org

Kearney, Missouri Parks and Recreation Department, 100 E. Washington, Kearney, Missouri 64060. (816) 903-4724.

Lawrence Parks and Recreation Department, 947 New Hampshire Street, Lawrence, Kansas 66044. (785) 832-3450. www.lprd.org

Leawood Parks and Greenway, 4800 Town Center Drive, Leawood, Kansas 66211. (913) 339-6700. www.leawood.org

Liberty, Missouri Parks and Recreation Department, 1600 S. Withers, Liberty, Missouri 64068. (816) 792-6009. www.ci.liberty.mo.us

Martha Lafite Thompson Nature Sanctuary, 407 N. LaFrenz Road, Liberty, Missouri 64068. (816) 781-8598. www.naturesanctuary.com

Missouri Department of Conservation, Kansas City Regional Office, 3424 NW Duncan Road, Blue Springs, Missouri 64015. (816) 655-6250. Anita B. Gorman Discovery Center, 4750 Troost, Kansas City, Missouri 64110. (816) 759-7300. www.mdc.mo.gov

Missouri Department of Natural Resources, 500 NE Colbern Road, Lee's Summit, Missouri 64086. (800) 361-4827. Anita B. Gorman Discovery Center, 4750 Troost, Kansas City, Missouri 64110. (816) 759-7300. www.dnr.mo.gov

Nature Conservancy, Kansas Chapter, 700 SW Jackson, #804, Topeka, Kansas 66603. (785) 233-4400. www.nature.org/kansas. Kansas City, Missouri Office, 1600 Genessee, Kansas City, Missouri 64102. (816) 221-8080.

Olathe, Kansas Parks and Public Ground, P.O. Box 768, Olathe, Kansas, 66051. (913) 971-6629. www.olatheks.org

Overland Park, Kansas Parks and Recreation, 8500 Santa Fe, Overland Park, Kansas 6621. (913) 327-6630. www.opkansas.org. Arboretum: (913) 685-3604.

Parkville, Missouri Parks Department, 1201 East Street, Parkville, Missouri 64512. (816) 741-7676. www.parkvillemo.com

Platte County Parks Department, 415 3rd Street, Platte City, Missouri 64079. (816) 858-2232. www.co.platte.mo.us/parks

Powell Gardens, 1609 NW Hwy 50, Kingsville, Missouri 64961. (816) 697-2600. www.powellgardens.org

Sugar Creek, Missouri City Hall, 103 S. Sterling, Sugar Creek, Missouri 64054. (816) 252-4400. www.sugar-creek.mo.us

U.S. Army Corps of Engineers, 601 East 12th Street, Kansas City, Missouri 64108. (816) 389-3632. www.nwk.usace.army.mil

U.S. Fish and Wildlife Service, Squaw Creek National Wildlife Refuge, P.O. Box 158, Mound City, Missouri 64470. (660) 442-3187. www.fws.gov/midwest/squawcreek

Unity Village Facilities Services, 1901 N.W. Blue Parkway, Unity Village, Missouri 64065. (816) 251-3569. www.unityvillagechapel.org

Authors Richard Ballentine, at left, and William Eddy.

ABOUT THE AUTHORS

Richard Ballentine

Co-author Richard Ballentine is a retired corporate attorney. He and his wife Emily have been residents of Fairway, Kansas for more than twenty-five years.

"I enjoy a variety of outdoor activities. They provide a balance to life, a time for contemplation and a great opportunity to be with friends and family," Ballentine said.

Ballentine, in retirement, volunteers and enjoys his hobbies: hiking, biking, traveling, photography and reading.

Ballentine and Eddy met while both were on the Board of Directors of Kansas City Consensus, a group that works to identify and provide solutions to issues affecting the community.

William Eddy

Co-author William Eddy is a retired faculty member and administrator at the University of Missouri-Kansas City. He is active in civic and outdoor organizations in Kansas City, where he has lived for nearly forty years. In addition to hiking with his wife Linda and their family and friends, Eddy's hobbies include music, environmental issues and visiting his grandchildren.

One of his favorite Walt Whitman poems reads:

> Afoot and light-hearted,
> I take to the open road,
> Healthy, free,
> the world before me,
> The long brown path before me,
> leading wherever I choose.